Higher Education
for the Public Good

Higher Education for the Public Good

Emerging Voices from a National Movement

Adrianna J. Kezar

Tony C. Chambers

John C. Burkhardt

JOSSEY-BASS
A Wiley Imprint
www.josseybass.com

Published by Jossey-Bass
A Wiley Imprint
989 Market Street, San Francisco, CA 94103-1741   www.josseybass.com

Jossey-Bass books and products are available through most bookstores. To contact Jossey-Bass directly
call our Customer Care Department within the U.S. at 800-956-7739, outside the U.S. at 317-572-3986
or fax 317-572-4002.

Jossey-Bass also publishes its books in a variety of electronic formats. Some content that appears in
print may not be available in electronic books.

Library of Congress Cataloging-in-Publication Data

Higher education for the public good : emerging voices from a national movement /
[edited by] Adrianna J. Kezar, Anthony C. Chambers, John Burkhardt.
    p. cm.
    Includes bibliographical references and index.
    ISBN 0-7879-7382-3 (alk. paper)
    1. Education, Higher—Social aspects—United States. 2. Education, Higher—Aims and
objectives—United States. 3. Common good. I. Kezar, Adrianna J. II. Chambers, Anthony C.
III. Burkhardt, John.
    LC191.94.H54 2005
    378'.015—dc22   2005000719

Printed in the United States of America
FIRST EDITION
HB Printing   10 9 8 7 6 5 4 3 2 1

The Jossey-Bass Higher
and Adult Education Series

Contents

Preface

Adrianna J. Kezar, Tony C. Chambers,
John C. Burkhardt

In this book, we examine what we believe to be one of the most significant challenges confronting higher education: a shift, and perhaps loss, within some institutions and sectors in the role higher education plays in serving the public good. The social charter between higher education and the public includes such commitments as developing research to improve society, training leaders for public service, educating citizens to serve the democracy, increasing economic development, and critiquing public policy. In return for these various social commitments, society provides tangible resources, political support, raw materials, and a guiding influence. The idea that higher education exists to serve the public good has been at the heart of the enterprise since its inception in the United States almost four hundred years ago. Although this commitment has shifted over time, evolving as society's understanding of what it needs and how best it can be served by colleges and universities has changed, higher education has always had an obligation to serve society in certain fundamental ways. We believe that these historical commitments have helped create a better society and are essential to a healthy deliberative democracy.

So what is happening? Why is this critical charter being altered, lost, or rejected? We believe that, for the most part, this charter is being lost as public policy and institutional decisions unintentionally focus more on revenue generation and the individual benefits of higher education rather than on its broader social role and benefits. The many subtle and small choices that erode the public commitment have cumulative effects. Some leaders may be altering the charter unintentionally as they try to grapple with declining state funds and state goals that may not prioritize higher education. Perhaps a few even reject this traditional charter and want higher education to be less active and involved in society. For these people, the production of workers is the primary goal of higher education. But, for the most part, we believe many of those in higher education too often make ill-considered choices in trying to respond to an environment in which the values and funding have changed. Most people realize the benefits that higher education brings to society and that the social, economic, and political success of the United States is largely attributable to our higher education, which is considered the premiere system in the world. It is considered premiere not because it educates workers, although this is an important component. It is revered around the world for the comprehensive ways it develops society—through knowledge production, leadership development, a literate electorate, and cultural and economic development, to name a few. Will the choices made over the last few decades erode this status as a premiere system of higher education?

Purpose and Focus

In recent years, several books concerned about this shift away from the public good have been published (for example, see Bok, 2003, and Kennedy, 1997). These books call attention to the emerging problem and try to make leaders aware of the consequences of recent choices. We wholeheartedly agree with these perspectives. Yet we approach this problem from a different angle.

In this book, we explore ways that higher education leaders can examine and build the role their institutions play in the larger public good. This book draws on the experiences of individuals and groups from all over the country that have been engaged in connecting the work of higher education with the social and civic needs of society. The goal then is to examine how we can build from existing approaches to serving the public good and reconstruct what has been eroded in recent years. This book describes ways that higher education contributes to the public good as well as ways that leaders can enhance their contribution through new policies and practices. In addition to institutional commitments, it also examines ways that the public, institutions, government, foundations, and individuals can be partners with higher education for the public good. These various levels and voices, we believe, constitute a movement that is likely to change higher education and society. In this book, we hope to capture the voices of the emerging movement as well as fuel the movement. Like any movement, backlashes occur, enthusiasm can be lost, or energies redirected and the movement can disintegrate.

In summary, our aim is to provide needed guidance and advice for how individuals and groups throughout the system of higher education can contribute to the public good. How can we move forward, who might be partners, and how can you get involved? We also hope the book is inspiring and creates enthusiasm for those who aspire to promote the civic and social values and commitments of their institutions.

Yet some may be cynical, wondering whether such a commitment is feasible in the current time of financial constraints and individualism, where individual benefits are seen as more important than contributions to the broader society. However, in this time of declining resources, government agencies, state legislatures, and foundations are looking for ways to cut costs and prioritize spending. One of the major criteria used by these organizations is the way that and degree to which institutions contribute to the public good. Commitment to social purposes has been rewarded in the past, and we believe that public dialogue and leadership can ensure that these efforts continue to be rewarded. Others may believe that we are merely in a time in which the overall public good is served by focusing on individualism or that higher education's contribution to the public good has not been eroded at all. We invite you to read the book and to reexamine your beliefs and assumptions. We also invite you into the dialogue and to help us reconsider our beliefs. The goal is to ensure that the public good is served, and open dialogue and exchange of views is critical to ensure this goal.

With these issues in mind, the three main purposes of the book are to

1. Give voice to an emerging movement in higher education related to the public good
2. Help educational and governmental leaders engage in a dialogue about the public good
3. Provide institutions with strategies to craft organizational cultures and environments that contribute to the public good

Although there has been an erosion of the traditional commitment to a social charter between higher education and society, there are many individuals and groups committed to civic engagement, community outreach and development, the leadership role of higher education in social policy, and the access and distribution of knowledge. In the chapters that follow, the voices of those committed to serving the public good are from every institutional sector—liberal arts colleges, universities, urban institutions, community colleges—and across every group from state officials to trustees to faculty to students.

Dialogue is an important place to begin, since a major reason that the social charter has been altered is that few people have come together to discuss the changes they see on their campuses. First, dialogues need to begin with an understanding of the problem at hand, which is why Part One is devoted to exploring the concept of the public good and social charter. Second, a dialogue is needed to understand what the public expects of higher education and for leaders in higher education to talk about opportunities for serving the public good. Lastly, dialogue can also help develop strategies and approaches for better serving the public good. The book is filled with ideas and questions for conducting such dialogues in your local community, state, or region.

In addition to providing guidance on how to structure meaningful dialogues, the book provides a host of ideas about ways to foster the public good. Some chapters focus on promising strategies such as service-learning, new approaches to training doctoral students, or civic education. Others address barriers to serving the public good such as faculty roles and rewards and institutional stereotypes. Others focus on reconceptualizing higher education with new modes of knowledge production or alternative views of liberal arts education. Since higher education is a decentralized system, efforts to enhance the public good must be instituted across various levels within and outside of higher education. The book is organized around many levels—individuals, institutions, disciplinary societies, national associations, and governmental and public entities. Each of these levels is critical in the partnership for creating higher education for the public good.

The book draws on existing literature about higher education's historic and current role related to the public good. The chapters draw on the expertise of leaders in the field who have created strategies, programs, and efforts to foster the public role of higher education. Many of these experts participated in a year-long national dialogue hosted by the National Forum on Higher Education for the Public Good (formerly the Kellogg Forum on Higher Education for the Public Good).

Audience

There are many different audiences for the book. First, legislators and policymakers will find this book useful for developing state and federal initiatives. Part Two focuses on how the policy sector can work to encourage a greater commitment to the public good. Second, presidents and boards who are responsible to external constituents can use this book to guide their decision making. There are two chapters devoted to the important role that board members play since they are entrusted with ensuring that institutions meet their missions. Boards help steer institutional direction and can be pivotal in realigning higher education with its historical commitment to the public good. Presidential leadership is also necessary for engaging campuses in a new direction or reinstating a commitment. Two presidents share their stories of creating campuses engaged in conducting work for the public good. Third, administrators, faculty, students, and individual change agents can use the book in order to help create change in their own domains. Part Five focuses on the role of individuals in creating campuses committed to the public good. There is a particularly strong opportunity to include faculty in this movement since there will be a 50 percent turnover of faculty by the year 2010, and new faculty appear to be more interested in service-learning and community outreach than their predecessors. Each chapter addresses various change agents throughout the system and the role they can play to redirect campuses.

There is practical advice across chapters for these specific campus groups. For example, administrators will learn how to develop campuswide steering committees to provide direction for efforts to create a larger role for their institution in the public good. Lastly, national and professional associations will be interested in this book as it focuses on a topic that is part of their national dialogues and for which they are seeking knowledge and resources. The public good is a critical question and concern in the liberal arts sector.

Concerns related to the public good have been part of the agendas of the American Council on Education, the National Association of State and Land Grant Colleges and Universities, and the American Association of Higher Education, to name a few.

Organization

As noted earlier, enhancing higher education's role in the public good will require the efforts of individuals throughout the system. The book is organized by the key entities: public policymakers (Part Two); national associations, disciplinary societies, and institutional sectors (Part Three); institutional governance and leadership (Part Four); and individual leadership (Part Five).

Part One sets the stage for the volume. It explains the key concepts, such as the public good and social charter. It places the discussion of the charter and public good in an historical and current context. In Chapter One, Tony Chambers defines and describes the significance of the social charter between higher education and society through a reflection on the work of the National Forum on Higher Education for the Public Good. In Chapter Two, Adrianna Kezar describes the current challenges to the traditional social and public charter and some of the aspects that have been eroded or lost within institutions and the system of higher education. In Chapter Three, Kezar reviews three movements—civic education, public service, and partnerships and collaboration—that have emerged that provide countervailing forces to the industrial model of higher education. These movements are elaborated on in the rest of the book. The main thesis of this chapter is that these divergent movements can become more powerful if they work in concert, and this book is an attempt to bring these voices together and to create a "meta movement."

Part Two focuses on public policy, as change in the charter will require work at the broadest level among legislators and trustees—those entrusted with the relationship between higher education and society. This section focuses on the policy transformation and strategies to achieve these alterations. In Chapter Four, David Longanecker describes three public policy directions: conjoining public with private interests, courting private gain, and privatization of higher education and its impact. He argues that public policy is likely to ignore the negative effects in the short term but sees hope in the long term. In Chapter Five, David Mathews focuses on a critical aspect of re-orienting higher education for the public good—carefully listening to local, regional, and national publics. This chapter describes approaches, such as forums, that have been used to foster communication related to public needs. In Chapter Six, Richard Novak and Susan Whealler Johnston present the role trustees play in maintaining a healthy and functioning relationship between higher education and society. They review a host of strategies for bridging the campus and community, monitoring the assessment of student learning, approving faculty policies that support civic engagement, and aligning the budget with service priorities. In Chapter Seven, Denise O'Neil Green and William Trent focus on how the new social charter that evolves through dialogue among state and institutional policymakers must include an understanding of the changed context—a diverse democracy. A new narrative about the public good must wrestle with and be inclusive of racial diversity. This chapter also examines the contemporary efforts made to articulate the importance of a diverse democracy for the public good and discusses the critical obligation that higher education institutions have to facilitate the public's awareness and understanding of our increasingly diverse society.

Part Three focuses on cross-sector issues that are often vexing to address because they are diffused across the system of higher education. These issues—knowledge production, the role of disciplines, and undergraduate education—are fundamental to the enterprise and are often overlooked and prevent change from occurring. For example, in Chapter Eight, Carol Geary Schneider looks at how the traditional notion of the liberal arts education needs to be redefined in order to support community engagement and civic education. The view of higher education as an ivory tower focused on abstract reflection has led the public to wonder about higher education's commitment to the public good. Schneider demonstrates how a redefined liberal arts education is consistent with and reinforces outreach and engagement. In Chapter Nine, Edward Zlotkowski examines how the disciplines—often considered barriers to change—can support efforts to embrace a new vision of the public good. He uses the example of the American Association of Higher Education's project

of working with the disciplines to institutionalize service-learning
nationally. In Chapter Ten, Judith Ramaley focuses on knowledge
production as a potential barrier to a social public charter. The academy has traditionally considered pure research to be superior to applied research, which prevents many faculty and institutions from
becoming engaged with the public good. She advocates the use of a
new model of knowledge production based on the book *Pasteur's
Quadrant* in which pure and applied research is blended and are no
longer seen as separate processes.

Part Four focuses on institutionwide leadership and governance. Most of the work in recreating the charter will occur at the
institutional level. Institutions need to work with legislators, trustees,
and communities, but most importantly leaders must work to transform the fabric of their own institutions. This section explores a
host of strategies for creating needed transformation. Chapter
Eleven focuses on the efforts of the University of Pennsylvania to
integrate service-learning in meaningful and deep ways into the institution. Lee Benson, Ira Harkavy, and Matthew Hartley review four
main strategies for institutionalizing a commitment to the public
good: refocusing undergraduate education, shaming and cognitive
dissonance, acting locally, and focusing on significant community-
based real-world problems. In Chapter Twelve, Kelly Ward explores
one of the main barriers to faculty conducting work for social and
public purposes. She notes how faculty are usually not rewarded for
institutional and local service in the community or innovative teaching and community-based research and community service-learning.
She notes that these are key ways faculty can serve the public good,
but which have been thwarted by current reward systems. Thus,
this chapter explores a new paradigm for rewards that serve the public good. In Chapter Thirteen, Barbara Holland describes a significant issue for institutional leaders: being blinded by institutional
stereotypes. Outreach, service, economic development, civic engagement, and other practices have a long history in land-grant
colleges, community colleges, and urban institutions. Because
these institutions are often considered less prestigious, the lessons
they have to offer for serving the public good are often overlooked.
She encourages research universities and liberal arts colleges to
consider the lessons these institutions have to offer. Additionally,

she describes some differences by sector in institutionalizing a new vision for the public good.

Part Five focuses on individual leadership that will help recreate the charter and create a more public mission. This section provides suggestions for individual change agents on ways to foster the leadership within institutions. In Chapter Fourteen, James Votruba describes his twenty-five years of experience leading institutions for the public good. Two qualities that he has found to be the most critical are: leaders need to be very clear about the outcomes that they want to produce and every element of the organization needs to be aligned to support those outcomes. In Chapter Fifteen, Ann Austin and Benita Barnes describe some of the barriers to faculty engagement in the public good, building on the work by Ward and Zlotkowski in previous chapters. They note that faculty finish graduate school with limited or no knowledge of the social purposes of higher education, and they receive mixed messages about what is valued and rewarded. Yet the new faculty are highly committed to doing work that is meaningful and will make a difference in the world. The authors offer a set of institutional strategies for doctoral preparation and orientation: articulating the core purposes of higher education and explaining what the public good means, explaining differences in institutional types, and teaching teamwork and collaboration skills. They provide specific examples of campus programs aimed at developing new skills in doctoral training and for orienting new faculty. In Chapter Sixteen, Stephen John Quaye reflects from a student perspective on what it means to contribute to the public good and the role students can and should play in fulfilling that aim. He uses his personal experience as a graduate student to provide a rationale for the importance of including students' voices in the dialogue on the public good. In Chapter Seventeen, Martha Gilliland offers advice from her career as chancellor of the University of Missouri-Kansas City and describes the role of vision, inspiration, values, and careful planning in creating campuses that serve the public good.

Part Six provides concluding comments and inspiration to individuals and informed networks involved in creating higher education environments that serve the public good.

We want to thank you for your continued commitment to higher education's role in serving the public good. We also want to thank each of the authors for sharing their wisdom and experience. We hope the lessons shared will contribute to your efforts to advance higher education's civic role in the United States and beyond.

Acknowledgments

We thank the National Forum participants for their ideas, passion, and commitment and continued work toward the public good. We also thank Stephen John Quaye for his editorial support on this project.

There are also some special people to whom we want to dedicate this book: Paul Viskovich, for your love and support; Lisa Chambers and our guys, Tony Jr., Kody, and Max for your love, energy, and infectious happiness; and Janis Burkhardt, a wife, friend, and partner who nurtures the best in everything around her.

And for our many students and colleagues, whose talents and commitment have already given hope to this work. If there is to be a movement to make higher education all it can be, it will be their movement and their creativity and faith that will sustain it.

References
Bok, D. (2003). *Universities in the marketplace.* Princeton, NJ: Princeton University Press.

Kennedy, D. (1997). *Academic duty.* Cambridge, MA: Harvard University Press.

About the Authors

Ann Austin is a professor in the Higher, Adult, and Lifelong Education (HALE) Program at Michigan State University. Her research and teaching are focused on faculty careers, roles, and professional development; reform in graduate education; the improvement of teaching and learning; and organizational change and transformation in higher education. With her colleagues, Jody Nyquist, Jo Sprague, and Don Wulff, she co-directed a longitudinal study of graduate students' development, sponsored by the Pew Charitable Trusts and the Spencer Foundation. Currently, she is co-principal investigator of the Center for the Integration of Research, Teaching, and Learning (CIRTL), a five-year National Science Foundation-funded project focused on improving teaching and learning in higher education in science, technology, engineering, and mathematics. Austin holds degrees from Bates College (B.A., history), Syracuse University (M.S., higher and postsecondary education), and the University of Michigan (M.A., American culture; Ph.D., higher education). She is the author or co-author of a number of articles on higher education and several books, including *Paths to the Professoriate: Strategies for Enriching the Preparation of Future Faculty* (co-edited with D. H. Wulff, Jossey-Bass, 2004). She has been a Fulbright Fellow in South Africa, and served as the 2000–2001 president of the Association for the Study of Higher Education (ASHE).

Benita J. Barnes is a doctoral candidate in the Higher, Adult, and Lifelong Education (HALE) program at Michigan State University. Her dissertation research examines how exemplary doctoral advisors understand and fulfill their advising role. Other research projects include further analysis of the 2000 National Doctoral Program Survey data. Barnes holds a bachelor's degree in psychology and master's degrees in adult and continuing education and measurement and quantitative methods—all from Michigan State. Currently, she is serving a second term as vice president for graduate welfare for Michigan State's Council of Graduate Students (COGS), and she is also currently serving as the executive coordinator, president, and CEO for the National Association of Graduate-Professional Students (NAGPS).

Lee Benson earned degrees at Brooklyn College, Columbia University, and Cornell University. He is Professor Emeritus of History and a Distinguished Fellow of the Center for Community Partnerships at the University of Pennsylvania. He collaborates there with Ira Harkavy on action-oriented research and teaching designed to exemplify their conviction that the primary mission of American universities is to practically help realize an optimally democratic society and world. He is co-executive editor of *Universities and Community Schools* and is the author or co-author of six books and dozens of articles. He has most recently completed (with Ira Harkavy and John Puckett) a book-length manuscript, *Progressing Beyond John Dewey: Practical Means to Realize Dewey's Utopian Ends.*

John C. Burkhardt is professor of higher and postsecondary education at the University of Michigan, and director of the National Forum on Higher Education for the Public Good, a partnership of institutions, scholars, and policymakers committed to making higher education more responsive to the needs of a changing society. He joined the University of Michigan faculty in September of 2000, after serving for eight years as a program director at the W. K. Kellogg Foundation, where he coordinated Foundation leadership grant-making and funded projects in education and leadership development around the world.

Tony C. Chambers is a senior fellow at the National Forum on Higher Education for the Public Good and faculty in the Program on American Cultures at the University of Michigan. He served as an administrator and faculty member at Michigan State University, University of Iowa, University of Missouri-St. Louis, University of Florida, and Illinois State University. He was also a program officer at the John Fetzer Institute. Chambers is a Woodrow Wilson Visiting Fellow, a senior fellow at the James MacGregor Burns Academy of Leadership at the University of Maryland-College Park, and a fellow with the Salzburg Seminars (Austria). He received the Kellogg National Fellowship from 1993 to 1996. He was inducted into the Illinois State University College of Education Alumni Hall of Fame. Chambers serves on the national advisory committee for the AASCU

American Democracy Project, and the Board of Trustees for the California Institute of Integral Studies. He received bachelor's and master's degrees from Illinois State University, and a doctorate from the University of Florida.

Martha W. Gilliland, chancellor of the University of Missouri-Kansas City, holds a doctorate in environmental engineering and systems ecology from the University of Florida, a master of science degree in geophysics from Rice University, and a bachelor of science degree in geology and mathematics from Catawba College. At UMKC, Gilliland has established a progressive and ambitious agenda for the urban campus of thirteen thousand students since April 2000 when she took office. Working in a highly collaborative process with the university community and the surrounding Kansas City community, Gilliland has outlined a five-year blueprint to transform UMKC into a twenty-first-century institution poised to realize the following goals by 2006: to be a national leader in scholarship and creative activity; to attract, nurture, and develop responsible community leaders; to be an essential community partner and resource; to be a workplace of choice; and to have the resources to fuel the university's vision. Gilliland, a leader in science and technology and cutting-edge business and leadership practices, is the author of numerous academic and popular journal articles. She authored the book *Energy Analysis: A New Public Policy Tool,* and is a coauthor on numerous other books. She is featured in the 2002 book *A Power of Her Own: Profiles of Kansas City Women of Power and Achievement.*

Denise O'Neil Green received her Ph.D. in public policy and postsecondary education from the University of Michigan, Ann Arbor. She is currently an assistant professor of higher education in the Department of Educational Organization and Leadership at the University of Illinois at Urbana-Champaign. To assist educational leaders in handling divisive issues, her research interests and publications focus on affirmative action, institutional engagement, campus diversity, and higher education policy and governance. In particular, her work on institutional engagement and affirmative action revealed salient dimensions (that is, activist leadership, mobilization strategies, and message development) that are important to higher education's successful engagement in the policy arena, as educational leaders promote the importance of diversity, democracy, and the public good. Green also serves as a research associate for several grant-funded projects that address access and campus climate issues, and has many years of experience in developing, directing, and evaluating undergraduate intervention programs for minority student populations. A native of Chicago, Illinois, she received her B.A. from the University of Chicago and her master's of public affairs from Princeton University. Green teaches graduate-level courses on various subjects, including college student development, diversity, policy, and qualitative research methods.

Ira Harkavy is associate vice president and director of the Center for Community Partnerships at the University of Pennsylvania. An historian, Harkavy teaches in the departments of history, urban studies, Africana studies, and city and regional planning. The West Philadelphia Improvement Corps (WEPIC), a twenty-year partnership to create university-assisted community schools that connect the University of Pennsylvania and the West Philadelphia community, emerged and developed from seminars and research projects he helps direct with other colleagues at Penn. With Lee Benson, Harkavy serves as co-executive editor of *Universities and Community Schools*. Under his directorship, the Center for Community Partnerships received the inaugural William T. Grant Foundation Youth Development Prize sponsored in collaboration with the National Academy of Sciences' Board on Children, Youth, and Families and a Best Practices/Outstanding Achievement Award from HUD's Office of Policy Development and Research.

Matthew Hartley is an assistant professor of education at the University of Pennsylvania. He earned an Ed.D. from Harvard University's graduate school of education in 2001. Prior to coming to Penn, he was an instructor for Hobart and William Smith Colleges as well as a teaching fellow and research assistant at Harvard University. He also served as co-chair of the editorial board for the *Harvard Educational Review*. Hartley's research and writing focus on organizational change at colleges and universities. He is currently involved in research examining how colleges and universities create and sustain civic engagement efforts.

Barbara A. Holland is the director of the National Service-Learning Clearinghouse, which is funded by the Learn and Serve America program of the Corporation for National and Community Service. She also holds appointments as a senior scholar in the Center for Service and Learning at Indiana University-Purdue University Indianapolis, and as adjunct professor at the University of Western Sydney and Australian Catholic University. Her research focuses on organizational change in higher education with special emphasis on the institutionalization and assessment of civic engagement programs, service-learning, and community-university partnerships. She also serves as executive editor of *Metropolitan Universities*, the journal of the Coalition of Urban and Metropolitan Universities. Her bachelor's and master's degrees were earned at the University of Missouri-Columbia School of Journalism, and she holds a Ph.D. in higher education policy from the University of Maryland-College Park.

Susan Whealler Johnston is vice president for independent sector programs at the Association of Governing Boards of Universities and Colleges, where she develops educational programs and services for trustees and institutional leaders of independent institutions. Prior to holding this position, she was professor of English and dean of academic development at Rockford College, where she also helped develop the college's service-learning program. Johnston's publications and presentations are in the areas of leadership, governance, and eighteenth-century literature. She holds a B.A. in English from Rollins College and an M.A. and Ph.D. in English from Purdue University. She has served on the boards of local social service agencies and currently is on the board of directors of the Association for Consortium Leadership and the board of trustees of Rockford College, alma mater of Jane Addams.

Adrianna J. Kezar is associate professor at the University of Southern California. She was formerly an assistant professor at the University of Maryland, editor for the ASHE-ERIC Higher Education Report Series, faculty director for the National Association for Women in Higher Education's (NAWE) Institute for Emerging Women Leaders in Higher Education, and director of the ERIC Clearinghouse on Higher Education. She holds a Ph.D. and M.A. in higher education administration from the University of Michigan and B.A. from the University of California, Los Angeles. Her scholarship focuses on higher education change and innovation, leadership, diversity issues, governance, and organizational theory. She is published in several journals, including *The Journal of Higher Education, The Review of Higher Education, Journal of College Student Development, NASPA Journal, Research in Higher Education, Innovative Higher Education, Community College Review, New Directions in Higher Education, New Directions in Institutional*

Research, and *About Campus.* Her most recent books include *Understanding and Facilitating Change in the 21st Century: Recent Research and Conceptualizations* (Jossey-Bass, 2001), and *Taking the Reins: Institutional Transformation in Higher Education* with Peter Eckel (Greenwood Press, 2003). Kezar has had six books and monographs published in the last five years. She is a senior fellow with the MacGregor Burns Leadership Academy and has been a fellow with the Salzburg Seminars. Her research has been used to guide the development of a national leadership institute for women administrators in higher education and a research center at the George Washington University related to educational leadership and change.

David Longanecker became executive director of the Western Interstate Commission for Higher Education (WICHE) in July 1999, working with WICHE's fifteen member states collaboratively to expand access to excellent higher education for all citizens of the West. Longanecker serves or has served on numerous national, state, and institutional commissions and boards, and has written extensively on a broad range of higher education issues. His primary interests are educational access and opportunity, higher education finance, preparing future teachers and faculty, the efficient and effective use of educational technologies, and international collaboration in higher education. Prior to joining WICHE, Longanecker served for six years as the assistant secretary for postsecondary education at the U.S. Department of Education, where he was responsible for developing, implementing, and managing national policy and programs providing more than $40 billion annually in student aid and $1 billion to institutions. Included within his purview were the federal Title III Developing Institutions program, TRIO programs, international education programs, the Fund for the Improvement of Postsecondary Education (FIPSE), and the new GEAR-UP and teacher education initiatives. Prior to that he was the state higher education executive officer (SHEEO) in Colorado and Minnesota. He began his public policy career as the principal analyst for higher education for the Congressional Budget Office. Longanecker holds a doctorate of education in administration and policy analysis from Stanford University, an M.A. in student personnel work from the George Washington University, and a B.A. in sociology from Washington State University.

David Mathews is president of the Charles F. Kettering Foundation. He served as secretary of Health, Education, and Welfare in the Ford administration. Between 1969 and 1980, he was president of the University of Alabama. At Kettering, he has steered the foundation's research toward studying the role of the public in our political system. He has authored numerous articles and several books on such subjects as southern history, public education, public policy, and international problem solving.

Richard Novak is vice president of public sector programs, with primary responsibility to direct the Center for Public Higher Education Trusteeship and Governance at the Washington, DC–based Association of Governing Boards of Universities and Colleges (AGB). The center's mission is to strengthen the relationship between public academic institutions and state governments by enhancing the performance and capacity of public governing boards. Funded by several major foundations, the center is staffed by three full-time professionals, a senior fellow, and two administrative assistants. Novak has written and consulted frequently on higher education policy and governance. He is also on the editorial board of the *Journal of Higher Education Outreach and Engagement.* Prior to joining AGB, he served for thirteen years on the staff of the American Association of State Colleges and Universities.

Stephen John Quaye is a research assistant in the Center for Higher Education Policy Analysis and a doctoral student studying urban educational policy at the University of Southern California. Quaye holds a B.S. in Psychology from James Madison University and an M.S. in College Student Personnel from Miami University of Ohio. His research interests include student activism, access and equity in higher education, critical theory and postmodernism, and the experiences of students of color on college and university campuses.

Judith A. Ramaley is assistant director, Education and Human Resources Directorate (EHR), the National Science Foundation (NSF). She is also Presidential Professor of Biomedical Sciences and fellow of the Margaret Chase Smith Center for Public Policy at the University of Maine. Prior to joining NSF, Ramaley was president of the University of Vermont (UVM) and professor of biology from 1997 to 2001. Before coming to UVM, she was president and professor of biology for seven years at Portland State University in Portland, Oregon. Ramaley has a special interest in higher education reform and has played a significant role in designing regional alliances to promote educational cooperation. She also has contributed to a national exploration of the changing nature of work and the workforce and of the role of higher education in the school-to-work agenda. She has played a national role in the exploration of civic responsibility and partnerships between higher education and society.

Carol Geary Schneider has been president of the Association of American Colleges and Universities since 1998. With a membership of about a thousand colleges and universities, AAC&U is the leading national association devoted to advancing and strengthening undergraduate liberal education. Since becoming president of AAC&U, Schneider has launched *Greater Expectations: The Commitment to Quality as a Nation Goes to College,* a multiyear initiative designed to articulate the aims of a twenty-first-century liberal education and identify comprehensive, innovative models that improve learning for all undergraduate students. Through *Greater Expectations,* AAC&U is championing civic engagement, both in a diverse democracy and in the global community, as an integral goal of liberal education for all students, whatever their background or choice of academic field.

William T. Trent received his doctorate in sociology at the University of North Carolina, Chapel Hill, and is professor of educational policy studies and sociology at the University of Illinois at Urbana-Champaign. He was a Fulbright senior scholar for 2003–2004 and was a visiting scholar at the College Board for 2003–2004. Trent's research centers on K–12 and postsecondary educational inequality. He is co-chair of the AERA-IES Postdoctoral Fellows Committee and also serves as a member of the Research Advisory Committee for the GATES Millennium Scholarship research program and a member of the Social Science Research Council's Postsecondary Transitions Project. He is currently principal investigator for a three-year, IES-funded project examining pathways to careers in the academy for students of color.

James C. Votruba became president of Northern Kentucky University, a fourteen thousand-student metropolitan campus located in the Northern Kentucky/Greater Cincinnati area, in August 1997. During his leadership, the university has achieved national recognition for its regional partnerships and public engagement. Votruba came to NKU from Michigan State University, where he was vice provost for university outreach and professor of higher education from 1989 to 1997. Prior to his tenure at MSU, he was dean of the College of Education and Human Development (1983–1989) at Binghamton University. He previously held faculty and administrative positions at the University of Illinois at Urbana-Champaign and Drake University. Votruba earned his B.A. in political science, M.A. in political science and sociology, and Ph.D. in higher education administration from Michigan State University. He is a frequent lecturer, author, and consultant in the areas of higher education leadership, strategic planning, and public engagement. Since 1995, he has been a faculty member in Harvard University's Institutes for Higher Education. In 2002, he chaired the American Association of State Colleges and Universities' Task Force on Public Engagement. He is also a faculty member in the AASCU New President's Academy.

Kelly Ward is an associate professor of higher education at Washington State University. Her research is focused generally on faculty life. She studies work and family concerns for new faculty, as well as related work-life policy environments, faculty involvement in service-learning, institutional service missions, and the development of a service ethic among faculty. Ward has held faculty positions at Oklahoma State University and the University of Montana. Her ideas about service and the public good are directly related to her administrative work with Montana Campus Compact and the office of Volunteer Action Services at the University of Montana. She is author of the monograph *Faculty Service Roles and the Scholarship of Engagement* (Jossey-Bass, 2002).

Edward Zlotkowski is a professor of English at Bentley College and the senior faculty fellow at Campus Compact. From 1995 to 2004, he served as general editor of the American Association for Higher Education's twenty-volume series exploring the relationship between service-learning and academic disciplines or disciplinary areas. He has also designed and facilitated professional development opportunities in service-learning for provosts and deans as well as a series of summer institutes for engaged academic departments. He has written and spoken extensively on a range of service-learning topics and regularly uses service-learning in his own teaching. In 2002, he edited *Service-Learning and the First-Year Experience: Preparing Students for Personal Success and Civic Responsibility*, and in 2004 served as lead author of *The Community's College: Indicators of Engagement at Two-Year Institutions*.

Higher Education
for the Public Good

Part One

Exploring the Public Good

Chapter One

The Special Role of Higher Education in Society

As a Public Good for the Public Good

Tony C. Chambers

> *Higher education has long occupied a special place in society. Viewed as the creator of knowledge, the producer of leaders, and the engine of the economy, higher education's role has been considered critical to society's well being. Equally if not more important, higher education has been seen as the intellectual conscience of society, above the marketplace throng. In return, higher education has received public support, been exempted from taxation, and often screened from the scrutiny of the public eye. Much of that has now changed. (Newman & Couturier, 2002, p. 6)*

The contributors to this book, along with many others, believe that we are giving voice to a movement that will challenge and reshape the relationship between our colleges and universities and the society of which they are a part. Collectively, even though we are giving voice to the movement, we alone do not constitute the movement. There are many others, including community partners, scholars and practitioners outside of the higher education sector, and students, who are central to the movement. Some of us who are a part of the movement differ on whether there is a movement or what kind of movement it is. However, we do share a common conviction that higher education is important to the future of our nation—indeed, our world. Many believe that higher education is more than a vehicle for providing economic opportunity for individuals and that without a determined effort higher education may soon forfeit its ability to be a major force in shaping the future of our world.

In this chapter, my main intention is to lay out a case for a movement that advances the notion of higher education as a "public good." In the following pages, I will discuss the significance of, what I believe to be, a movement that strengthens the public relationship between the system of higher education and American society. Within the broader discussion of the movement's significance, I will talk about the social benefits of higher education beyond those that are primarily individual and economic. In addition, I will briefly explore some of the antecedent events that contributed to this movement and conclude with a discussion about the work of the National Forum on Higher Education for the Public Good (formerly the Kellogg Forum) as one toehold from which the movement can advance.

Significance of a Social Movement to Strengthen the Public Relationship Between Higher Education and American Society

Before discussing the relationship between higher education and society, I will first explain what I mean by the key terms *movement, covenant,* and *charter.* These contentious terms are not easily defined yet are often used to express our sense of what is and what should happen in regard to higher education's relationship with society.

Are We Experiencing a Social Movement?

> *Social movements can be viewed as collective enterprises to establish a new order of life. They have their inception in the condition of unrest, and derive their motive power on one hand from dissatisfaction with the current form of life, and on the other hand, from wishes and hopes for a new scheme or system of living. (Blumer, 1939, p. 199)*

> *A social movement is a collective acting with some continuity to promote or resist a change in the society or organization of which it is a part. As a collectivity, a movement is a group with indefinite and shifting membership and with leadership whose position is determined more by informal response of*

the members than by formal procedures for legitimating
authority. (Turner & Killian, 1987, p. 223)

There is an entire discipline and science built around the study of social movements. Based, at least, on the assertions of Blumer (1939) and Turner and Killian (1987), the range of definitions of a social movement depends on who is considered a part of the movement, what the social circumstances are surrounding the movement, and what the goals of the movement are. For purposes of this chapter, I resonate with the work of Mario Diani (1992), the Italian sociologist from Scotland, who was introduced to me by Elizabeth Hollander, the executive director of Campus Compact (Hollander & Hartley, 2000). According to Diani, social movements consist of informed networks of actors (organizations, groups, and individuals) engaged in conflict for the control of material or symbolic stakes, on the basis of shared identities (Diani, 1992, 2000). The common characteristics that distinguish a social movement are that (1) they arise to address societal problems, (2) members are bound by a "shared set of beliefs and a sense of belongingness," and (3) they consist of "networks of informal interaction" (Diani, 1992, p. 7). My sense of what currently exists and what continues to emerge among higher education institutions, communities, and other social institutions is a movement that shares the elements articulated by Diani. Hollander and Hartley (2000, 2003) and Kezar in Chapter Three provide detailed reviews of literature and practices that support the position of an existing movement to strengthen higher education's civic role in society. It is not my intention in this brief chapter to attempt the same level of detail. For a more thorough review of social and public movements that focus on reinvigorating the public relationship between higher education and American society, see Hollander and Hartley (2000, 2003), as well as the Web site for Campus Compact at www.compact.org.

My experience through the work of the National Forum on Higher Education for the Public Good suggests that there is a substantial, and growing, network of informed individuals and groups that are coalescing around a common sense of what a democratic society should look like; what citizens of that society should know, understand, and be involved in; what common purposes all social institutions in democratic societies should share; and what policies, practices, and social values support democracy. Since the events of

September 11, 2001, a host of unimaginable social and global challenges have stimulated the formation of interacting networks within and outside of national borders to think about and act more systemically on problems that once might have been considered the province of a single nation, institution, or individual. In a sense, the movement to connect informed networks with common interests and shared identities to address social problems has expanded beyond definable boundaries to what some might consider a new social movement (Melucci, 1994; Offe, 1985; Calhoun, 1993; Diani, 2000). Higher education's place as a major player among these informed networks is vital. The challenge for higher education, as it has been throughout its history, is to maintain the core values of its mission while pursuing its mission differently within a rapidly changing social and global context. Another challenge for higher education in the new social and global context is to continue to shape its own boundaries to allow for partnerships across and between different types of institutions to address public issues. A focus inward at its own practices, values, and social relevance and outward at its social impact, networking flexibility, and collaboratively-inspired innovations will be required of higher education as a network in the movement to strengthen higher education's covenant with society.

Why the Terms *Covenant* and *Charter*?

Throughout this book, the term *charter* is used to describe the relationship between higher education and society. At the National Forum, we borrowed the term *covenant* from the Kellogg Commission on the Future of State and Land-Grant Universities (2000) to describe what we believe to best frame the relationship between higher education and society. Within this brief section on terms, and throughout this chapter, my position is that both notions, *covenant* and *charter*, though holding distinct qualities, reflect a complex relationship and set of public agreements between higher education and society.

The term *covenant* may connote religious, moral, or spiritual images. *Charter* has a corporate, transactional connotation that brings to mind legalistic and historically stable, maybe rigid, qualities. Both sets of images have a place in my use of the terms *covenant* and *charter*. *The American Heritage Dictionary of the English Language* (1982) defines *covenant* as "a binding agreement made by two or more persons or parties; a compact; contract. 2. A solemn agreement or vow made . . . to defend and support its members' faith and doctrine." The dictionary's definition of *charter* includes "a document issued by a sovereign, legislature, or other authority, creating a public or private corporation, as a city, college, or bank, and defining its privileges and purposes." I use these terms to express the moral, enduring, reciprocal, and socially articulated nature of the relationship between colleges and universities, as social institutions, and the public(s) that create and support them.

The publicly aimed, if not publicly mandated, relationship between higher education and society has both transactional (contractual) and transformational (moral and mutually developmental) qualities embedded within it. To be clear, covenants and charters require all parties to embrace particular sets of responsibility. Within the context of a relationship and public agreement between higher education and society, the Kellogg Commission (2000) laid out the responsibilities, or commitments, of higher education as those supporting:

> Educational opportunity that is genuinely equal because it provides access to success without regard to race, ethnicity, age, occupation, or economic background
>
> Excellence in undergraduate, graduate, and professional curricula
>
> Learning environments that meet the civic ends of public [and I would add, private] higher education by preparing students to lead and participate in a democratic society
>
> Complex and broad-based agendas for discovery and graduate education that are informed by the latest scholarship and responsive to pressing public needs
>
> Conscious efforts to bring the resources and expertise at our institutions to bear in community, state, national, and international problems in a coherent way
>
> Systems and data that will allow us periodically to make an open accounting of our progress toward achieving our commitment to the public good. (pp. 10–11)

The relationship between higher education and the societies of which it is a part requires a collective reshaping of the ways in which all partners in the relationship understand the needs, resources, challenges, and visions of the others. This dynamic and complex relationship also requires a collective, less competitive, approach to fostering an environment in which public policy and public support are born out of the democratic spirit toward the public good. Finally, the covenant or charter of which I speak has to move the partners away from the old language of "us" and "them". . . . away from thinking and speaking of higher education as separate from the public, and toward a consciousness and practice of higher education as part of the public, as a part of society.

Higher Education's Broader Social Benefits

Perhaps the two greatest challenges to the relationship between higher education and society are the general public's limited understanding of the benefits of higher education beyond those that are individual and economic and higher education's limited articulation of its own broad social benefits beyond those of an individual and economic nature.

This section will briefly examine this double-sided challenge. I will also offer a few words of caution about ways in which social outcomes are ascribed and interpreted. Many of the ideas in this section are expanded upon in subsequent chapters of the book.

The vast majority of Americans view higher education as important and valuable to building and sustaining the democratic life that distinguishes America around the world. Recent polls reveal high approval ratings for higher education by overwhelming majorities of Americans (Immerwahr, 2004; Selingo, 2003; National Forum on Higher Education for the Public Good, 2002). Scores of reports and scholarly publications also acknowledge higher education's central and essential role in America's future (Association of American Colleges and Universities, 2002; Barber, 1992; Brademas, 1987; Chambers & Burkhardt, 2004; Giroux, 1999; Kellogg Commission, 2000; Southern Regional Education Board, 2000; Wingspread Group on Higher Education, 1993). However, this seemingly universal public validation of American colleges and universities masks an imbalance in society's understanding of the broader public and private benefits of higher education. This imbalance in public understanding signals a more complicated and fragile dynamic regarding the values, concerns, and fears of a diverse American public (Immerwahr, 2004; Kellogg Commission, 2000; Smith, 2003).

The Kellogg Commission's (2000) observation and urging is of particular poignancy here. "The irreducible idea is that we [American higher education] exist to advance the common good. As a new millennium dawns, the fundamental challenge with which we struggle is how to reshape our historic agreement with the American people so that it fits the times that are emerging instead of the times that have passed" (p. 9). Complicating the challenge to reshape higher education's "historic agreement" with society is the reduction of public support as reflected by state financial appropriations for higher education. However, Smith's (2003) critique of the growing financial difficulties within higher education suggest that the problems are the product of a more complicated and seemingly persistent social situation. His position is that there is a fundamental "decline of the public sphere in American life" (p. 61), and "that this decline has been accompanied by a lowering of regard for the institutions that have been most significant in creating and maintaining the public sphere" (pp. 61–62). None of these institutions, he goes on to say, are more prominent than higher education. Smith further challenges institutions and systems of higher education to clearly, intentionally, and publicly place the prosperity of society over that of individual institutions: "To gain public support, we must insist on the academy's importance to a democratic society—rather than on the importance of the academy's own values, values that are increasingly seen outside universities as having been constructed by and for the advantage of academics. . . . We must make it clear that a healthy, dynamic public sphere is essential to the well-being of the nation and that public [and private] higher education is essential to the well-being of the American public sphere" (p. 62).

While higher education is rarely near the top of Americans' public policy and social issues agenda, historically, among those who have been asked about its importance, most have acknowledged that it's a "good thing and it's a worthy topic of public debate" (Lorenzen, 2002). The issue, however, has been that the public values the individual and economic benefits of higher education, with less recognition, and perhaps less concern, for the nonmonetary benefits of higher education. One of the greatest disappointments, however, has been the complicity with which higher education leaders have supported this lopsided message by repeating the mantra of lifetime earning potential of college graduates, without a balanced articulation of the broader social benefits of higher education. Howard Bowen's (1977) early analysis of the individual and public benefits of higher education in America laid out a conceptual framework for others to embrace and develop further (Behrman & Stacey, 1997; Institute for Higher Education Policy, 1998, 1999; Council of Ministers of Education in Canada, 1999; Duderstadt & Womack, 2003). Bowen and others identified four major intersecting dimensions, with related areas of impact, that frame the broad individual and social benefits of higher education—public, private, economic, and social. (See Figure 1.1.)

A word of caution is in order when attempting to attribute specific social outcomes to higher education alone and categorizing particular benefits into discrete and neat domains. Clearly, many institutions contribute to any measure of social success whether economically, educationally, civically, personally, or otherwise. I also recognize that many scholars have empirically explored the private

Figure 1.1. The Array of Higher Education Benefits.

	Public	Private
Economic	• Increased tax revenues • Greater productivity • Increased consumption • Increased workforce flexibility • Decreased reliance on government financial support	• Higher salaries and benefits • Employment • Higher savings levels • Improved working conditions • Personal / professional mobility
Social	• Reduced crime rates • Increased charitable giving / community service • Increased quality of civic life • Social cohesion / appreciation of diversity • Improved ability to adapt to and use technology	• Improved health / life expectancy • Improved quality of life for offspring • Better consumer decision making • Increased personal status • More hobbies, leisure activities

Source: The Institute for Higher Education Policy (1998). Used by permission.

and societal, nonmonetary benefits of education (Behrman & Stacey, 1997; Wolfe & Zuvekas, 1997; McMahon, 1998). However, I would nonetheless caution higher education colleagues, community partners, and policy leaders from making limited cause-and-effect judgments when aligning higher education with particular social outcomes. The danger of attributing any social outcomes to higher education alone is the potential to create division and competition among the many institutions that are interconnected in any social success. For example, is higher education primarily responsible for an educated citizenry and their civic participation? How about the role and contribution of elementary or secondary education? Churches, families, and the media? The complication regarding attribution of social outcomes is clear. Another danger with singular attribution is the potential for increased public expectation for the wrong things. The more social outcomes are attributed solely to higher education, the more the public expects higher education, alone, to deliver on those outcomes. Employment and personal income is an example in this case. While several factors contribute to employment and personal income (availability of relevant positions, competition for particular positions, adequate preparation for positions, and so on), the message linking college degrees with personal earnings and employment further fuels the public's expectations that a college degree alone guarantees employment and sufficient personal finances for life. It would be more accurate to acknowledge that a college degree is one factor contributing to issues of life quality including employment, health, security and safety, civic participation, and so on.

The other caveat is about categorizing social and individual benefits into discrete domains (that is, public, private, economic, and social). Simply put, the world does not work in discrete boxes. Like every other part of life, who receives benefits and how they receive them is multicontextual. Private benefits contribute to public benefits and vice versa. The same is true for economic and social benefits. Private economic and social benefits often translate into public economic and social benefits. The confluence of factors influencing outcomes toward the public good is many and is shifting regularly. In addition, many of these factors remain unknown, thus defying categorization. The caveats about categorizing benefits and attributing social outcomes to higher education alone are not intended to discourage action on the part of those of us in higher education, and elsewhere, who seek ways to improve society in the broadest ways possible. Although collaborative networking is demanded in this new social movement, higher education, like the other partners, has a unique role and set of contributions. William Bowen's (1999) position on higher education's social role is clear:

> Higher education plays a unique role in our society. The obligation of a university is to the society at large over the long run, and, even more generally, to the pursuit of learning. Although this may seem amorphous, there is no escaping a university's obligation to try to serve the long-term interests of society defined in the broadest and least parochial terms, and to do so through two principle activities. Those activities are: advancing knowledge and educating students who in turn will serve others, within this nation and beyond it, both through their specific vocations and as citizens. Universities therefore are responsible for imparting civic and democratic values that are essential to the functioning of our nation. (p. 1)

Generally, the American public believes that higher education is a positive force in society. The challenge, however, is to frame the scope of higher education's social impact in broader terms and to do this in collaboration with other institutions and individuals in society. A parallel challenge is for higher education institutions to act in accordance with their missions to serve society through their unique set of resources and relationships. The consequences of limiting the story told about the social benefits of higher education are real and can lead to significant retrenchments in public support, resulting in financial, political, educational, and civic losses for higher education and society.

Critical Points in the Evolution of the Movement

Historically, higher education has partnered with public and private entities to address many of the pressing issues in America and around the world. Often these partnerships have experienced considerable tension over who determines the particular issues to address and how those issues are ultimately addressed. It is safe and appropriate to say that while the historical relationship between higher education and American society has been extremely positive, it remains, to this day, a relationship requiring ongoing negotiation and compromise. Colleges and universities have contributed to their historical pact with the public by preparing students with traditional and contemporary knowledge, skills, and sensitivities to advance national economies and civically vibrant social infrastructures; providing expanded access to a growing American population as well as significant numbers of future leaders across the globe; providing research outcomes that advance the frontiers of science, health, technology, economics, as well as the depths of human consciousness and behaviors; serving as places and resources for cultural and social development through the availability and dissemination of multiple art and literature forms; and providing financial, technical, and institutional leveraging support to communities, states, and beyond to build on their existing assets or completely reshape the economic and social base of their environments. Throughout history, many efforts by higher education have been made possible by the significant support and involvement of networks of people, institutions, and groups in society. A brief review of historical events contributing to the public relationship between higher education and society can serve as a foundation for the current movement and beyond.

Higher Education and Society: A Historical Overview

The early colonial colleges were founded out of a need to provide the fledgling European settlements with a class of learned men and professionals that would enable their new society to survive. The teachers, physicians, lawyers, ministers, and businessmen who received training in the colleges of the seventeenth and eighteenth centuries were instrumental in creating and sustaining the political, social, economic, cultural, and religious institutions and infrastructure that enabled the survival and eventual growth of the colonies.

Once the new nation was founded, its early leaders developed a framework for expansion of the country to the West. Their vision included the important public service role that education would serve in the further development of the American experiment; this was articulated quite clearly in the Northwest Ordinance of 1787, which stated "religion, morality and knowledge being necessary to good government and the happiness of mankind, schools and the means of education shall forever be encouraged." Early public colleges, such as those in Virginia, Michigan, and Indiana, were founded with the understanding that they would provide leadership for the development of a general system of education beginning with the primary grades and continuing to the university level. The nineteenth century also brought the involvement of various Protestant denominations and Catholic orders in the establishment of colleges to provide for the moral and religious development of young citizens.

The Morrill Acts of 1862 and 1890 led to the creation of land-grant colleges and universities, which focused on providing "practical" education in the agricultural and mechanical arts. As a result, universities were engaged for the first time with conducting research to improve the efficiency and productivity of farming and domestic practices, while training engineers, draftsmen, and other professionals to design and build the developing nation. During this same period, states began creating "normal schools," or colleges specifically designed for the preparation of elementary and secondary school teachers—necessary for the burgeoning public school movement that was seen as critical to the advancement of society. Urban institutions such as the University of Chicago, Columbia University, and Johns Hopkins University assumed a more active role in embracing their surroundings and working to improve the lives of local citizens. This was exemplified in the settlement house movement, in particular through the leadership of Jane Addams, whose Hull House on the near west side of Chicago became a model for grassroots urban community development and helped to form ties between the city and the university.

In the early twentieth century, a new type of public service mission was realized at the University of Wisconsin with the development of a statewide extension service. The "Wisconsin Idea" brought university professors and staff into the communities of the state to provide resources, training, and consultation for farmers, homemakers, businessmen, and local leaders. A new emphasis was brought to campus-based research, with a focus on helping to advance local interests by devoting resources toward the political, economic, and social needs of the state. The Wisconsin Experiment became the model for the development of public service extension systems by flagship universities in the Midwest and other states.

Two significant phenomena expanded the civic and social engagement role of higher education after World War II. The first was the growth of a largely federally funded research enterprise within universities. While universities had been conducting significant research for decades, the federal government—through various agencies primarily related to defense, health, and the sciences—began to direct huge amounts of money to institutions for research in the national interest. Second, major demographic changes would forever change the mission and nature of higher education. Returning soldiers entered colleges and universities in record numbers, while more women, persons of color, and nontraditional-aged individuals pursued college degrees.

The civil rights movement and social activism of the 1960s and 1970s brought new social and civic engagement responsibilities to universities. Institutions located in urban centers discovered that they could not insulate themselves from the economic decline, crime, and violence that often plagued their nearby neighborhoods, leading many colleges and universities to appoint community liaison officers and develop outreach and development programs, such as the Joint Educational Project at the University of Southern California. An increasingly diverse and empowered student population demanded curricular and program offerings that they considered more relevant to their experiences and needs and reflected a more multicultural and international perspective, leading to the establishment of ethnic and area studies and human relations programs. The omnipresence of the Cold War and conflicts and unrest in southeast Asia led many to reconsider the role and place of the United States in the world, leading to the expansion of international education and study abroad programs.

After a long period of growth in enrollment and in state and federal resources, higher education began a period of budgetary austerity and retrenchment in the late 1970s. State governments and accrediting agencies became more active in pushing for accountability in the areas of student learning outcomes and fiscal expenditures, partly as a result of public demands for higher education to be more responsive to the needs of a rapidly changing society. The lingering disillusionment with institutions engendered by political scandals and the Vietnam War and a rethinking of the hedonism and self-centeredness of the "me" generation promoted in popular culture contributed to a gradual reorienting toward issues of social welfare and community outreach.

During the 1980s two major student community action organizations were founded. The first, the Campus Outreach Opportunity League, or COOL, began in 1984 when recent college graduate Wayne Meisel visited more than seventy campuses on a walk from Maine to Washington, DC, to motivate students to get involved in their communities and counter the prevailing perception of student apathy and materialism. Based in Boston, the national not-for-profit organization assists in the development of campus infrastructure, resources, and support for effective student engagement and campus-community partnerships. Soon afterward in 1985, the presidents of Brown, Georgetown, and Stanford Universities, along with the president of the Education Commission of the States, joined together to form Campus Compact, a coalition of college and university presidents whose primary purpose is to help students develop the values and skills of citizenship through participation in public and community service. Based at Brown University in Rhode Island and with nearly eight hundred institutions in forty-eight states holding memberships, Campus Compact has since broadened its mission to include faculty, presidential, and institutional involvement in community service and civic engagement. These two organizations served as catalysts by providing the resources, infrastructure, technical assistance, and perhaps most importantly, the imprimatur to enable hundreds of colleges and universities to develop programs of varying depth and scope in student volunteerism and community and academic service-learning.

The 1990s and beyond brought additional programmatic initiatives and scholarship in service-learning and other forms of civic engagement, including federal support for Americorps and other service programs, and the involvement of the Kellogg Foundation and other philanthropic organizations in encouraging state and land-grant universities to return to their roots of public and community service. Today, an increasing emphasis is being placed on infusing the values of social and civic engagement throughout the core functions of colleges and universities. But while nearly every campus can claim to have some form of community outreach initiative or service-learning program, fewer are integrating the essence of civic engagement into the foundational elements of the institution: courses, research, and faculty work. As Caryn McTighe Musil of the Association of American Colleges and Universities notes, institutions "inadvertently model a mode of civic involvement that occurs off-stage or after hours. Such a bifurcation between the work of the classroom and the life of the college prepares students all too well for the larger societal schizophrenic predicament in which adults are to 'care about community' after 5:00 p.m. or on weekends" (Musil, 2003, p. 4).

Current and emerging social trends will continue to shape, and be shaped by, the public role of colleges and universities. Just within the past four years, America, and by extension the world, has been inexorably altered by the events on and after September 11, 2001. Wars in Iraq and Afghanistan, regular announcements of terrorist threats and acts, challenges to the civil liberties of American citizens, weakened relations and tainted perceptions of Americans abroad, creeping unemployment, disempowering state and federal financial circumstances, and increased fear of losing a safe and better future for youth, the elderly, and the environment are all part of the emerging reality in the twenty-first century. These new realities, along with expansions in technology and telecommunications, advances in genetics research and the life sciences, the growing recognition of diversity as a social asset, and new international dialogue around a growing understanding of the interdependence and fragility of our global ecosystem, create an exciting and risky confluence of dynamics that, if addressed boldly and with a spirit of innovation and cooperation, can open unforeseen opportunities for higher education and other social institutions to create new forms, principles, and practices to serve the public good.

The National Forum on Higher Education for the Public Good

The National Forum (formerly the Kellogg Forum on Higher Education for the Public Good) was established in 2000 at the University of Michigan with a grant from the W.K. Kellogg Foundation. The National Forum evolved out of deep concern for the shifting role that colleges and universities were playing in addressing important social issues and preparing their students for the civic, economic, and cultural demands of this and future generations. Also, we were concerned about the projected drift of public support and public policy away from higher education and the resulting impact the drift would have on access and success in higher education and society.

Those of us at the National Forum recognized the many important initiatives already addressing these issues from various perspectives. What we wanted to do was align the many efforts in, what we have come to call, a movement and amplify the collective voice of those of us in the movement through various initiatives, gatherings, documents, public presentations, and informed networks.

The mission of the National Forum is to "significantly increase awareness, understanding, commitment, and action relative to the public service role of higher education in the United States" (National Forum on Higher Education for the Public Good, 2004). The principle approach of the National Forum in carrying out its mission, goals, and activities is through collaboration with broad networks of individuals and organizations, within and outside of higher education. In addition, the National Forum sponsors activities within three main strategic areas: leadership dialogues, connecting research to practice, and public policy and public stewardship.

Leadership Dialogues

The Forum sponsored a series of national dialogues, in different parts of the country, on specific topics that dealt directly with higher education's role in society. The dialogue series was followed by a national summit, including all of those who participated in the dialogue series, to move the lessons learned and recommendations offered in the dialogues to the action stage. The main product of the summit was the *Common Agenda to Strengthen the Relationship Between Higher Education and Society.* The Common Agenda is a "living" document that identifies commitments of individuals to specific actions on behalf of the public good. The Common Agenda serves as a basis for a three-year Wingspread Conference Series to assess the progress of committed actions and to determine collective future directions of those in the larger movement. The Forum also sponsored dialogues among state legislators and college and university leaders around issues of partnerships to strengthen higher education's civic role.

Connecting Research to Practice

The National Forum sponsors the annual Rising Scholars Award to Advance Research on Higher Education for the Public Good. Each year, the National Forum, in partnership with the American Association for Higher Education (AAHE), the Association for Institutional Research (AIR), the American College Personnel Association (ACPA), the American Educational Research Association (AERA), and the Association for the Study of Higher Education (ASHE), selects and provides support to advanced doctoral students or early-career professionals to complete a proposed original research project that focuses on higher education's public good role. The selected scholars are also invited to the National Forum's Intergenerational Research Symposium that convenes senior researchers and rising scholars to discuss critical research issues related to the public service mission of higher education. The Intergenerational Research Symposium is sponsored in partnership with the Higher Education Research Institute at UCLA and the Center for the Study of Higher and Postsecondary Education at the University of Michigan. Students and others are also provided opportunities and resources to engage in research projects, evaluation studies, and paper presentations at national and state conferences that address issues pertaining to higher education and society.

Public Policy and Public Stewardship

The Forum has initiated a statewide effort focused on public deliberation using the approach of the National Issues Forum to involve a wide range of citizens in Michigan in community-level discussions about a series of public issues including the purposes of higher education. The initiative, *Access to Democracy,* is working with leaders in many public and private sectors in the state (education [K–16], libraries, nonprofit agencies, businesses, philanthropies, and various civic groups) to train facilitators, host the community discussions, and translate the outcomes of the discussions for public policy leaders in the state. The staff of the National Forum has partnered with two public policy firms in Michigan to provide research support for the work of the Cherry Commission on Higher Education and Economic Growth that was established by Governor Jennifer Granholm in March of 2004 with the goals of (1) doubling the number of college graduates from Michigan colleges and universities in the next ten years, and (2) more closely tying higher education to economic growth in the state of Michigan.

Hopefully these efforts will stimulate new and more advanced efforts among multiple networks to strengthen the relationship between higher education and American publics.

Summary

In this chapter, I made a case for a movement to advance the notion of higher education as a public good and set the foundation for a more detailed and focused discussion of critical issues central to the movement in the chapters that follow. In the next two chapters within this section, Adrianna Kezar will closely examine many of the evolving challenges to higher education as a public good, as well as the various "forces" that contribute to the growing movement to strengthen the relationship between American higher education and society.

References

American heritage dictionary of the English language (1982). Boston: Houghton Mifflin.

Association of American Colleges and Universities. (2002). *Greater expectations: A new vision for learning as a nation goes to college.* Washington, DC: Author.

Barber, B. (1992). *An aristocracy for everyone: The politics of education and the future of America.* New York: Ballantine Books.

Behrman, J. R., & Stacey, N. (1997). *The social benefits of education.* Ann Arbor: University of Michigan Press.

Blumer, H. (1939). Collective behavior. In R. Park (Ed.), *An outline of the principles of sociology.* New York: Barnes and Noble.

Bowen, H. (1977). *Investment in learning.* San Francisco: Jossey-Bass.

Bowen, W. G. (1999). *Postsecondary education's roles in social mobility and social justice. Transforming Postsecondary Education for the 21st Century: Briefing Papers.* Denver: Education Commission of the States.

Brademas, J. (1987). *The politics of education: Conflict and consensus on Capital Hill.* Norman: University of Oklahoma Press.

Calhoun, C. (1993). New social movements of early 19th century. *Social Science Journal, 17,* 387–427.

Chambers, T., & Burkhardt, J. (2004). *Fulfilling the promise of civic engagement.* Washington, DC: Association of Governing Boards of Universities and Colleges.

Council of Ministers of Education in Canada. (1999). *A report on public expectations of postsecondary education in Canada.* Toronto: Author

Diani, M. (1992). The concept of social movement. *The Sociological Review, 40,* 1–25.

Diani, M. (2000). Towards a network theory of new social movements. *European Journal of Social Theory, 3*(4), 387–406.

Duderstadt, J. J., & Womack, F. W. (2003). *Beyond the crossroads: The future of the public university in America.* Baltimore: The Johns Hopkins University.

Giroux, H. (1999). Schools for sale: Public education, corporate culture, and the citizen-consumer. *The Educational Forum, 63*(2), 140–149.

Hollander, E., & Hartley, M. (2000). Civic renewal in higher education: The state of the movement and the need for a national network. In T. Ehrlich (Ed.), *Civic responsibility and higher education.* Phoenix: Oryx Press.

Hollander, E., & Hartley, M. (2003). Civic renewal: A powerful framework for advancing service–learning. In B. Jacoby (Ed.), *Building partnerships for service-learning.* San Francisco: Jossey-Bass.

Immerwahr, J. (2004). *Public attitudes on higher education: A trend analysis, 1993 to 2003.* San Jose: The National Center for Public Policy and Higher Education.

Institute for Higher Education Policy (1998). *Reaping the benefits: Defining the public and private value of going to college.* Washington, DC: Author.

Institute for Higher Education Policy. (1999). *Contributing to the civic good: Assessing and accounting for the civic contributions of higher education.* Washington, DC: Author.

Kellogg Commission on the Future of State and Land-Grant Universities. (2000). *Renewing the covenant: Learning, discovery, and engagement in a new age and different world.* Washington, DC: National Association of State Universities and Land-Grant Colleges.

Lorenzen, M. (2002). Education: Public or private goods? Available at www.michaellorenzen.com.

McMahon, W. W. (1998). *Knowledge for the future: Measuring the returns to investment in education and research at the University of Illinois at Urbana-Champaign.* Urbana-Champaign: University of Illinois Office of the Vice President for Academic Affairs.

Melucci, A. (1994). A strange kind of newness: What's "new" in new social movements? (pp. 101–130). In E. Larana, H. Johnston, & J. Gusfield (Eds.), *New social movements.* Philadelphia: Temple University Press.

Musil, C. M. (2003). Educating for citizenship. *Peer Review, 5*(3), 4.

National Forum on Higher Education for the Public Good. (2002). *The role of higher education in promoting civic engagement and public discourse: A presentation of findings from four focus groups and national survey questionnaire at the national leadership dialogue series.* Ann Arbor, MI: Author.

National Forum on Higher Education for the Public Good. (2004). Mission statement. Available at http://www.thenationalforum.org/mission.shtml.

Newman, F., & Couturier, L. K. (2002). *Trading public good in the higher education market.* Report from the Observatory on Borderless Higher Education. London, UK: Observatory on Borderless Higher Education.

Offe, C. (1985). New social movements: Changing boundaries of the political. *Social Research, 52,* 817–868.

Selingo, J. (May, 2003). What Americans think about higher education *Chronicle of Higher Education, 99*(34), A10.

Smith, W. D. (Summer, 2003). Higher education, democracy, and the public sphere. *The NEA Higher Education Journal,* pp. 61–73.

Southern Regional Education Board. (2000). *Changes in changing states: Higher education and the public good.* Atlanta: Author.

Turner, R. H., & Killian, L. M. (1987). *Collective behavior.* Upper Saddle River, NJ: Prentice Hall.

Wingspread Group on Higher Education. (1993). *An American imperative: Higher expectations for higher education.* Racine, WI: Johnson Foundation.

Wolfe, B., & Zuvekas, S. (1997). Nonmarket outcomes of schooling. *International Journal of Educational Research, 27*(6), 491–501.

Chapter Two

Challenges for Higher Education in Serving the Public Good

Adrianna J. Kezar

In recent years, leaders across the country such as Donald Kennedy (1997), Derek Bok (2003), and Clark Kerr (1998) have expressed concern that higher education is no longer serving the public good in ways that it has in the past. They worry that higher education is forgoing its role as a social institution and public role in society and is functioning increasingly as an industry. Traditionally, higher education's public role has included educating citizens for democratic engagement, supporting local and regional communities, preserving knowledge and making it available to the community, working in concert with other social institutions such as government or healthcare in order to foster their missions, advancing knowledge through research, developing the arts and humanities, broadening access to ensure a diverse democracy, developing the intellectual talents of students, and creating leaders for various areas of the public sector. The values undergirding this social mission include equality, service, truth, justice, community, academic freedom, and autonomy.

Commentators suggest that these traditional purposes and values are being eroded as higher education becomes driven by business or corporate values and predominantly economic goals. Although the aims of higher education have shifted over time, this dramatic alteration is taking place seemingly without dialogue or awareness among the major constituent groups. This alarming trend has precipitated the emergence of the National Forum on Higher Education for the Public Good (formerly the Kellogg Forum on Higher Education for the Public Good). The goal of the Forum is to first examine the above trend and then work to reestablish the preeminence of the social charter. The purpose of this chapter is to describe the manifold symptoms that compromise the social charter and to use these to raise questions that will help higher education reestablish its commitment to serving the public good.

The orientation to the market and economic goals is a worldwide phenomenon and is even more extreme within developing countries where economic advancement has become the cornerstone of political and educational agendas. The governing powers in these countries are redefining the public good as private advancement and economic attainment rather than long-standing missions of social development, social justice, and democratic engagement. Astute observers connect the change in the social charter to larger societal forces, for example, neoliberalism, the philosophy that the common or public good emerges from a focus on protection of individual rights and freedoms; the accumulation of private goods; the trend toward greater individualism and a move away from community involvement; privatization and corporatization of public services as represented by the HMO system in medical care; and further commercialization and marketization of public life, in part due to supply-side economics of the 1980s and 1990s. (For a more detailed discussion of these forces please see Kezar, 2004; portions of this chapter were printed in that article.)

The result of these complex forces is that the social charter between higher education and society is being rewritten. Publicly funded colleges and universities are now encouraged to privatize some activities, becoming for-profit entities with economic engines and with private and economic rather than public and social goals. In exchange, universities receive less funding but increased opportunities for entrepreneurial sources of revenue. The broader notion of social accountability (such as preservation of knowledge or development of the arts) has been thinned down and replaced with responsiveness to the market.

The notion of the social charter suggests that higher education and society are always renegotiating their appropriate relationship. Its current manifestation, many critics suggest, encourages ethical and educational compromises that are potentially harmful for higher education and the general public, especially to the historic mission of fostering democracy and important values such as equality, academic freedom, or pursuit of knowledge. The current charter informed by the industrial model of higher education needs articulation (provided in this chapter) and attention by government, the private sector, students, parents, and educational leaders.

Sociologists have identified the notion of a "tipping point" as the point at which a phenomenon moves so far in one direction that it cannot be reversed or restored to its previous state. Once some areas become so distorted (toward economic gain or commercialization in this instance), they reach a tipping point where turning the trend back becomes difficult, if not impossible. Big-time college athletics, an area where commercialization has gone so far as to distort the purpose of this activity at Division I schools, should serve as a warning to all of higher education. Many other activities on campus are moving toward this tipping point, so there is urgency to addressing this issue and for dialogue among leaders.

Losing the Social or Public Charter

Since the 1950s, advanced economies have increasingly tied economic development to higher education's "production" of workers especially in fields such as science, technology, and engineering (Kerr, 1998). In the United States, this has led to growing partnerships and connections between higher education and industry, particularly the corporate sector (Kerr, 1998). Higher education has always served the labor market in one way or another and to one degree or another, but production of workers was never the primary goal of higher education. In addition, higher education has become a "market" in which individuals purchase goods for their personal benefit. Reaganomics of the 1980s and 1990s created an intensely market-oriented environment, more than at any other time period in the history of the United States. Policy decisions were being made based on neoliberalism and economic rationalism where economic goals and outcomes are at the center, markets and commercialization are best for fulfilling society's goals, privatization of the public sector is encouraged, and creation of corporate structures and deregulation fulfills these ends (Currie & Newson, 1998; Slaughter & Rhoades, 1993).

There are many disturbing effects of unbridled neoliberalism and economic rationalism on higher education's social charter. Several of these can be documented and measured empirically, but others avoid easy detection and categorization. Therefore, the full magnitude of the problem is likely to be deeper than is currently appreciated. The shift in the social charter has been difficult for campuses or individuals to identify because many of the changes are occurring at the state, federal, or intrainstitutional level. There are some who will argue that the benefits of the changes (additional funds to higher education, contributions to economic growth, engendering greater public support of job creation) outweigh the disadvantages and problems. However, even if higher education continues to increase its corporate and commercial orientation to maximize these benefits, the ethical problems must be addressed and the social and public benefits should be bolstered so as not to be lost. Understanding these changes is critical in being able to create a new vision for higher education that respects a balance between market forces and the public good.

This section outlines the ways in which the mission shift (from public-social to private-economic) has affected core activities of higher education, such as administration, curriculum, research, governance, financing, policy, as well as constituents including faculty and students. A review of how the shift in mission has affected the values of the academy, such as community or academic freedom, illustrates the depth of the effects of the new social charter. These changes threaten the core characteristics and nature of higher education institutions. If trends are allowed to continue and modifications are not made soon, even if we want to alter the social charter, it may not be possible to revitalize lost areas of the public good.

Corporatized Governance and Leadership

In the last two decades, a corporate revolution hit higher education replacing collegial and shared governance and leadership on most campuses (Bessant, 1988; Giroux, 1999). Because private investment in colleges and universities has increased, often through trustees' corporate connections, activist trustees are now demanding increased input into institutional governance and in some cases circumventing traditional shared governance structures (Kerr, 1998). Trustees often do not have the expertise about educational issues to make sound decisions, and institutions are suffering from decisions that negatively affect the teaching and learning environment. Furthermore, activist trustees and administrators have centralized power and decision making, altering traditional democratic processes on campus that serve as models for students about how democratic communities operate (Giroux, 1999; Gumport, 2000; Kolondny, 1998). Several studies demonstrate that in the past twenty years, decision making has become increasingly centralized (boards and presidents), issues are selectively opened up for consideration in the governance process, and that less consultation takes place, especially related to strategic decisions such as for-profit spin-offs and distance education (Bessant, 1988; Currie, 1998; Mingle, 2000). Within this corporatized environment, presidential leadership has also suffered over the years. Presidents spend the majority of their time fundraising and developing entrepreneurial activities; their previous role as intellectual and moral leaders for their communities and for the nation has waned (Kennedy, 1997; Kerr, 1998).

Competitiveness, efficiency, and cost effectiveness have become the overriding criteria in decision making. Many commentators have noted that corporate language and practices are replacing traditional academic administration that holds that educational values are central to decision making (Daalder, 1985; Gumport, 2000; Rollin, 1989). One corporate strategy used in higher education institutions is outsourcing university jobs and services to private companies. In some instances, this practice has been successful; for example, with bookstores or food services. In others, the result has been disastrous, such as with residence halls or facilities where the service was too close to the learning mission of the institution and jeopardized core goals of the institution (Gumport, 2000). Corporate strategies can work in limited sets of situations, but too often those who adopt this belief system use it unilaterally. The same critique has been directed at responsibility-centered budgeting and user fees (students or a division pay to use a campus service); in some circumstances these policies make sense, but in many instances they inequitably affect a particular group of students, department, or program.

Vocationalized Curriculum and Teaching

The education available to students is increasingly vocational and focused more on training or information-based delivery rather than on developing higher-order intellectual skills (Slaughter, 1993). Fostering wisdom and higher-order thinking, not just memorization and bytes of information, has been a hallmark of higher education

(Giroux, 1999). Most agree that a quality education should prepare students for public life, not just for a career. This has been a key element of higher education's contribution to the public good. Broadly educated individuals vote and are involved with political organizations (citizenship), join community organizations and volunteer their time (community development), and are healthier (reduced medical costs for society). Vocational and market-oriented programs often favor distance education that can be offered more efficiently (Giroux, 1999). Yet distance education also tends to stress information delivery over critical thinking.

This shift in the curriculum and teaching affects the social good and the traditional charter. First, the humanities and non-applied social sciences fields as well as holistic and critical thinking pedagogies are essential for citizenship education and the education of leaders (Ehrlich, 2000). Second, learning suffers. During the last twenty years, the academy has been wrestling to overcome lecture-driven pedagogies, which have proven ineffective for student learning; yet corporate management promotes weak lecture methods due to cost effectiveness (Currie & Newson, 1998). In addition, studies about college student development demonstrate the benefits of students developing multidisciplinary knowledge (Pascarella & Terenzini, 1991). Students receiving a vocationally oriented curriculum are much less likely to have exposure to a variety of disciplines. Third, preservation of knowledge is compromised when certain fields are underfunded or closed. Fourth, advancement of knowledge is threatened since fewer disciplines can be brought to bear on any problem. Many studies have shown that complex problems such as poverty are best addressed through multiple disciplines (Bok, 1982). At a time when the scientific community realizes the value of bringing more disciplines and new ways of thinking to challenging social dilemmas, there are fewer faculty in these programs to conduct research, and their numbers are continuing to shrink. These are just a few of the ways that the public good is being undermined.

Privatization and Commercialization of Research

Perhaps the most significant problem related to commercialization and distortion of the social charter is research. As already mentioned, advancement of research is compromised since disciplines that do not serve the market are being dramatically underfunded within institutions and receive fewer external grants (Gumport, 1993; Slaughter & Rhoades, 1993). Also, corporate funders and government provide less support for research on general topics that do not have immediate results or serve commercial interests (Bok, 1982; Soley, 1995). So areas such as poverty, education, adult literacy, and the like receive minimal resources and attention. Without a constant and substantial flow of funds, good scholars and students will not be attracted to these fields and intellectual progress is inhibited.

Another threat to the public good has been the move to privatize and commercialize research. The Bayh-Dole Act of 1980, legislation that was part of the supply-side economics of the 1980s, allowed universities and small businesses to retain title to inventions developed with federal research and development monies (Slaughter & Rhoades, 1993). The intent of this act was to increase collaboration between universities and commercial interests. It encouraged universities to become involved in technoscience and applied research and to privatize and profit from research initiatives. Policymakers came to see high technology as a national resource central to success in a global marketplace. Areas such as medical research have become big business with technology transfer offices that sell research findings to pharmaceutical or biotech firms (Soley, 1995). Different surveys of industry show substantial increases each year in numbers of collaboratives and funding. For example, the Association of University Technology Managers reported a tripling of funds in 1997 and 1998, and patents were up 26 percent (Mingle, 2000). There are many ways that higher education-industry collaboratives are beneficial to both parties. Corporations draw on university expertise, gain necessary employee training, and provide growth opportunities for employees who teach at universities (Business–Higher Education Forum, 2001). Corporations provide students, additional funding, facilities that allow universities to reduce their expenditures, and corporate faculty to serve as adjuncts for universities.

However, the conflicts of interest are dramatic and problematic (Business–Higher Education Forum, 2001; Cichy, 1990; Mangan, 1999; Moynihan, 1998):

• A move toward applied research (already a shift in place based on government contracts)

- A decline in basic research (critical to advances in science)
- A reduction in the importance of teaching on many campuses (often called conflict of commitment)
- Conflicts of interest such as faculty having financial interests in their research, which has affected the integrity of academic journals
- Loss of community intellectual property
- A shift in graduate student research foci to more applied topics with marketable orientations
- Refocused research agendas for faculty

Other problems that have emerged are even more disturbing, such as secrecy of findings or interpreting research results so that they will not reflect unfavorably on the sponsor (Business–Higher Education Forum, 2001). The scope of these problems is mostly unknown, but the implications could be profound. Furthermore, such university-industry partnerships have led some universities to adopt more corporate values (such as being profit driven) that can violate educational values and mission (such as community, equality, or justice) (Dunn, 1987; Mangan, 1987, 1999; Tierney, 1998). Many campus leaders now acknowledge that this move to commercialize research has compromised the traditional role of universities as arbiters of knowledge and guarantors of objectivity in the public interest (Business–Higher Education Forum, 2001; Mingle, 2000).

One area is worth elaboration since it is so dramatically altering the social charter—intellectual property (Bok, 1982). Within the global economy, research discoveries that are not patented by industry benefit the entire global community. Economic rationalists purport that countries will fail if they do not commodify and privatize discoveries to benefit their own interests (Brown & Schubert, 2000; Currie & Newson, 1998). Thus, corporations and states have sought to privatize and commodify research through intellectual property rather than develop a free contribution to the international community of scholars. This philosophy and concurrent legislation moved intellectual property from being a by-product of the quest for knowledge to being the goal of science. In the past, basic research was supported by the state and remained public property since it was uncertain who the beneficiaries of the research would be (Slaughter & Rhoades, 1993). Yet technoscience makes the lines of beneficiaries so clear that the public and others are starting to question funding for all forms of research.

An example of how the research process and enterprise has changed helps demonstrate this shift. Slaughter and Rhoades (1993) illustrated how the state of Arizona enacted policies throughout the 1980s that made the state increasingly the owner, organizer, and producer of commercially relevant scientific products and reduced any faculty claims to patent royalties. Over that same time period, a massive number of contract faculty were hired, and the system operated more like a private enterprise with managers controlling commercial research activities with oversight and faculty activities. Since faculties had contract appointments, they had less control over what was done with research or the direction of research. Arizona State law came to define the public interest as best served by the pursuit of private profit. This is certainly far afield from traditional notions of research being freely shared and for everyone's benefit within the global community. Although research discoveries are being privatized to serve specific corporate interests, there has been minimal discussion related to how the public good is compromised.

Privatization and Marketization of Financing Higher Education

Although funding for higher education has always been diversified among many different sources and private funding has been a major source of revenue, several forces have coalesced making higher education more focused on revenue generation in recent years (Leslie, 1995; Slaughter, 1998). As state budget and public monies declined in the 1980s, presidents sought other sources of support, often through corporate trustees who served on their boards (Kerr, 1998). Industrial parks, real estate investments, and contract research emerged to help provide additional funding within state budget shortfalls. Yet these ventures focused on the research function, which further compromised faculty commitment to teaching and skewed institutional resources even further toward research and a possible commercial payoff (Kerr, 1998; Slaughter, 1998).

Tuition, another source of revenue, rose at rates well above inflation throughout the 1980s and 1990s (Institute for Higher Education Policy [IHEP], 1998; Leslie & Slaughter, 1995). But higher tuition restricts access and limits the public good of making higher education available to all qualified students. Ironically, this may only be a perception of cost since students may be able to obtain aid packages to cover most of the tuition. However, less-well-off institutions often leave students with a financial aid gap, and research indicates that low-income students are affected by "sticker shock" and are also the most hesitant to take out loans. The shift away from grants and toward loans in financial aid has negatively affected those most in need of aid to attend college.

A second shift in financial aid policy has also pushed higher education toward an industry model and has led to a focus on private and economic interests. The reallocation of financial aid directly to students beginning in the early 1970s was the beginning of the competitive model and market orientation (Leslie & Johnson, 1974). Although positive in providing students choice and power in college selection, reallocation of financial aid led to a new orientation among institutions (competition) and students (as consumers). *US News & World Report* rankings, college guides such as Peterson's, and other consumer reports developed in the 1970s further fostered the notion of higher education as a product that students purchase. Fears associated with predicted declines in student enrollment in the 1980s intensified discourse about the student as consumer since there would be even greater competition for students (Institute for Higher Education Policy, 1998). Institutions consider students to be consumers who they bid for in the competitive marketplace. Enrolled student-consumers are encouraged to think of themselves as purchasers of services rather than as members of communities (Institute for Higher Education Policy, 1998).

This market model was also exacerbated by state funding mechanisms changing to performance approaches rather than the traditional, egalitarian, across-the-board funds for all institutions (Leslie & Slaughter, 1995). With the introduction of performance funding, institutions compete against each other for resources, vying for students, financial aid dollars, and other state funds. Furthermore, with the growth of for-profit providers of education, competition has been introduced within another sector (Kerr, 1998). As higher education increasingly sees itself as an industry, it has diverted its attention from the public good toward competing for business (Brown & Schubert, 2000; Kerr, 1998; Leslie, 1995).

Compromise related to funding is not new; higher education has long adapted its priorities to those established by foundations, government, corporations, and other donors (Kerr, 1998). Today's environment presents a unique challenge. As public higher education becomes increasingly private, what will be the effect on the public good? Will the corporate good replace the public good? Since funding so strongly determines mission, values, and priorities, the increasing privatization and marketization of funding seems especially disconcerting.

Disenfranchised Faculty

There are many significant ways that faculty lives have been altered by corporate practices. First, the nature of the academic labor market has changed dramatically in composition in the last twenty years. There are now over 50 percent part-time faculty compared to less than 15 percent two decades ago, and the number of contract faculty has risen from almost 0 percent to over 20 percent of the faculty (Anderson, 2002). This dramatic rise in part-time and contract faculty is a result of efforts to decrease costs, a major emphasis within corporatization practices. The impact of the growth in part-time and contract faculty has been less student advising, limited student-faculty contact (known to be one of the most important predictors of learning among students), decreased involvement in campus governance, among other outcomes (Baldwin & Krotseng, 1995; Currie, 1998; Giroux, 1999; Kerr, 1998; Marginson, 2000). As money for faculty salaries and lines declined, the number of administrative staff rose over the past two decades (Slaughter & Rhoades, 1993). The rise in administration is partly due to staffing for research collaboratives and regulatory offices that are for private and less mission-driven activities.

As noted in the section in curriculum, faculty hires are now concentrated in the applied fields, science, and those aligned with growth in labor rather than the traditional, liberal arts areas. Slaughter (1993, 1998) notes that this is particularly disturbing since the social sciences and humanities have much larger numbers of women and students of color, so these groups are disproportionately affected by redeploying faculty. Faculty engaged in commercial science are compensated more highly than other faculty. In addition, faculty are being rewarded for and encouraged to seek external funding from consulting and research, so that their salaries are not being paid for by the institution (Slaughter, 1998). It has been suggested that this alteration in the composition in faculty (away from the social sciences and humanities) and change in role (to seek external support for their positions) has decreased the role of the faculty as social critic. There are fewer social scientists, and they no longer engage in general critiques of society; instead, they are encouraged to develop consulting practices for corporations and industry (Altbach, Gumport, & Johnstone, 2001; Currie & Newson, 1998; Giroux, 1999). This is particularly problematic since economic rationalism has also affected the media, and they too are losing their voice as a trusted social critic. Corporate takeovers of media outlets have resulted in stories critical of companies or industries, such as tobacco, not being released.

Diverting time, thought, and energy away from teaching and basic research has been labeled "commitment conflict." Commitment conflict has been reinforced by corporate managers who have increased funding for research and lessened expenditures toward instruction in the last fifteen years (Leslie & Slaughter, 1995). The many changes in faculty contracts, terms of employment, alteration of load, and the like have led to unionization among many faculty, a trend likely to continue in the coming years (McCollow & Lingard, 1996). Faculty unionization is only problematic in that it can often make faculty input to governance difficult since it is considered outside the purview of their collective bargaining contracts. Because faculty are necessary to make sound institutional judgments, this trend could portend trouble for institutions. The public good affected by the changes in faculty work are serious: loss of faculty within key areas to conduct research and within the realm of governance, decreased student learning, decline in public service, slowing growth of women and minority faculty, and minimized faculty role as social critic.

Careerist Students

In an environment where private and economic goals are stressed, students adopt consumerist and careerist attitudes that are not balanced with ideas about the public good (Riesman, 1980). In 2000, over 80 percent listed "to be able to get a better job" as highest among reasons for going to college, up from 45 percent in 1966 (Institute for Higher Education Policy, 1998). Student enrollments have shifted from liberal arts areas to professional areas (also affecting the curriculum). Not only are students careerist, but student engagement and interest in politics is at an all-time low (Ehrlich, 2000). In the last twenty years, there has been a shift in financial aid programs from grants to loans (Currie & Newson, 1998; Institute for Higher Education Policy, 1998). Studies have shown that this shift encourages students to enter high-paying fields where they are better able to repay their large loans and discourages entry into lower-paying fields that serve the larger social and collective good (Slaughter, 1998). For example, undergraduate enrollments in business more than doubled between 1980 and 1995 (Slaughter, 1998). In other countries, students who enter careers in areas that serve the public good are forgiven their loans.

Economic Public Discourse

The Institute for Higher Education Policy (IHEP) documented how the public dialogue about higher education during the last twenty years has emphasized the private and economic benefits over the social and public benefits. As evidence, IHEP notes the media's exclusive attention to graduates' job prospects but with no attention to the broader social benefits of employability. Focus groups conducted by the American Council on Education suggest that Americans believe the most important benefit of college to be job attainment (far above any other benefits). While improving economic prospects, especially for those with few opportunities, is important, conceiving of higher education as merely a means to employment neglects the other essential components and negates powerful effects they can have in improving society (Leslie & Slaughter, 1995). At the broadest level, the social charter has been altered, and the general public no longer perceives the social and public benefits of higher education as the most salient aspect of its purpose. Perhaps social and public benefits are not considered salient at all.

Academic Values

Altering the administrative, teaching, research, funding, and learning environment challenges the values that undergird the traditional mission, such as public service, academic freedom, community, truth, equality, and justice. First, public service is becoming less of a priority, yet it has always been the keystone of the public trust (Bok, 1982;

Tierney, 1998). Public service has declined as a value in recent years; fewer institutions engage communities, schools, or social agencies. Certainly, higher education's commitment to public service has fluctuated over time, but it is currently at a low point. It could be argued that higher education's service role is to the market, but it is important that legislators and educational leaders decide if that is the only or predominant service role of the academy.

University-industry partnerships have compromised independence of inquiry, often termed "academic freedom" (Slaughter & Rhoades, 1993). One of the core values of the academe is "academic freedom," the right to pursue whatever research interests the faculty member desires and choose the appropriate teaching materials for a class. Faculty were provided academic freedom because their research was done for the public's interest, not for private and commercial interests (Dunn, 1987; Slaughter & Rhoades, 1993). Scientific and professional codes were based on assurances that knowledge was developed for the community in a disinterested way. The "communism of science" is characterized by a belief that the substantive findings of science are a product of social collaboration and are assigned to the community. Even though producers do not profit from the findings, they are awarded academic freedom and autonomy to pursue research interests. As faculty and the academic community continue down the path of commercialization and privatization, academic freedom and the historic autonomy may be altered within the social charter. Society may not grant this right if there is not the concomitant responsibility to the public good.

Closely tied to the notion of academic freedom and independent inquiry is the value of truth. An aspect of the social charter is that higher education will develop rigorous, impartial knowledge or truth for society's benefit (Soley, 1995; Young, 1997). Although the notion of truth is widely disputed, many scholars believe that rationalism, empiricism, and pragmatism can offer windows into truth (with a small *t*) to separate it from spiritual notions of Truth. Therefore, truth (with a small *t*) is seen as changing and contextual (Young, 1997). Some researchers might say they are trying to develop understanding, rather than truth, but there is an essence among most researchers that they are attempting to follow a rigorous and ethical process in order to develop insight. Even postmodernists who believe that truth and impartiality do not exist and that research is affected and biased by the researcher would be concerned about privatizing research and creating perhaps even deeper levels of bias fueled by economic self-interest. Related closely to truth is the notion of neutrality or disinterested research. In the academy, this has resulted in faculty freely critiquing political, economic, and social systems. While many scholars would argue that researchers inevitably bring some bias to their inquiries, research methodologies are designed to mitigate, or at a minimum reveal, such biases. But biases caused by corporate sponsorship and economic motivation are especially troubling and too easily ignored (Mangan, 1999). This problem, combined with the growing number of part-time faculty without protection of academic freedom and needful of income, is alarming (Fairweather, 1996). Together, they are threatening the time-honored role of professors as social critic.

Community has always been a deep and abiding value of higher education (Boyer, 1987). Learning is best facilitated in a social environment that is safe for debate and challenge. The changes to faculty life and role, the downsizing and restructuring of the curriculum, the redirection of faculty to industry partnerships and consulting, and the corporatization of governance and management has resulted in decreased campus community (Bilik & Blum, 1989; Daalder, 1985; Giroux, 1999; Gumport, 2000). A Canadian study (Currie, 1998) over a ten-year period documented the sense of community on campuses before the implementation of corporate management practices and then looked at what happened in the seven years thereafter. Faculty have less interaction with each other as they spend more time off campus. Administrators and faculty have not only less interaction but the nature of their relationships has become more contentious. Market-oriented funding approaches have also eroded community on campus (Leslie, 1995). The competition for dollars mentioned earlier has had an impact on collaboration among higher education institutions. It has led to the further decline in community already happening due to conflicts between faculty and administrators. This loss of community on campus has been shown to negatively affect learning among students as well as faculty morale and commitment.

Equality is the assurance of freedom and opportunity through the formation of certain rights; it encompasses economic, political, cultural, intellectual, scientific, and moral matters (Young, 1997). Today's environment compromises equality since only economic gains are stressed, and not all individuals are provided the critical or transformatory education necessary to participate in political and social life. Since knowledge is a form of community property that is being privatized, equality in terms of individual rights to knowledge is being compromised.

There are many examples of ways that justice (the principle of fairness) is also at stake. Research is conducted for primarily commercial purposes, marginalizing social purposes. Moreover, the salaries of faculty vary dramatically, leaving certain fields impoverished and others with generous private sector salaries (Slaughter & Rhoades, 1993; Slaughter, 1998). Justice is compromised, as students are unable to afford tuition based on market-driven competition and decline in public funds. The list could go on, but the main point is that core values supporting higher education are in jeopardy, thereby threatening the ability of institutions to fulfill their vital mission of serving the public good.

Summary

Some argue that these ethical issues and problems will be resolved over time as market forces stabilize, and that the effect will eventually be positive (Zemsky, 1993). Yet the example of Australia suggests that problems will not diminish with the passage of time. In the 1980s, the Whitlam and Hawke governments brought higher education and industry in close connection to conduct applied research, altered the mission of higher education to focus on training rather than education, vocationalized the curriculum, increased student fees, adopted corporate management strategies of downsizing and outsourcing, and instituted accountability and efficiency principles for measuring faculty work (Currie & Newson, 1998). Over time, community has not only not been restored on campus but has become more fragmented: the vocational curriculum and faculty supplanted the liberal arts tradition, careerism among students and parents is growing, and basic research and social critique has declined (Currie & Newson, 1998).

Several countries have resisted economic rationalism and successfully maintained more community-oriented, humanistic, and democratic approaches to higher education. For example, South Africa developed a white paper to inform higher education national policy; it outlines the public as well as private benefits of higher education (Currie & Newson, 1998). Labor market responsiveness was brought into alignment with other goals and reinforced by national policies that temper the move toward marketization of higher education that many leaders saw emerging. French higher education reform provides an example for the United States of resisting the excesses of marketization—liberal arts remains well supported, faculty are unionized against the erosion of academic labor, and students have rioted against commercialization and commodification of education. At the same time the French have expanded access, academics still have a strong say in the governance of the institution, and basic research is still strongly supported. Countervailing voices and movements helped to shield the South African and French higher education systems from becoming a tool of market forces and overemphasizing private and economic interests. The French and South African systems are not perfect and can learn much from the United States, but they have effectively created balance and drawn boundaries between private-public and social-economic goals. South Africa and France have confronted pressures for change but have been critical of certain alterations that seemed to threaten what had traditionally been aligned with the public good. The American colonies used France as a model to shape democratic ideals for the emerging United States. Perhaps this is another time when we need to learn from external models.

I do not mean to suggest that we retreat to a golden age or model of higher education and not continue to evolve as external forces change. However, I argue that successful change needs to be thoughtful, intentional, and fair or just in terms of its effect on groups in society. In the next chapter I examine movements that provide hope for a different vision for higher education from one driven solely by economic rationalism and neoliberalism.

References

Altbach, P., Gumport, P., & Johnstone, B. (2001). *In defense of American higher education*. Baltimore: Johns Hopkins Press.

Anderson, E. (2002). *The new professoriate*. Washington, DC: American Council on Education.

Baldwin, R. G., & Krotseng, M. V. (1995). *Incentives in the academy: Issues and options*. New Directions for Higher Education, no. 51. San Francisco: Jossey-Bass.

Bessant, B. (1988). Corporate management and the institutions of higher education. *Australian Universities' Review, 32*(2), 10–13.

Bilik, L. J., & Blum, M. C. (1989). "Déjà vu all over again": Initiatives in academic management. *Academe, 75,* 10–14.

Bok, D. (1982). The corporation on campus: Balancing responsibility and innovation. *Change, 14*(6), 16–25.

Bok, D. (2003). *Universities in the marketplace: The commercialization of higher education.* Princeton, NJ: Princeton University Press.

Boyer, E. (1987). *College: The undergraduate experience in America.* New York: HarperCollins.

Brown, R., & Schubert, J. D. (Eds.) (2000). *Knowledge and power in higher education: A reader.* New York: Teachers College Press.

Business–Higher Education Forum (2001). *Working together, creating knowledge. The university-industry research collaboration initiative.* Washington, DC: American Council on Education.

Cichy, K. A. (1990). Ethical implication of for-profit corporate sponsorship of research. *Journal of the Society of Research Administrators, 22,* 23–27.

Currie, J. (1998). Globalization practices and professoriate in Anglo-Pacific and North American universities. *Comparative Education Review, 42,* 15–29.

Currie, J., & Newson, J. (Eds.) (1998). *Universities and globalization: Critical perspectives.* Thousand Oaks, CA: Sage.

Daalder, H. (1985). Trends and dangers of increased bureaucracy in higher education: A view from below. *International Journal of Institutional Management in Higher Education, 9,* 35–43.

Dunn, M. (1987). *The effects of corporatization on academic medical centers.* Paper presented at the Annual AERA conference, Washington DC.

Ehrlich, T. (2000). *Civic responsibility and higher education.* Washington, DC: ACE-Oryx Press.

Fairweather, J. (1996). *Faculty work and the public trust: Restoring the value of teaching and public service in American academic life.* Boston: Allyn & Bacon.

Giroux, H. A. (1999). *Corporate culture and the attack on higher education and public schooling.* Phi Delta Kappa Fastback 442. Bloomington, IN: Phi Delta Kappa International.

Gumport, P. (1993). The contested terrain of academic program reduction. *Journal of Higher Education, 64*(3), 283–311.

Gumport, P. (2000). Academic restructuring: Organizational change and institutional imperatives. *Higher Education, 39,* 67–91.

The Institute for Higher Education Policy [IHEP]. (1998). *Reaping the benefits: Defining the public and private value of going to college.* Washington, DC: Author.

Kennedy, D. (1997). *Academic duty*. Cambridge, MA: Harvard University Press.

Kerr, C. (1998). *Troubled times for American higher education*. Albany: State University of New York Press.

Kezar, A. (2004). Obtaining integrity?: Reviewing and examining the charter between higher education and society. *The Review of Higher Education, 27*(4), 429–459.

Kolondny, A. (1998). *Failing the future*. Durham, NC: Duke University Press.

Leslie, L. L. (1995). What drives higher education management in the 1990s and beyond?: The new era in financial support. *Journal for Higher Education Management, 10,* 5–16.

Leslie, L. L., & Johnson, G. P. (1974). The market model and higher education. *Journal of Higher Education, 45,* 1–20.

Leslie, L., & Slaughter, S. (1995). The development and current status of market mechanisms in United States postsecondary education. *Higher Education Policy, 10*(3/4), 239–252.

Mangan, K. S. (1987, July 29). Institutions and scholars face ethical dilemmas over pursuit of research with commercial value. *Chronicle of Higher Education,* 11–12.

Mangan, K. S. (1999, June 4). Medical professors see threat in corporate influence on research. *Chronicle of Higher Education,* A14–15.

Marginson, S. (2000). Rethinking academic work in the global era. *Journal of Higher Education Policy and Management, 22,* 23–35.

McCollow, J., & Lingard, B. (1996). Chancing discourses and practices of academic work. *Australian Universities' Review, 39,* 11–19.

Mingle, J. R. (2000). *Higher education's future in the "corporatized" economy*. Paper presented at the Symposium on Research and Scholarship on Higher Education Governance, Trusteeship and the Academic Presidency sponsored by the Association of Governing Boards of Universities and Colleges and the University of Virginia, Curry School of Education (Charlottesville, VA, December 5–6, 1999).

Moynihan, D. P. (1998). On the commodification of medicine. *Academic Medicine, 73,* 453–459.

Pascarella, E. T., & Terenzini, P. T. (1991). *How college affects students*. San Francisco: Jossey-Bass.

Riesman, D. (1980). *On higher education: The academic enterprise in an era of rising student consumerism*. San Francisco: Jossey-Bass.

Rollin, R. (1989). There's no business like education. *Academe, 75,* 14–17.

Slaughter, S. A. (1993). Retrenchment in the 1980s: The politics of prestige and gender. *Journal of Higher Education, 59,* 241–262.

Slaughter, S. A. (1998). Federal policy and supply-side institutional resource allocation at public research universities. *Review of Higher Education, 21,* 209–244.

Slaughter, S. A., & Rhoades, G. (1993). Changes in intellectual property statutes and policies at a public university: Revising the terms of professional labor. *Higher Education, 26,* 287–312.

Soley, L. C. (1995). *Leasing the ivory tower: The corporate takeover of academia.* Boston: South End Press.

Tierney, W. (1998). *The responsive university: Restructuring for high performance.* Baltimore: Johns Hopkins Press.

Young, R. (1997). *No neutral ground.* San Francisco: Jossey-Bass.

Zemsky, R. (1993). Consumer markets and higher education. *Liberal Education, 79*(3), 14–18.

Chapter Three

Creating a Metamovement
A Vision Toward Regaining the Public Social Charter

Adrianna J. Kezar

While market forces have always affected higher education in the United States, countervailing forces have emerged to balance these forces when they became extreme. This chapter reviews current countervailing forces including service-learning, the K–16 movement, community-college partnerships, and new notions of faculty work life. I suggest that these movements be seen together as one larger metamovement. Yet, they tend to operate in isolation of each other. If we are to truly revive higher education's role in the public good and perhaps even expand it, the various movements need to work in concert.

Several movements have come to fruition in recent years that focus on public and social issues rather than on economic or market concerns. Many individuals, groups, institutions, and associations have become concerned about the move away from the social and public orientation of colleges and universities. Some of the major movements are described in this chapter, and other chapters in this volume also describe these important directions. Unfortunately, many of these movements operate independently and are not aware of each other's work toward similar goals, which may diminish the capacity for long-term impact. Hollander and Hartley (2000) recently suggested that a national network be established among these many similar initiatives to bolster the public good since little communication and coordination occurs across these various initiatives.

It is the intention of the National Forum that these various efforts be aligned in order to create an even stronger and broader countermovement to the private and economic interests that have been such a powerful force in the last twenty years.

These movements have been headed by major leaders in higher education such as Derek Bok (1982, 2003), Ernest Boyer (1987, 1990), and Donald Kennedy (1997). Many of these initiatives emerged from critiques that higher education did not take the knowledge and skills invested in teaching and research into the community to provide a broader social benefit related to poverty, homelessness, healthcare, or education reform. Bok (1982) elegantly argued that service must be defined more broadly than economic responsiveness and also maintained that universities should not be seen in purely instrumental terms, "which can weaken the conviction of faculty about the intrinsic worth of learning, undermine its intellectual standards and values, expose it to endless petty distractions and corruptions from the outside world . . . and undermine the value of intellectual inquiry for its own sake" (p. 8). These leaders developed convincing arguments for balancing utilitarian interests such as service (and although they did not discuss commercial interests, it could be included) with higher education's focus on liberal learning. The three major themes in these movements are civic education (which counters economic emphasis), public service (which counters economic and private emphasis), and collaboration (which counters individualism and private focus). Many of these themes overlap. Public service is often described as a component of civic education, and learning communities are considered an approach to civic education, while civic education is desired as part of the engaged, public service–oriented campus. Each movement shares a decidedly public and social focus and provides a vision for beginning to rethink the current social charter.

Civic Education and Fostering a Diverse Democracy

Perhaps the most organized and active movement has been toward enhancing citizenship education. Within this volume, Mathews, Schneider, and Greene and Trent provide more detailed elaborations on this movement. Organizations such as the Kettering Foundation were concerned about the low voting rates, lack of civic engagement, and lack of public service. The foundation developed dialogues and publications to foster an awareness of these problems and to encourage higher education to help prepare students for participation in public life. In order to address these problems, education needs to stress the art of public argumentation, interest in public affairs, the curiosity to listen closely, and the ability to work with others different from ourselves. A variety of pedagogical innovations have been developed in order to foster this type of education including community-based learning (which ties experiences in the community to theory in the classroom) and service-learning (described in greater detail in the public service section).

As London (2001) notes, "A new movement is taking shape in American higher education, one aimed at educating for democracy, nurturing community, and promoting civic participation. Across the country, colleges, universities, and academic associations are striving to make civic engagement an integral part of the way they do their work" (p. 17).

Several Washington-based higher education associations have projects to increase civic or democratic engagement including the American Association of Higher Education, the Council of Independent Colleges, the American Council on Education, and the Association of American Colleges and Universities. Individual campuses are being engaged in this effort through conferences such as "Renewing the Civic Mission of American Research Universities" that assist them in devising ways that their institution can change teaching and programs to focus on civic education. New approaches to institutional accreditation have also begun to support civic development among undergraduates. The National Project of the American Academy for Liberal Education identifies civic virtue as one of five categories of student achievement that should be assessed within accreditation reports.

The civic education movement is conceptualized differently than in the past. In recent years there has been an emphasis on the importance of diversity to enhance the democratic and social goals of higher education. Green and Trent review this trend in Chapter Seven. Barry Checkoway (2000) notes "that democracy is about the participation of the people, and the people are increasingly diverse, then education in democracy must include education for diversity" (p. 28). Students need to learn how to engage different types of people—the capacity to engage, respect, and negotiate the claims of multiple and disparate communities and voices is critical to being civically literate. Several recent projects focus on enhancing a diverse democracy. The Association of American Colleges and Universities' American Commitments project focuses on the improvement of civic education in a pluralistic society. In addition, the federal government has supported a recent study led by Sylvia Hurtado, Preparing College Students for a Diverse Democracy, to examine the relationship of diversity to learning outcomes, with particular attention to civic and social goals.

Public Service: Engaged Campus, Scholarship Reconsidered, College-Community Partnerships, and Community Service-Learning

The social and public benefits of higher education have often been demonstrated through public service. Public service can vary tremendously: from conducting research in the community, teaching a distance education course within a community, helping to reform schools in the local area, to a faculty member serving on a community board. Since World War II, many institutions have emulated research universities, ignoring their service mission. On other campuses, service and partnerships had become marginalized and outside the normal course of institutional activities. In recent years there has been a reinvigoration of the service role. For example, the Kellogg Foundation supported an effort headed by national associations such as the National Association for State and Land-Grant Colleges and Universities (NASLGCU) toward reinvigorating the service mission within these sectors.

In 1997, Campus Compact attempted to "re"-institutionalize the public service mission of higher education. Their notion of the "engaged campus" was an attempt to broaden and deepen the campus service role, engaging all members of the campus (faculty, students, and staff). Community engagement can vary tremendously by the mission of the institution, but the goal is to encourage a deeper and more systemic engagement across the campus. In this new vision of engagement, the university extends resources and expertise to the community as well as receiving input and expertise from the community in ways that serve both institutional and community needs. Judith Ramaley's chapter provides a detailed review of this movement.

Perhaps one of the most profound movements related to the public service mission of higher education was lead by Ernest Boyer. His groundbreaking work *Scholarship Reconsidered* (1990) helps rethink and broaden the role of faculty and redefines scholarship. Boyer argued for a shift from a dominant focus on basic research (emphasized in particular at research universities) where teaching was less regarded to a new value system where research, teaching, integration (synthesis of what we know), and application were regarded equally. He conceptualized teaching, integration, and application to be areas of scholarship. For example, applying a new social theory within a community setting should be conceptualized as a form of scholarship. This new articulation of faculty roles made public service more prominent and developed a way to institutionalize this new vision within faculty roles and rewards (see Chapter Twelve by Ward for more details).

Over the past several decades, national associations have helped sponsor and develop partnerships between colleges and communities. The Council of Independent Colleges and the National Society for Experiential Learning developed networks among institutional partnerships to increase their impact. College-community partnerships reach beyond the institutional level and have received federal support. For the past decade, the Department of Housing and Urban Development has awarded over 150 community-college partnership grants to encourage collaborations that help foster development of communities in need. In addition, federal GEAR UP grants (Gaining Early Awareness and Readiness for Undergraduate Programs) support hundreds of colleges and communities working together to develop early intervention college programs for high school students. Many community-college partnerships have also been supported through private giving or foundations. New public service collaboratives have emerged recently, including those bringing together ten to twelve social institutions (hospitals, governments, schools) and higher education institutions across focused areas (such as San Diego County) to address public concerns such as poverty, health, or the environment.

One of the most successful ways that the public service mission has been reinvigorated has been through community service-learning (see Chapter Eleven by Benson, Harkavy, and Hartley). This movement focuses on incorporating community service into academic course work so that students gain experience with issues they are studying such as poverty. Community service-learning provides social benefits by having students work to change communities and therefore contribute to the public good. Students rise above their own self-interests in career or knowledge development. A number of organizations have helped to foster and support the service-learning movement in the last decade including Campus Compact, an organization of college and university presidents; COOL—Campus Opportunity Outreach League, an organization of student leaders; and the Corporation for National Service, a government office that supports Americorps volunteers and provides seed money to hundreds of campus-based service efforts. Over six hundred universities or colleges are now members of Campus Compact and have made a commitment to increase the public service role of higher education through service-learning or community partnerships.

These four movements provide a new vision for higher education in public service; they are embedded across institutional processes, reciprocal with communities, and tied more to the educational mission of the institution. The public service movement is discussed throughout this book.

Collaboration: Learning Communities, K–16 Movement, Multidisciplinary Research, Student and Academic Affairs Partnerships

An emerging vision for higher education is based on a more collaborative and community-oriented enterprise, in which partnerships and connectedness that support the public good are held above private, individual interests. Learning communities, a pedagogical innovation, are one way that community is reemerging. Most commonly, "learning communities" refers to a curricular restructuring that links or clusters classes around an interdisciplinary theme and enrolls a common cohort of students. Programs vary in form and content, but they are all an intentional restructuring of students' time and credit to foster greater intellectual connections between students, between students and faculty, and between disciplines. Students learn that knowledge is developed with others and that groups often develop better ideas than individuals. Learning communities facilitate students' engagement in community life, which is critical to a democracy. Chapters Seven and Eight allude to the importance of collaboration for the public good.

Many campuses are realizing that collaboration between academic and student affairs is an important technique for enhancing student learning and for re-creating community on campus. Research illustrates that the separation of academic and student affairs has a negative impact on student learning and that collaboration between these groups enhances student learning by creating a more seamless learning environment that connects in- and out-of-classroom learning. Much of the learning occurring outside the classroom is essential for public service and civic education, including leadership and volunteerism.

There are many groups advocating the importance of inter- and multidisciplinary research, which is based on the assumption that each area of inquiry—humanities, social sciences, and physical and biological sciences—are needed to advance knowledge. Multidisciplinary research brings scholars together across various fields of inquiry to address pressing societal problems; scholars work in partnership to serve critical public needs. Many scholars have criticized traditional research methods based in a single discipline as being inadequate to understand complex problems in the real world. Increasingly, multidisciplinary teams (such as sociology, biology, anthropology, religious studies, and physics) are conducting research projects addressing community and societal issues. Another aspect of multidisciplinary research is the growth of public policy centers and institutes, which are becoming a more visible part of many universities. These centers are a cross between think tanks and academic units that provide public service; they focus on policy research and facilitation of public discourse.

The emerging national K–16 movement further illustrates a renewed interest in collaboration and the need for public service. Educational policymakers and practitioners agree that a seamless transition from high school to college is important and that this can only be achieved through collaboration between these sectors. Greater collaboration between K–12 and higher education creates students who are better prepared for college. Additionally, faculty members have a better understanding of the type of learning occurring before college, such as the greater reliance on technology for delivery of knowledge. The American Association of Higher Education has been a strong advocate of the partnership movement, one result of which was the development of the Education Trust. Through several national and state initiatives, schools and colleges are now in dialogue with each other, reaffirming their interdependence. The K–16 movement also illustrates the importance of higher education's service role to the community.

The Current State of Affairs as a Threat to a Social and Public Vision of Higher Education

If the current state of affairs is not checked, it could become entrenched as our new social charter between higher education and society, well beyond the tipping point and difficult to change. The goal of the National Forum is to ensure that as society and higher education continue to negotiate a new social charter, the public good remains a key ingredient. Ernest Boyer, a strong advocate for community service-learning, community engagement, learning communities, and citizenship education, worried about the effect of current trends such as fragmentation of campus community and the redefining of faculty roles to meet the needs of the labor market. He was one of the first leaders to identify the trends that were destroying the vision of higher education for the public good. The current climate, marked by fewer faculty in humanities and social sciences, deemphasizes citizen skills such as political awareness, leadership, and diversity, portending difficulty for groups interested in fostering civic education. The emphasis on low interaction pedagogies, such as distance education or the lecture methods favored by corporate management and vocationalized curriculum, also deemphasize the interactive pedagogies necessary for citizenship education. Student consumerism works against efforts to interest students in course work or pedagogies that emphasize education for citizenship.

Public service is eroded in many different ways. For example, service-learning is threatened if faculty continue to be drawn away from traditional social science and humanities areas where the majority of service-learning is currently concentrated (although it can be incorporated into all disciplines) and pulled toward applied, commercially oriented research. Furthermore, faculty commitment conflict (away from teaching) and the increasing numbers of part-time faculty (who typically do not engage in service-learning since it is based on long-term engagement with the community) stand in the way of many colleges and universities institutionalizing service-learning or being involved in public service. Current trends in student consumerism and vocationalism may work against student involvement in either service-learning or public service in the future, although recent increases in high school service have made community service-learning rise temporarily on campuses. Unfortunately, it is difficult to know if this trend will be sustained. Trends toward commercial research affect faculty time and interest in conducting research for social purposes.

Lastly, collaboration is threatened. Corporate management techniques thwart collaboration between academic and student affairs, provide minimal funding or support for learning communities, and do not support costly K–16 partnerships. Campuses are becoming increasingly fragmented, affecting interest and ability to create collaboration. Even with these formidable barriers, some campuses have created more engaged campuses, but will engagement continue to spread with all these systemic barriers?

While the above mentioned movements have focused on revitalizing an aspect of the social or public good, other forces are emerging that attack the heart of the market- and consumer-oriented higher education culture. The National Survey of Student Engagement, a new institutional survey that will perhaps replace or supplement the *US News & World Report* rankings, is directly addressing student consumerism. *US News & World Report* focuses on traditional market-oriented criterion such as resources and reputation and emphasizes individual benefits for students. The National Survey of Student Engagement focuses on student learning, engagement in campus, active learning such as learning communities or community service-learning, and the development of the whole student. This instrument can help students and parents identify institutions that offer an education that is broadly defined with social and public benefits. It attempts to transform the dialogue from private and economic to public aims. Perhaps other movements of this kind are afoot and can help to counterbalance the emphasis on private and economic goals.

Closing Thoughts on a Metamovement

In summary, several public, social, and community-oriented movements have emerged that counter the private and economic orientation that has been so forceful in the last two decades. These movements also present the beginning of a new vision for higher education—rather than just reclaiming the role of civic education, this new vision for the public good combines civic education with preparation for a more diverse democracy. Rather than seeing service as the university bringing its expertise to communities, service is now seen as reciprocal and more permanent. Furthermore, service is no longer relegated to an extension office but is becoming part of the core of the institution through community service-learning, Boyer's new notions of scholarship, and the engaged campus. Creating genuine, sustained collaboration within and between institutions and engaging students in learning communities is critical to modeling and practicing the "social aspect" of the public good. This promising, emerging vision needs sharpening and further dialogue. The new civic, public service, and collaborative elements of the vision balance the current focus on private and economic benefits, which often threatens the ability of higher education to serve a public role.

It is important to understand that these movements alone cannot transform the current climate and mold a new social charter. First, most of these movements work at the institutional level, the exception being community service-learning, while the whole system needs to be altered. The trend toward privatization and commercialization is difficult to identify and resolve since it is not operating at a systemwide level. Second, the reciprocal nature of the charter (society's responsibility to higher education) is not engaged by these current movements. Society's commitment and input are critical to a renegotiation of the social charter. Third, no movement has worked with or engaged the private and economic interests in a discussion in order to reconcile competing missions and values. For example, service-learning and community-college partnerships will, most likely, languish if the trend toward corporatized management or part-time and contract faculty is not tempered. Corporate, government, and college and university leaders who reinforce economic and private interests need to be engaged in a discussion about balancing priorities.

References
Bok, D. (1982). The corporation on campus: Balancing responsibility and innovation. *Change, 14*(6), 16–25.

Bok, D. (2003). *Universities in the marketplace: The commercialization of higher education.* Princeton, NJ: Princeton University Press.

Boyer, E. (1987). *College: The undergraduate experience in America.* New York: HarperCollins.

Boyer, E. (1990). *Scholarship reconsidered: Priorities of the professoriate.* Princeton, NJ: Carnegie Foundation for the Advancement of Teaching.

Checkoway, B. (2000). Public service: Our new mission. *Academe, 86*(4), 24–28.

Hollander, E., & Hartley, M. (2000). The civic renewal in higher education: The state of the movement and the need for a national network. In T. Ehrlich (Ed.), *Civic responsibility and higher education* (pp. 345–366). Washington, DC: ACE-Oryx Press.

Kennedy, D. (1997). *Academic duty.* Cambridge, MA: Harvard University Press.

London, S. (2001). *The civic mission of higher education: From outreach to engagement.* Dayton, OH: Kettering Foundation.

Part Two

Public Policy and the Public Good

Chapter Four

State Governance and the Public Good

David Longanecker

States clearly see higher education as a public good—right? After all, they invest heavily in higher education, providing the lion's share of funding for the enterprise—more than $70 billion annually. In every state, higher education is one of the most significant areas of public expenditure, generally ranking either second or third behind elementary and secondary education and medical services (Medicaid, indigent care, and public health). Our states have built an infrastructure of more than two thousand public institutions, which evolved over the last century into the best and most expansive national system of higher education in the world. This is strong evidence that states see higher education as serving the public good.

But what, exactly, do these disparate states envision as *the public good*? Traditionally, this concept simply referred to the betterment of individuals and society. The public good was served when better-educated citizens advanced both their own lives and the standard of living within their communities. By advancing civilization and helping to drive economic development, higher education served the public good. It was as simple as that.

Economic development has always been seen as part of the public good derived from higher education. By creating "human capital" to fuel economic growth and by providing the research engine to drive innovation and economic revitalization, higher education contributed to the economic, social, and civic vitality of the states.

The financial resources that states poured into higher education reflected an investment in this public good.

Yet today we hear concerns from many corners that the states and their public institutions of higher education are losing their way—that the ability of higher education to serve the public good is being eroded. State policymakers (governors and legislatures) worry that their public institutions are forsaking public purposes for private interests. Meanwhile, leaders of public higher education institutions (governing boards, institutional and system CEOs, faculty, and others) fear that state policymakers no longer value higher education as a public good—as evidenced by what they see as reduced financial commitments to the enterprise. The rhetoric and actions of both policymakers and institutional leaders contribute to these very different views of the situation. Their disparate perspectives create a dissonance that makes it difficult to define what the public good is and who is responsible for protecting it.

So who's right? Who truly speaks for "the state"? And what exactly is "the public good"?

Letting the Market Decide

Contemplating the appropriate balance between public and private purposes—as well as the appropriateness of public-sector entities co-opting private-sector tactics—is all the rage these days. The National Forum on Higher Education for the Public Good bears witness to this high level of concern. On one side of the issue, Robert Zemsky, CEO of the Learning Alliance, whose *Policy Perspectives* have improved our understanding of many higher education issues over the years, has provoked discussion and concern with his stimulating, seminal work on higher education markets, which builds the case for colleges and universities to be "market smart and mission centered." While Zemsky (1998) does not argue against higher education focusing on serving the public good, his work encourages institutions to be guided by private-sector principles, including being savvy of market forces. The Mellon Forum on Higher Education, at the dawn of the new millennium, focused on the theme of "Competitive Advantage and Common Purpose in Higher Education." Robert Berdahl and Terrence MacTaggart (2000) have promoted the concept of charter colleges as a way to provide public

colleges and universities with greater autonomy from state governance and intrusive oversight. Meanwhile, Colorado has adopted a
radical new "market-driven" approach to funding higher education,
providing the bulk of state funds to students in the form of vouch-
ers rather than to institutions in the form of state subsidies for services rendered.

But not everyone likes this market-focused approach. The late
Frank Newman's work with the Futures Project at Brown University helped raise concerns about whether higher education was
"losing its way" through its infatuation with privatization (Newman,
Couturier, & Scurry, 2004). And in his 2001 farewell speech as outgoing president of the American Council on Education, Stan Ikenberry
(2001) expressed concern about "the risk that market forces will become the controlling force in setting academic and public policy."

Obviously, the issue of public versus private purposes is a timely
and important issue.

But why? What has brought us to this new world where states
weigh public good versus private gain, seeking a new *balance,* where
balance previously wasn't even a consideration?

Back in the old days, the story was much simpler: higher education served the public interest, and that was that. Without doubt,
there was private gain associated with public purposes: college-
educated individuals benefited greatly in many dimensions of their
lives; communities with college-educated people benefited from
the enhanced quality of life that an educated citizenry brought;
and business and industry benefited, too, from a highly educated
workforce and university research, both of which enhanced their
productivity. But these private benefits were not the *reason for being*
of our public institutions; they were simply logical and serendipi-
tous by-products of our investment in serving the public good.

Today, however, the story has begun to change. This evolution
from "supporting public higher education as a public good" to
"finding a balance for public higher education between its public
and private purposes" has evolved along a trio of distinct paths.
Each of these paths has consequences for how higher education
and public policy are responding today to the need to serve the
public good—and for how they'll respond in the future. In each
case the move away from a strict and singular focus on serving the
public good began innocently enough, sometimes intentionally

and sometimes not, but nonetheless it has evolved into a real and possibly irreversible shift toward serving both public and private purposes.

The Three Paths

The evolution of public policy from "serving the public good" to "balancing public and private purposes" has proceeded along three different paths:

- The conjoining of public activities with private interests
- The courting of private gain to achieve the public good
- The privatization of the public enterprise

The first path, reflected in both the rhetoric and action of the public higher education and public policy communities, began with a perception that *public activities could be conjoined with private interests* to more effectively advance public purposes. State colleges and universities began hiring the private sector to run some of their more peripheral activities, such as food service, printing services, security services, and so on. They did so simply because the costs and benefits made this worthwhile. Institutions could get service at a lower cost from private vendors that was as good as or better than what they could provide. These activities were not truly related to their core business of education and research, so building a public-private partnership and saving money that could better be spent on core activities made good business sense.

Public policy was quite supportive of this. If we could provide these essential, but noncore services through private partnerships, even though there was clear private gain for our partners, that was fine because it contributed to the public good. At least it was fine so long as it was on our terms—that is, so long as we (the state) remained the captain of our destiny.

Over time, however, this concept of private-public partnerships has evolved well beyond its initial focus on noncore activities. Today, many public colleges and universities contract with private companies, not only to build and manage residence halls but even to manage residence life activities, thus essentially abdicating their traditional *en loco parentis* responsibilities to private vendors. Many public institutions hand over other core activities to private vendors as well. Private companies like e-college.com, BlackBoard, Web CT, and others now actually develop and manage portions of the curriculum for these institutions. Fellow institutions, such as Regis University and the California State Universities (through its Merlot project), franchise their curriculum to other institutions. While these private partners ostensibly meet high standards in the integrity of the products they provide, our public institutions have nonetheless granted others a strong hand in shaping their core business; we are no longer the captains of our destiny in the same way we were when we controlled all of our core activities.

Most public policymakers have remained quite supportive of these ventures. In part, this is because they have seen this shift as inevitable in a rapidly changing higher education marketplace; one in which public institutions with limited resources for new ventures rely on private-public partnerships to infuse new life into a resource-constrained public system. Why not let the private sector risk the venture capital and then buy their proven products down the line?

Beyond these practical reasons, however, philosophical shifts have also contributed to the change in policymakers' perspectives. Increasingly, policymakers have themselves become more enamored with using nonpublic vendors to provide public services, often believing that private vendors can "do the job better" than public institutions. Higher education leaders often reinforce this perspective by bemoaning their inability to foster high productivity from state employees imbedded in a lethargic state bureaucracy.

The first path away from relying on public institutions to provide for the public good, then, is driven by both practical and philosophical considerations; by contracting for services instead of providing them, institutions seek "a new balance" between the public and the private—one that has clear benefits for them.

The second pathway to balancing public and private agendas reflects a new focus within states *to aggressively court private gain for the public good*. Two examples of this courtship are customized training and customized research.

Customized training is now nearly universal in community colleges throughout the United States and increasingly popular within public four-year colleges and universities as well. It provides private businesses with customized worker training, generally as a tax-subsidized benefit designed to retain or attract business to the community in which the college resides. In the standard model, the college "works with" a firm to design a customized curriculum that will provide specific skills to prospective or current workers to accommodate the firm's manufacturing requirements. Sometimes these customized training programs are paid for from state or local economic development funds, and sometimes businesses actually pay some or all of the costs, but seldom are these activities financed through the regular state subsidy garnered through a higher education appropriation. In a radical version of this, all public higher education institutions in Colorado have abdicated the task of designing curriculum for high-tech programs to a new state institution, the Colorado Institute of Technology (CIT), which will develop programs that are more responsive to the state's technology industry than what higher education has developed in the past.

So what's the big deal? Does it really denigrate serving the public good if we become more directly responsive to the communities we serve? Isn't this really just an extension of what we have always been about, but with a more direct link to one of our ultimate customers—the business community? Clearly, the economic development that results serves a public purpose by enhancing the community's economic vitality.

Or have we sold our soul? At the very least, with customized training we are no longer the captain of our ship; rather, the businesses we serve share in the control of our curriculum, which is our destiny. Furthermore, some community colleges are now chasing this infatuation with customized training at the cost of serving well their original and core mission of providing broad-based, high-quality general and technical education, particularly to those students who have traditionally been disenfranchised from the rest of higher education. Who will serve these students when community colleges leave them behind?

With respect to customized research, the activity is a bit different but the story is about the same. Public higher education has always engaged in applied research. While basic research has been an important part of the mission of our public universities, we've always wanted our research to be valued for its utility. Our magnificent land-grant universities literally changed the landscape of America through their research in agriculture and mechanics. Virtually every agribusiness owes its wealth and success to the publicly funded research conducted by these great universities. Even our most modest land-grant universities would rank amongst the best research institutions when compared to similar institutions around the world.

This research served the public good. And it was publicly funded, either by the states or by the federal government. Today, that is changing too. An increasing share of research funds at public institutions are coming from private enterprises that clearly have proprietary, not public, purposes in mind.

But again, what's the problem? Sure, these private entities have private purposes in mind, but does this really corrupt the public good being served? How is it different when General Mills, Exxon, or Lilly contract directly with a public university? Certainly the research still serves the public interest, even if it was conducted for the proprietary interest of the sponsoring company. Some argue that there is a chance that the research results may be stifled, but institutions that recognize they serve the public good can protect against such nefarious outcomes. Just because research may be narrowly focused to attend to proprietary interests doesn't mean that it has no value. In fact, it is pretty strong evidence of the utility of the research.

On the other hand, courting the private sector, once again, hands control of our destiny to others. We are no longer captain of our ship, though we may fool ourselves into believing we are. Furthermore, private gain isn't wholly consistent with the public good. Although much privately sponsored research does contribute to the public good, mounting evidence demonstrates that research results can be "influenced" by the source of financial support, in terms of which findings are shared and which are not. While the public good often supports private interests, private interests don't always serve the public good. In becoming less public our great universities risk sacrificing the public good.

Despite the potential problems with this *courtship* between public institutions and the private sector, public policymakers, just like public institutional leaders, have reached out to embrace this new partnership. Indeed, states and the federal government often subsidize such activities, either directly or indirectly. A recent trend at the federal level has been to encourage public-private partnerships in federal grant requests. Some programs within the Fund for the Improvement of Postsecondary Education (FIPSE), for example, require or strongly encourage public-private partnerships.

There are telltale signs of the dangers of this approach, however. Much of the ambiguity in current discussions centers around whether higher education is primarily a public or a private good, or whether it is both at the same time. As supporters of public higher education, we have made the case for the great value of higher education, often by touting the huge returns on investment, both in terms of personal income and research productivity. And we have made the case that this public good justifies the substantial public investment in higher education. But some policymakers argue that we have confused correlation with causation—that we see the equation backwards. Thanks to our own arguments, some state policymakers now appear convinced that what used to be considered a public good actually provides more private than public gain and thus should be financed primarily from the private beneficiaries. If the students are the primary beneficiaries of the education they receive, perhaps it is in the public interest to have them pay for the product. Our recent increases in tuition suggest that students, at least those who can afford it, will pay appreciably more for this service than they have in the past; many current policymakers believe a more market-based system makes sense—because we inadvertently taught them so. With respect to research, the same argument can be made: let those who want the research pay for it. Our recent successful efforts to attract more privately funded research indicate that many industries are quite willing to contract for such research services.

So policymakers are left to wonder. Perhaps the paradigm has shifted. Or perhaps our rhetoric has just been too successful in convincing folks that the paradigm has shifted, when in fact it has not.

Which leads to the third and final path by which state governance has tipped the balance between the public good and private gain in recent years: *by taking the public enterprise private*. This is happening in a variety of ways.

One way state public policy has tipped the balance is by transferring the governance of public institutions, subtly or not so subtly, away from public ownership. The charter college movement, espoused to free public institutions of the burdens of public management, has been adopted for institutions in a number of states, including Colorado, Maryland, Massachusetts, and Oregon. While charter institutions generally remain *governed* by publicly appointed boards, their "charters" often carry little language that speaks to the ways in which they'll serve the public good. Promoters of the concept contend that the responsibility of charter institutions to the public good is implicit in their creation—but implicit expectations are subject to interpretation.

Similarly, a number of states, including Arizona, Colorado, Hawaii, and Oregon, have flirted with the concept of transitioning their public institutions from "public agency" to "public enterprise" status, thus allowing them to escape state bureaucracy and become more entrepreneurial, as private business is.

Another "rebalancing" effort has some public institutions actually venturing into for-profit activities. The University of Maryland's now-abandoned effort to establish an online for-profit subsidiary reflected such a venture. The quick exodus of the University of Maryland and other private universities, when they did not turn a quick profit, suggests that these institutions were unclear about whether their mission was to serve the public or private good. Similarly, many public institutions now have stock positions in profit-oriented research and education ventures that they have spawned through their own research and economic development activities. That may make sense, given it was often a public investment that led to the profitable returns. Yet it is another example of public institutions looking for private gain.

Rebalancing Act

Why do our public institutions pursue such for-profit ventures? In part they do so to compete in the market-driven world of American higher education. Virtually every governor, legislature, and public governing board is encouraging the public universities with which they work to garner more resources from nonpublic venues. In part, public higher education is eschewing its publicness to become more private because it is being told to do so by state policymakers. But in doing so, it risks losing its contribution to the public good.

In part, higher education is "rebalancing" because it is more fun and more profitable than simply focusing on serving the public good. This is particularly true for public governing boards and for the CEOs of institutions. Willie Sutton, the famous bank robber, is reputed to have said when asked why he robbed banks, "It's because that's where the money is." It's much the same situation in public higher education today. The public good clearly isn't "where the money is"—particularly when you compare it to other less publicly oriented activities. The jollies for a president or a public higher education board come from scoring big on a new research contract or directed gift, not on trying to cajole the governor into recommending more funding for higher education in her or his budget request or in begging the legislature for sustaining support (and often losing).

Much of this evolution away from serving the public good is so new that it is hard to know how public policy will respond over the long term. Currently, for the reasons discussed, the shift or "rebalancing" as I have politely referred to it, seems to be sitting quite well with most policymakers, many of whom simply believe that the public good can be better served by being less public.

Yet evidence suggests that we face substantial potential risks by diminishing the expected attention to the public good by public institutions.

First, when public institutions increase their focus on serving privately beneficial economic development—both for individual students and for the communities in which they live—they may also provide an excuse for diminishing public investment in them. Indeed, the declining share of state funding for higher education has persuaded some within our institutions that this has already occurred—though continuing increases in funding on a per student basis contradict this impression. Whatever the actual case, diminishing "the publicness" of public higher education could well diminish the perceived public good being served—and it is the public good that justifies the public investment.

Indeed, this could extend well beyond simple reductions in direct state appropriations. How will the IRS and state revenue departments perceive future tax exemptions for higher education, including the huge current value of property tax exemptions, if the enterprise becomes viewed more as a vendor of private services than a provider of public ones? This question becomes more significant as for-profit educational providers enter the higher education community and argue that they provide equivalent service but at a distinct disadvantage—because of the many explicit and implicit subsidies provided to their publicly owned, nontax-paying competition.

Perhaps an even greater and more imminent calamity, however, is the possibility that higher education will simply begin fooling itself—that it will begin to redefine the public good in such a way as to claim success in serving it when it is actually failing to do so.

A Distinct Difference

There is, in fact, a difference between the public good and private gain. In a civilized society, one way we serve the public good is by caring about the least fortunate; serving the public good means that we make sure our least fortunate individuals are served. Yet there is no compelling private interest for a vendor of educational services to serve these individuals because there is no private gain in doing so. Absent public intervention to serve this public good, the least fortunate will be left out. Historically, public institutions have recognized this obligation, in part because of their mission but also in great part because they were recompensed for doing so. If public resources to support the public good disappear, public institutions will lose their incentive to serve the disenfranchised. And that will be a loss of the public good. Unless, of course, we redefine the public good so that the least fortunate are no longer our concern, or shift responsibility for them (at least rhetorically) onto others. Isn't this, in fact, what we do whenever one of our public colleges or universities redefines its mission to become more selective, or (as Bob Zemsky puts it) when they become "market smart," thus excluding the least fortunate individuals in order to enhance their mission and image?

Another way we serve the public good is by protecting and ensuring the quality of the educational experience we offer. Yet the quality of our overall educational enterprise could also be jeopardized if we lose our focus on the public good. Though the mantra of privatization is that it fosters greater competition and thus improves quality, too often, that's simply bunk. What competition often fosters is more *marketing* of product, not higher quality. The essence of marketing is market segmentation and sales. On the other hand, quality is enhanced when *better,* not *marketing,* information is available to the consumer (real economists speak of providing perfect information, but I would settle for simply better information). Marketing that focuses on serving private gain and not the public good, however, essentially relies on the art of deception—it pretends to offer quality whether it exists or not. A BMW may be of substantially higher quality than a Honda but not of such high quality that it justifies the substantial price differential; yet that's not the story BMW portrays in its marketing campaign.

Caring for the least fortunate and assuring a high-quality education are just two ways we serve the public good. Fostering civic engagement, imbuing democratic principles, and advancing the general quality of life are some others. The point is that the concept of *serving the public good* has a real and distinct meaning in our world, and it signifies something very different from the concept of *serving private purposes*.

What does this all bode for state policy and governance with respect to the balance between the public good and private gain?

In the short-term, evidence suggests that states will continue to react as they have during the past few years: with a combination of benign indifference and some active support in shifting the balance from serving the public good to embracing private gain. Why?

- First, because it is cheaper, and currently there is tremendous pressure within state government to reduce state services so that the states can reduce tax burdens.
- Second, because it fits a privatization philosophy that has gained great credence within many state policymakers.
- Third, because higher education actually likes this philosophy, too. While many leaders within public higher education decry the perceived disinvestment in their public mission, they nonetheless enjoy the idea of gaining greater autonomy. Furthermore, many have themselves become enamored of the nonpublic revenue streams that have become increasingly available to them (and with which they can do nonpublic things).
- And fourth, because it will take a while before we witness the damage caused by our divestment of support in the public good. As Al Yates, former president of Colorado State University once pointed out, and I paraphrase, dismantling higher education is like dismantling a ship at sea. Plank by plank the ship can be dismantled, with the removal of no single plank

suggesting the demise that lies ahead. Ultimately, however, the ship will become unseaworthy.

This, of course, could bode ill, not only for higher education but for our society at large. If we lose sight of serving the public good, the very fabric of our civilization will erode. Yet we may not even recognize it.

Though this danger exists, I believe the longer term holds a different and more optimistic outcome. Most state policymakers do, in fact, know the difference between the public good and private gain, and they appreciate the difference. When it becomes obvious that chasing private gain has jeopardized our ability to support the public good, public policy will come alive again to protect the public good. Access to higher education will be protected. Quality will be assured. Research in the public interest will be supported. Whether states do this by establishing new institutions, as the Western governors did in creating the Western Governors University, or by reigning in their established public institutions through new regulatory and financing models, is not yet known. In the end, however, I trust that the states and their policymakers will protect the true public good.

In his farewell speech, Stan Ikenberry (2001), outgoing president of the American Council on Education, said, "The problem is not a lack of agreement on core values and purpose. We enjoy a widely accepted consensus. While we agree on these values and precepts, however, it gets harder every day to strike the right balance between the practical and ideal: will the market eventually crowd higher education leaders out of the driver's seat?"

Ikenberry had it almost right—but he may have feared the wrong culprit. While it is common and convenient for those of us working in higher education to place blame for the shift away from serving the public good on others, particularly state policymakers, it may well be that Pogo had it right: "We have met the enemy and he is us." Our higher education leaders may not be crowded out of the driver's seat but may instead become comfortable steering public higher education along this new path.

This is not a conundrum, however. There are ways to put the ship back together again. Perhaps one new model will not be to *conjoin* or *court* or *take our publicness private* but rather to *co-opt private gain for the public good.* Perhaps, through crafty public policy, we will incentivize private businesses to enter into more co-op educational partnerships, in which students from less fortunate backgrounds can earn and learn at the same time. And perhaps we can convince the private sector to develop and market quality assessment tools that help us all better understand student learning.

Harold Enarson, former executive director of the Western Interstate Commission for Higher Education, president of Ohio State University, and current sage of American higher education, once said that those who attempt to achieve perfect public policy will suffer the same fate Don Quixote did, tilting at windmills—perhaps even with the same false sense of success in the battle. He suggested that to be successful in the public policy arena, policymakers should seek more modest objectives, that true success in public policy will be achieved only by "disciplining the inevitable." This is wise counsel as we seek today to find the balance between serving the public good and following our current infatuation with private gain, for both individuals and institutions.

References

Berdahl, R. O., & MacTaggart, T. J. (2000). *Charter colleges: Balancing freedom and accountability.* Boston: Pioneer Institute for Public Policy Research.

Ikenberry, S. O. (2001, 20 February). *Mission and market: A leadership struggle for presidents.* Plenary session speech, 53rd annual meeting of the American Council on Education.

Newman, F., Couturier, L., & Scurry, J. (2004). *The future of higher education: Rhetoric, reality, and the risks of the market.* San Francisco: Jossey-Bass.

Zemsky, R. (September 1998). A very public agenda. *Policy Perspectives, 8*(2).

Chapter Five

Listening to the Public
A New Agenda for Higher Education?
David Mathews

The topic for this chapter fits logically in a book that deals with higher education's responsibilities to the public good. "Listening" reflects a proper sensitivity to consulting with people instead of assuming what they want and then providing what some institution believes is good for them. Yet the title might give the impression that I am going to write about a better way of divining what Americans want in order for colleges and universities to serve them better—some technique that is more effective than polling or focus group research. I am not going to do that. And I don't want to endorse the consumerism that might be implied in the notion that higher education's role in a democracy is "serving the needs of the people." There is nothing wrong with providing services, but I don't believe it meets all of academe's responsibilities to a sovereign public. These obligations grow out of the nature of the work that must be done by the public in order to exercise its sovereignty responsibly.

Words like *public* and *good* have a wide variety of acceptable meanings; so for me, the first questions before taking on the topic of listening and serving the public good are what *public* and what *good* are we talking about? How higher education understands its obligations to democracy is determined by how institutions answer those two questions (Mathews, 2000). In what I am about to propose as civic engagement, the word *public* refers to a citizenry actively engaged in the work that self-government requires. I understand *good* in a democratic society to be what citizens determine is most valuable in their common life—more precisely, what actions people deem most consistent with the things they hold dear. The public, as I see it, is constituted by these collective decisions and the collective actions that follow from them. From this perspective, the public does not appear as a constituency, audience, or market. Rather, it shows itself as a dynamic entity more like electricity than a light bulb, more a set of interactions or practices than a static population.

Choice Work

I believe that the quintessential work of self-government is choosing. To be free is to be able to make choices. People who would rule themselves have to make countless collective decisions: which policies will result in the greatest good, which candidates for office will best represent us, which projects will most improve our community. Every one of these issues can be addressed in several ways, so citizens have to make judgments, not only about what to do but also about what is most important. The fate of a democratic society is determined by the soundness of these decisions.

Focusing on the work of self-rule makes the broad issue of higher education's obligation to promote the common good less abstract. If the work of the public involves making collective decisions, then what can academic institutions contribute to the task of making sound judgments? Is it enough for them simply to educate students and provide a wealth of factual information on policy issues? Instruction, research, and service are certainly necessary but, I think, not sufficient. Nor is a response from any one part of an institution or any one group (faculty, students, administrators, alumni, or trustees). If American higher education is to recover its sense of a democratic mission, these sometimes estranged parties have to come together as civic actors.

Democratic decisions aren't solely matters of rational choice; they have to do with what *should* be—with matters on which there are no experts. These decisions require people to consider what is truly valuable—imperatives that have emerged from centuries of attempts at self-government. Equity and freedom are two. The difficulty people face when they are confronted with having to act in a particular way on a particular problem in a particular set of circumstances is that the many things they hold dear lead them to different responses. A collective action to protect a community from an external threat may have impinged on individual freedom or compromised standards of justice. That is why collective decision making is often called *choice work*, even though the more precise term for doing this work is *deliberation*. Its Latin roots give us the image of an old-fashioned scale with two arms (the scale that is now used as a logo for the judiciary). It is an apt image because choice work consists of fairly weighing different options for public action, on one side, against what citizens hold most dear, on the other.

Unlike weighing produce on a scale, however, where one side has a fixed weight, when there are decisions to be made about "what should be done," both sides of the scale have to be determined by deliberation. What is most valuable in a particular situation has to be weighed or judged and so does the appropriateness of the actions being considered. Struggling with the tugs and pulls of all that we hold dear is inescapable in self-government. We have to decide what we should do when terrorists threaten our country, when costs limit our access to healthcare, or when some schools fail our children. We can't predict which conclusions will be the right ones because we can't see into the future. So we consider decisions sound when the actions we plan to take are judged consistent with those things that we hold to be truly valuable. That is never easy, not only because we can't see into the future but also because each of us places a different weight on what is valuable—even if we all value the same things.

That is the reason collective decision making in a pluralistic democracy seldom ends in total agreement. Yet the choice work done by citizens can provide a general sense of direction or at least a delineation of what people will and won't do to solve a problem. The shared and reflective judgments that emerge when we deliberate together can give rise to what might be called a "public voice," which is more coherent than the cacophony of special interest pleadings that fill the airwaves. That is no small achievement. One of the most serious complaints Americans make about the political system—one of the reasons people say they distrust politics—is because the balance between particular and general interests has been lost. As people put it, moneyed interests rule; citizens don't. The question of what higher education has to contribute to the formation of public judgment, then, is not merely "academic." It goes to the heart of a critical problem in contemporary democracy.

Another Role for Academics?

Let me restate the question of higher education's contribution to public decision making in a way that emphasizes the production of knowledge, which is one of the functions of the academy. If one of the sovereign responsibilities of a democratic public is to judge what should be done, then what kind of knowledge is needed? Will the answer become evident if academics simply listen more attentively to what citizens say to them? I think not. The knowledge the public needs can only be produced by the dynamic engagement of citizens with citizens. Scholars have to find ways to relate to the process of forming sound judgments. (That could be one kind of "public scholarship.") The nature of what the public needs to know is different from academic knowledge and so is the process for generating public knowledge. Actually, *knowledge* is not the right word; the Greeks had a better term when they described the outcome of public deliberations as *phronesis* (practical wisdom). Simply put, *phronesis* is knowing how to act, knowing what should be done. *Phronesis* is the sagaciousness or prudence that grows out of purposeful thinking and ends in resolve. In the fourth century, Isocrates provided one of the first accounts of practical wisdom when he distinguished *phronesis* from scientific knowledge, philosophy, and popular opinion. Isocrates believed that humans had a particular mental faculty that they could use in making political decisions—the ability to distinguish between wise and unwise action, which is captured in the word *judgment* (Isocrates, 2000).

Because questions about what should be done politically can be answered in more than one way and, therefore, require the exercise of judgment, they have to be addressed in a particular fashion, in which the full range of people's concerns, perceptions, and experiences are shared. In other words, practical wisdom is socially constructed in a highly interactive exchange. The interaction itself is instructive, which prompted Athenians to call a deliberative dialogue "the talk through which we teach ourselves." Practical wisdom, therefore, consists of things that people can only know when they are together—never alone.

Even though cursory, this description of what is involved in producing practical wisdom shows that the question of what academic disciplines and bodies of professional knowledge have to offer is not self-evident. Answering the question is quite a challenge. Providing objective data and relevant information certainly serves the interest of all; so does professional expertise. Yet they cannot substitute for practical wisdom nor are they produced in the way that *phronesis* is.

I haven't posed this challenge so that I could present my own answer, and I don't know of one that is entirely satisfactory. However, I am aware of a number of academics who are interested enough in the challenge to have taken it up in a series of articles in the Kettering Foundation's *Higher Education Exchange,* an annual publication that publishes case studies, analyses, news, and ideas about efforts within higher education to develop more democratic societies. The articles suggest, for instance, that public deliberation might be well served if scholars practiced more of what Immanuel Kant describes as "thinking aloud" with other citizens. Given that practical wisdom has to be produced *with* people rather than *for* them, Kant's notion seems worth exploring.

Equally intriguing, recent papers from deep within the epistemological wellsprings that feed academe have had obvious implications for deliberative practice. An example: Christopher Smith's (2000) article on consultative reasoning. He insists that certain realities can only be heard. Compare the impact of seeing your mother's name written with what happens when you hear her say, "This is your mother calling." Public deliberation is more dialogic than logic, more discursive than "an exercise of pure reason." The power of the spoken word, grounded in collective experiences, forms practical wisdom.

If public discourse is essential to the creation of the knowledge people need to exercise their sovereignty, then where scholars and institutions stand in relationship to the deliberation of citizens is critical. By *stand,* I mean both the physical place they occupy and the way they relate to the interaction among citizens. Merely standing to listen isn't enough; institutions must stand in places that enable them to facilitate the practice of choice work.

Standing in the Practice

In 2002, The Ohio State University's Civic Life Institute was called to Cincinnati to help in dealing with racially charged issues. A year earlier, the Economic Development Institute at Auburn University became involved in a small, rural community, Smalltown, Alabama, which was caught in a web of wicked social and economic problems. Neither institution went into the communities offering professional or expert knowledge. Instead, what each did was informed by an understanding of public deliberation and practical wisdom. Ohio State helped frame the issue of race relations so that it would be easier for citizens to weigh options for actions that would reduce conflict and restore justice. Auburn posed questions for town meetings. In both communities, citizens directed their own decision making; the universities were only catalysts.

Cincinnati has had more than 150 deliberative forums involving nearly 2,000 citizens. Some people just talked; others began to organize in order to act. Have all racial problems been overcome? No. Yet according to the *Cincinnati Enquirer*, the community has developed a stronger sense of its civic capacity to deal with these problems, which is reflected in the slogan "Cincinnati Can." In addition, a new grass-roots movement called Neighbor to Neighbor has emerged to follow up on the forums.

Has Smalltown made dramatic progress socially and economically? Not really, at least not yet. But there is now a new civic organization that, project by project, is beginning to change the town's physical and political environment (Economic Development Institute, 2002; Battle, 2003).

The Auburn faculty is also doing longitudinal research on what is happening in Smalltown. It fits what I think of as "public scholarship." Their first case study has been well received at the Southern Growth Policies Board, and a Spanish translation is being done for the Inter-American Foundation. Both organizations are intrigued by the insights into the economic consequences of social and political conditions in a community. The Auburn study is related to the research being done in institutional economics, where informal norms of cooperation, levels of trust, and standards of ethical conduct are studied for their impact on economic innovation and development—as well as their effect on the production of those public goods that facilitate economic growth (Burki & Perry, 1998).

In addition, Auburn has developed new standards for determining if Smalltown-type research can be considered for tenure and promotion. That is significant because it shows both a recognition that public scholarship is distinct and, at the same time, a willingness to give it a place in the regular academic system.

Institutions placing themselves as a catalyst in the dynamics of public work not only contribute to the formation of more shared, reflective, and hopefully sound judgments but also contribute to the formation of the public itself. A group of individuals becomes a public when they begin to do public work. Institutions like Auburn and Ohio State have moved beyond simply "serving the public" to assisting in the creation or strengthening of the public, which is essential because the dynamic processes that constitute the public are seldom in perpetual motion. To return to the electrical analogy, the switch may not be on in some communities or the current may be too weak to light the bulb.

Auburn and Ohio State are not alone in efforts to assist in the creation of practical wisdom. There are more than thirty new institutes and projects that engage citizens as they carry out the work of self-government. These projects can be found all over the country in almost every kind of academic institution, from community colleges to private research universities. Not all of the institutes are focused exclusively on public deliberation. Some are interested in what has to come before collective decision making is possible and what must result from it. Choice work has to be preceded by naming and framing issues in public terms and followed by collective action, then evaluation or civic learning.

Some of the institutes' projects are on their own campuses as well as in distant communities. The universities where they are located are concerned about problems in the collegiate culture and about what kind of civic skills their students will have. Miami University, for example, is using student deliberations to devise strategies for combating alcohol abuse on its Oxford, Ohio, campus. Purdue, which has done the same thing, reports a significant reduction in its alcohol-related problems. Wake Forest is testing to see if experience in public deliberations, coupled with classroom instruction, will affect students' cynicism about their ability to make a difference in politics.

Is Civic Engagement a Movement or a Passing Fad?

New institutes like those at Ohio State and Auburn and campus initiatives like those at Wake Forest stand out because of the concept of the public and democratic politics that is implicit in what they are attempting. Yet what is happening at these institutions is only part of what may be a genuine movement to recover the civic mission of higher education.

The public scholarship at Auburn, for instance, is but one of many types of research being done under this rubric. Recently, I have been invited to meet with several faculty senates and ad hoc academic groups at the University of Minnesota, Penn State, and other institutions where discussion of a more publicly relevant scholarship has been on the agenda for several years. In fact, so much is going on around this subject that a book of case studies is being compiled by Scott Peters (in press) at Cornell University, which will be published by the Kettering Foundation Press. Some of this scholarly work deals specifically with the difference between the way issues appear from an expert or professional perspective and the way citizens see them. For example, Dr. Douglas Scutchfield at the University of Kentucky Medical Center is looking into this discrepancy on health issues in collaboration with the Owensboro, Kentucky, community.

New ventures in public scholarship may have something in common with recent investigations into the public purpose of traditional disciplines. Claire Snyder's (2001) paper on the civic mission of political science is an example. So is William Sullivan's project on professional education at the Carnegie Foundation for the Advancement of Teaching. These efforts are already having an effect. James Carey's research on the role of the media in public life, for example, has helped stimulate a movement called "public journalism" (Munson & Warren, 1997). Despite the controversy in the profession over public journalism, the University of Southern California, the University of South Carolina, Kennesaw State University, and the University of Kentucky are getting a closer look at the role of the press in a democracy.

What do all these efforts add up to? Do they add up at all? Are they evidence of a return to higher education's civic mission? Real movements usually have features that distinguish them from mild groundswells. They are radical, they get at the root of problems, and they involve more than institutions doing good things in better ways. Successful movements also result from a confluence of forces that give shared meaning to what otherwise would be independent and unrelated phenomena. In higher education, significant changes typically come from linkages with political and social movements outside the academy.

At signal points in their history, American colleges and universities have encountered an aroused polity—a citizenry that would rule itself. And these encounters have given the institutions a political sense of their mission. It happened around the time of the American Revolution. Colonial colleges taught piety and the classics until politically sensitive presidents like Ezra Stiles of Yale encouraged students to debate the issues of independence (Tucker, 1974). It happened in Jefferson's time, when state legislatures began to charter universities to prepare leaders for the new nation. It happened in the late nineteenth century, when land-grant institutions were created to serve America's working citizens—its farmers and mechanics. The mandates of historically black institutions and community colleges have emerged from similar encounters.

Are academic institutions today in touch with the citizenry that is angry about being shut out of the political system? Is there any connection between the quest for a more "engaged" university and the efforts at public engagement going on in government agencies, schools, and mainline civic organizations? Maybe the use of the same terminology is just coincidental or evidence of a popular jargon that has little substance. Rumblings in the body politic don't always resonate with what is happening in academe.

A case in point: the response of the academy to the political upheaval in the late 1960s and 1970s. In 1976, at the bicentennial of the country's birth, Americans had just witnessed the success of the civil rights movement, new voices from women and ethnic minorities were finding expression in politics, and campuses were alive with young activists. But the records of a conference of leading academics assembled at Airlie House in Warrenton, Virginia, in December of 1976 suggest that the political turbulence was more a worry than an inspiration in much of the academy (Mathews et al., 1977).

Charles Frankel, one of Columbia University's preeminent philosophers, opened the conference by voicing concerns about "the new egalitarianism," which stimulated a discussion of access and equality. References to democratizing higher education (largely meaning a greater emphasis on pluralism) competed with remarks on the importance of research, the place of the liberal arts, and other to-be-expected subjects (Mathews et al., 1977). Much of what was said had a defensive tone, which was understandable; after all, colleges and universities had been singled out for attack in recent student uprisings. Social "relevance" was one of the slogans during those years, and it raised concerns about degrading academic standards—a major issue for faculties, which were gaining more power within institutions. The implications of this change in the governance of higher education for its external relationships has been described by Christopher Jencks and David Riesman (2002) as an "academic revolution," and it has been discussed more recently by Alan Wolfe (1996).

Despite some comments made at the Airlie conference about higher education serving the nation, the records of this 1976 gathering don't show a movement toward greater civic engagement. Almost the contrary. Participants like Earl Cheit, who was dean of the business school at the University of California-Berkeley, recalled with some nostalgia a time when the interaction between the academy and society had been more "vibrant." Cheit repeated one of his favorite themes: educators had forgotten "that for most of its history, higher education . . . was a movement, not a bureaucracy" (Mathews et al., 1977).

In the 1970s, there was more a clash of forces than a confluence. The emphasis was on protecting traditions; "radical" was a bad word. The citizenry had mixed feelings about the academy—as did the academy about the citizenry. So what about today? Is something radical going on in the cases discussed in this book? I think there may be in projects based on the idea that a democratic public is a dynamic entity different from a constituency or audience. The notion that such a citizenry is constituted by the deliberative practices of what Harry Boyte (1995) calls "public work" envisions people as producers of civic goods rather than consumers. And projects that assume a deliberative citizenry can speak in a more public voice means there could be ways to redress the imbalance between particular and general interests, which is at the root of much of the public's frustration with politics.

The prospects for a confluence of forces? I am intrigued by the common chords coming from inside academe—from public scholars, from institutes making space for the public to form, from student groups testing a more deliberative form of democracy, from philosophers grappling with public ways of knowing, and from disciplines reexamining their civic purposes. I am also struck by the openness of these initiatives. Their receptivity makes it possible for energy coming from different sources to flow together. Anyone who wants to join in seems welcome; there are few definitional barriers.

The critical question for me is whether a common cause will be made with efforts *outside* campuses. There are citizens who are determined to reengage their institutions, and there are public schools, government agencies, and civic organizations eager to reconnect to the public. If colleges and universities look at what is happening around them, I think democratically inclined academics will find they have a lot of company. What are the chances of that happening?

The Missing Link?

Who is in a strategic position to forge ties between higher education, citizens trying to reengage their institutions, and organizations attempting to reengage the public? What about boards of trustees? Having argued earlier that no one group in higher education is able to do all that civic engagement requires, I couldn't very well put the entire responsibility on trustees. And yet it would be odd to write about everyone else and say little about people who are in an ideal place to listen to the citizenry—their own representatives. Boards have a history of a democratic mission that is worth recalling. It is a history that sheds considerable light on how institutions came to have a civic mandate.

Not long after the American Revolution, the democratic notion that trustees should be citizens who were representative of and answerable to the public challenged the colonial tradition of independent, self-appointing board members. The most famous case in which these two conceptions clashed occurred in 1816 at Dartmouth College, where the trustees were still the successors of men appointed under the authority of the King of England. William Plumer, New Hampshire's governor, with support from Thomas Jefferson, wanted to bring the Dartmouth board under the control of the state assembly and end the policy of self-perpetuation. Even though Dartmouth's objections to Plumer's plan were sustained in court, the Jeffersonians eventually won the war. Plumer's views on trustees became the norm. Higher education was to be the servant of American democracy whether or not legislators appointed board members. Jefferson made the winning argument quite forcefully in a letter to the governor: "The idea that institutions established for the use of the nation cannot be touched nor modified, even to make them answer their end . . . is most absurd" (Crane, 1963, p. 64). In a democracy, colleges and universities were to serve the public interest, and the primary function of trustees was to see that they did.

Trustees were quite visible in their public roles during the founding of the state universities, which were patterned after Jefferson's University of Virginia. They had to build these institutions from the ground up and hire a faculty. And they were responsible for bringing public purposes to bear on academic predilections as was demonstrated in the case of the land-grant movement. In the twentieth century, trustees moved more to the background, usually operating behind the scenes. Some lapsed into micromanagement and used their positions to serve personal rather than public interests, prompting some chief executives to criticize boards for, as one put it, directing "internal details which, in all successfully conducted institutions are delegated to the president and faculty" (Sellers, n.d., p. 6). Trustees were also litigants in court cases brought by faculty members who were dismissed for what today would be considered lack of due process and sufficient cause. Between 1894 and 1914, boards won most of these legal contests, but the faculty then began to shift the balance of power in its favor using new organizations like the American Association of University Professors (AAUP).

Although board members still had absolute legal authority, they had to consider their relationship to both the internal and external constituencies of their institutions. Governance was becoming an increasingly contentious issue. How it was to be resolved was uncertain. One of the AAUP's founders, Professor J. McKeen Cattell, proposed combining internal and external constituencies in a unified governance system, an arrangement I always thought had considerable merit. He advocated an inclusive corporation of professors, administrators, alumni, and even "members of the community who wished to pay dues to belong." I don't think of such a "United Nations" as an alternative to student, faculty, alumni, and other associations but as useful common ground. But Cattell's colleagues in the AAUP rejected his plan, opting instead for "an organization that they would control" (Metzger, 1955, pp. 198–199).

During the late nineteenth and early twentieth century, trustees often formed governing alliances with strong presidents, and they dominated higher education until the faculty gained the upper hand in the late twentieth century. The victory of the faculty was sealed, according to Alan Wolfe's (1996) study, by the growing dependency on those who could attract the federal funds that were becoming a larger and larger part of the budget. The significance of the change for the civic mission of higher education was profound. According to Wolfe, it spread meritocratic norms in society as institutions became more professional in character and national in outlook. Only community colleges and a few other institutions retained an allegiance to communities and citizens' organizations (Wolfe, 1996).

The implication of Wolfe's analysis, as I interpret it, is not that trustees should have taken control from a self-interested faculty that was indifferent to the public good. To the contrary, the scholars who were doing more and more contract work for the government could have argued that they were serving the national interest in a very direct and useful fashion. Trustees were delighted with the prestige and funding the faculty provided. The faculty who excelled in government research may have simply defined *public* and *good* in ways different still from those who had informed earlier concepts of civic engagement and different from notions that became prominent on campuses in the late 1960s and early 1970s.

Reflecting a nationwide loss of confidence in authoritative institutions and troubled by the expanding war in Vietnam, college students in the late 1960s called for abolishing grades and "free universities." By the mid-1970s, however, the next generation of collegians used different tactics in hopes of making their institutions more socially relevant. More involved off campus and in a broader range of issues, they were "less idealistic but more realistic . . . less moralistic but more ethical" (Schulman, 2001, p. 158). Their proposals weren't really that radical: greater diversity in the student body, more choices in the curriculum, and the creation of internships and clinical programs. Some of these students won seats on governing boards, but I haven't found an account showing that they changed the orientation of trustees.

Much of what students advocated by the late 1970s would qualify as civic engagement today, yet the student movement as a whole touched off a strong reaction, which I have already noted. Writing when student unrest was teeming at Columbia University, Dean Jacques Barzun (1968) penned what proved to be the obituary for the movement in *The American University*. Barzun dismissed the watchword of reform, "relevance," as an "illusion," even though he acknowledges that some of the reformers' complaints, such as attacks on "a petrified curriculum" (pp. 71–72, 74) were justified.

What role did trustees play while these shifts in power were going on internally and students were calling for changes that would make institutions more responsive to external issues? What happened to the tradition of boards as stewards of the public interest? Barzun (1968) only devoted three pages of his book to the trustees. He described them as "men of business," whose job was to attract endowments and exercise financial control. Presidents also seemed to have been drawn more into internal issues. The days of powerful political and educational leaders like Nicholas Murray Butler, who presided over Columbia University from 1902 to 1945, were over. The next generation of presidents would describe their lives as "running for office every day" (Wolfe, 1996, p. 55).

Two trends are evident in this brief history. First, there is a clear precedent for trustees serving as intermediaries between their campuses and society at large. Second, in the latter half of the twentieth century, board agendas appear to have been filled with managerial and financial matters rather than with issues arising from the public and its problems (Brint & Levy, 1999). Nonetheless, a University of South Carolina trustee, William Hubbard, encourages his university to be more active in identifying issues of concern to the public, promoting open discussions, and listening to what results (Brown, 2001). Surely he is not alone. Because the history of the civic responsibilities of trustees parallels the history of the civic engagement of colleges and universities, I see enormous potential in connecting the two. Board members could be the natural allies of the democratically inclined at their institutions—the leaders of the new institutes I mentioned, the public scholars, the administrators, and faculty who are concerned about what kind of citizens their students become. Yet the earlier precedent is strong enough, I believe, that trustees could balance their fiduciary responsibilities with greater attention to their civic responsibilities. Some already have recognized that trustees have dual obligations.

What Legacy?

One hundred years from now, I hope historians will find that today's civic initiatives did, in fact, coalesce into something larger. I hope this will prove to have been an era when higher education returned to its democratic moorings. I hope civic engagement will have come to mean more than simply attracting greater support from the citizenry or providing better services. I hope ours will be remembered as a time when colleges and universities made a common cause with the Americans struggling to create a more meaningful place for themselves within the republic. If all that happens, those whose work is celebrated in this book will have been part of the greatest movement of all—one that dates back to the origins of this country—the movement to govern ourselves in freedom and justice.

References

Barzun, J. (1968). *The American university: How it runs, where it is going*. New York: Harper and Row.

Battle, D. (2003). *Neighbor to neighbor: How people used deliberation to ease racial tensions*. Report to the Kettering Foundation. Dayton, OH: Kettering Foundation.

Boyte, H. (1995, Spring). Beyond deliberation: Citizenship as public work. *Good Society, 5*, 15–19.

Brint, S., & Levy, C. S. (1999). Professions and civic engagement: Trends in rhetoric and practice, 1875–1995. In T. Skocpol & M. P. Fiorina (Eds.), *Civic engagement in American democracy* (pp. 163–210). Washington, DC: Brookings Institution Press.

Brown, D. (2001). On the role of trustees: An interview with William C. Hubbard. *Higher Education Exchange*, 38–42.

Burki, S. J., & Perry, G. E. (1998). *Beyond the Washington consensus: Institutions matter* (pp. 11–12). Washington, DC: World Bank.

Crane, T. R. (Ed.) (1963). *The colleges and the public: 1787–1862*. New York: William Byrd Press.

Economic Development Institute. (2002). Auburn University shared learning research project: Report of 2001–02 activities and findings. Report to the Kettering Foundation. Dayton, OH: Kettering Foundation.

Isocrates. (2000). Antidosis. In George Norlin (Trans.), *Isocrates* (Vol. 2). (pp. 179–365). New York: G. P. Putnam's Sons.

Jencks, C., & Riesman, D. (2002). *The academic revolution*. New Brunswick, NJ: Transaction.

Mathews, D. (2000). How concepts of politics control concepts of civic responsibility. In T. Ehrlich (Ed.), *Civic responsibility and higher education* (pp. 149–163). Phoenix: Oryx Press.

Mathews, D., et al. (1977). *The changing agenda for American higher education*. Washington, DC: U.S. Government Printing Office.

Metzger, W. P. (1955). *Academic freedom in the age of the university*. New York: Columbia University Press.

Munson, E. S., & Warren, C. A. (Eds.). (1997). *James Carey: A critical reader*. Minneapolis: University of Minnesota Press.

Peters, S. (Ed.) (in press). *Realizing the engaged institution: Practice stories of civic engagement and public scholarship in land grant education*. Dayton, OH: Kettering Foundation.

Schulman, B. (2001). *The seventies: The great shift in American culture, society, and politics*. New York: Free Press.

Sellers, J. B. (n.d.). *The history of the University of Alabama: 1900–1935* (Vol. 2). Unpublished manuscript.

Smith, P. C. (2000). The uses of Aristotle in Gadamer's recovery of consultative reasoning: Sunesis, sungnômê, epieikeia, and sumbouleuesthai. *Chicago-Kent Law Review, 76,* 731–750.

Snyder, R. C. (2001, June). Should political science have a civic mission? An overview of the historical evidence. *PS: Political Science and Politics, 34,* 301–305.

Tucker, L. L. (1974). *Connecticut's seminary of sedition: Yale College*. Chester, CT: Pequot Press.

Wolfe, A. (1996, Winter). The feudal culture of the postmodern university. *Wilson Quarterly, 20,* 54–66.

Chapter Six

Trusteeship and the Public Good

Richard Novak, Susan Whealler Johnston

Discussions of higher education and the public good rarely include meaningful analysis of the contributions boards of trustees can make to this national effort. In a recent conversation, a college president, someone who is personally committed to service and civic engagement and whose campus is actively seeking purposeful connections with the surrounding community, said he saw no place for his board in the college's efforts to serve the public good. Based on a recent review of publications, this president is not alone in his opinion. The review located references to trustees as potential sources of funding for community service activities, as reviewers of new curricula involving service-learning, and as handy leverage points for presidents interested in building faculty involvement in civic renewal. Each of these references was brief and rare—one sentence or less in only a handful of essays, chapters, and books. One exception to this cursory treatment of governing boards in the context of higher education and the public good is *Fulfilling the Promise of Civic Engagement* (Chambers & Burkhardt, 2004). Written for an audience composed largely of board members, this essay identifies ways in which trustees can provide leadership and support for institutional efforts to serve communities and the public good. This essay, however, is one of the only exceptions in the thirty years of discourse about higher education and the public good.

Why is this? Why are trustees not seen as significant parties in the national discussion of civic engagement? By excluding trustees from this discussion, what opportunities has higher education missed, if any? Is the work of governing boards too far removed from the aims of higher education's civic engagement movement to make meaningful contributions? Is the public good an inappropriate topic for trustees to consider, or is it beyond their ability to contribute to or affect higher education's work in this area? Is the public good simply out of their line of vision? In *The Future of the Public University in America: Beyond the Crossroads,* James Duderstadt and Farris Womack remark on the highly politicized environment in which governing boards, especially boards of public universities, function. As a result, they argue, boards are "focusing more on oversight and accountability than on protecting and enhancing the capacity of their university to serve the changing and growing educational needs of society" (2003, p. 179). For some institutions and some boards, this is no doubt true, especially if conditions on the campus or in the state are particularly challenging. Yet given the responsibilities of trustees and the nature of their service as board members, in many ways they are in the perfect position to advance higher education's efforts to address public needs. Rather than limiting their engagement or assuming a lack of interest or usefulness, it is important to ask what more can be accomplished by including trustees in higher education's efforts to fulfill its obligation to serve the public good, and how might their engagement be achieved effectively.

Trustees' Responsibilities

To see how board members can contribute to the current struggle for higher education to serve the public good, it is important to understand the role they play in the life of a college or university. Whether they are on boards of public or private institutions, large or small, trustees are volunteers with fiduciary responsibility for the institutions they serve. They approve the mission, set policy, and oversee matters of academic quality and financial health for the institution or system they serve. By state charter, statute, or constitution, governing boards have legal authority for their institution. They have the responsibility to ensure the continued existence of the institution and, particularly in private institutions, the continued availability of the endowment to support the institution and its students in perpetuity. They are responsible for hiring, supporting, and, if necessary, firing the chief executive. Trustees are responsible for ensuring that strategic planning is done and that adequate resources are available to support the institution's work. All trustees, whether public or private, are advocates for all of higher education, and as a group they are responsible for ensuring that legislators, communities, taxpayers, and others shoulder the responsibility for the continuation of a sound and strong system of higher education.

Lastly—and most importantly—trustees represent the broader community to the college or university, and they represent the institution to the community. In several important ways, they are guardians of the public trust. Trustees are guardians of the public trust in that boards of trustees, rather than government officials, govern our colleges and universities. They are responsible for ensuring that the institutions will serve the purpose for which they were designed, that they will fulfill their missions and serve the public good by creating an educated citizenry, contributing to the creation of knowledge, and preserving cultural heritages. Trustees protect and control the institutions that are established to provide education for our nation and are charged with ensuring that those institutions are not used for political or propagandistic purposes. They are advocates for academic freedom and freedom of speech, and while they typically have no training in governing within an academic environment and little prior knowledge of higher education beyond their own educational experiences, they fulfill a critical function when they serve as the bridge between higher education and society. That function is elemental to the discussion of higher education and the public good.

Trustees "are duty-bound to be attentive to the political, economic, and other priorities of their states and communities and to be actively engaged in the search for solutions to society's problems" (Association of Governing Boards of Universities and Colleges [AGB], 2003, p. 15). They should ensure that society's interests, current and future, are being served by the work of colleges and universities. This latter is especially critical for public institutions, created by the state to serve the needs of the state in a particular way that no other business or industry can. As Patricia Gumport says, "the legacy of service" for public institutions is a particularly practical one, with benefits for local, national, and international society (2001, p. 86). The nature of this service changes as priorities evolve and new challenges emerge. Jane Wellman points out that colleges and universities "have broad civic purposes at the core of their missions," purposes that are reflected in the combined "civic education and institutional service roles" of institutions (1999, p. 8). It is challenging for institutions which, in addition to meeting broad public purposes such as the education of students and the preparation of citizens, should also seek to engage with their external constituents by providing assistance such as applied research, technical assistance, policy analysis, and lifelong education opportunities. And fulfilling aspects of this responsibility presents its own challenges for governing boards. However, trustees can play a valuable role, by understanding the nature of public service and civic engagement within higher education contexts, by establishing policies that recognize and reward such activities, and by ensuring that such programs are effective and successful extensions of the college's or university's mission.

The Context for Higher Education Trusteeship

Today, the context for higher education trusteeship is replete with challenges. The economic heyday of the 1990s was followed by a period of financial crisis in most states, with budgets for public higher education slashed. For private institutions, endowment earnings tumbled to record lows at the same time that charitable giving by individuals stagnated. And all of higher education found that the financial support previously received from private and corporate foundations was deployed to other sectors, most notably preK–12 education. Because tuition income does not come close to paying the real cost of education, these economic factors have been of critical significance to governing boards that have had to make hard decisions to preserve their institutions' financial health and ensure access for growing numbers of college-bound students. These growing numbers are another area of concern for many boards, especially in the public sector, where for years access to higher education has been assumed for students with ability. In the confluence of declining financial support for higher education and rising numbers of students seeking that education is the "double whammy" identified by Jane Wellman (2002). As Wellman points out, just when a new, large population of students is approaching college age, economic conditions have arisen that seriously affect institutions' ability to provide appropriate access.

One of the biggest challenges resulting from decreased state funding for public universities is to what extent they will remain "public." As state dollars decline and private gifts, corporate sponsored research, and tuition dollars increase, will the public university, particularly the public research or flagship university, engage on public issues to the extent it has in the past and as its original charter and mission intend? Or will responding to market forces lead it to serve a narrower, more homogeneous band of students? Will it continue involvement with less able communities and constituents systematically or grow increasingly unresponsive? Such dilemmas for major public institutions are recognized in the work of the Kellogg Commission on the Future of State and Land-Grant Universities (1999) and in a recent paper by David Breneman (2004) on institutional independence and privatization for the Association of Governing Boards of Universities and Colleges.

Another condition affecting higher education, and therefore affecting the work of governing boards, is the much decried consumerism that has resulted in students' unwillingness to pay the price for education despite their desire for the personal benefits they derive from it. There are the demands from students and parents for more and better services and accoutrements on campus, often not even related to the academic experience. This consumerism is also driving institutions into the campus equivalent of an arms race, with more expensive facilities being developed in an effort to court potential students. Rising enrollments, declining dollars, and the drive for colleges to offer the best possible services and facilities have led to sharp tuition increases at both public and private institutions. At the same time that students and their parents are demanding more value for their tuition dollars, the public is questioning the price of higher education. There is a growing public intolerance for high tuition and a growing demand for institutional accountability. State and federal government officials have joined the chorus, making the environment surrounding university finances, tuition setting, and salaries more politically charged than ever.

Are Duderstadt and Womack right? In this environment, with eroding state support for public higher education, a turbulent economy playing havoc with colleges' endowments, surges in demand in many parts of the nation, and waning public trust in higher education's fiscal management, are boards so focused on "oversight and accountability" that they simply cannot attend to "the changing and growing educational needs of society" (Duderstadt & Womack, 2003, p. 179)? Given the obligations of trustees to serve as the bridge between college and community, to ensure the quality of the educational experience of their current students, and protect the future of the institutions they serve, the answer must be no. Trustees in states such as California where demand for admission is outstripping space grapple with issues of the public good regularly, as do trustees in Michigan, the epicenter of the most recent challenge to affirmative action, when they struggle to make higher education accessible to growing numbers of minority students. So too the growing numbers of private college boards that attempt to balance socially responsible investing and the challenge of intergenerational equity. In fact, by virtue of their volunteer status, their responsibility to link the institution and the community, their fiduciary obligations, and their seat at the conflux of the varied forces currently at work in higher education, trustees are in a perfect spot to play an active role in higher education's ongoing effort to serve the public good.

What Boards Can Do

Board interest, advocacy, and support can make a huge difference in institutional priorities, and there are a number of things boards can do to ensure that colleges and universities are serving the public good. In fact, some of these things are the exclusive authority of the board, and others can be affected significantly by board involvement.

Setting the Institution's Mission

It is the board's responsibility to set the mission of the institution. At regular intervals, the board should revisit the mission to ensure that it remains appropriate for the institution and that the mission informs the critical functions of the institution. In the past few decades, many institutions were found guilty of "mission drift," typically in the addition of departments, centers, and degree programs that go beyond the institutional mission. For example, in the 1970s and 1980s, many liberal arts colleges added business and other professional programs. A small group of these institutions adopted the classification "New American Colleges," with missions that intentionally and fruitfully blend liberal and professional education, but for many other institutions, the addition of professional programs had a splintering effect that continues today. Aware of this "mission drift," boards are generally mindful of the need to monitor adherence to mission. Tied to assessment discussions and reaccreditation visits, trustees should expect reports on how the mission is being fulfilled. Because most institutions have mission statements that mention service to the community or the public, this is an ideal place for boards to enter the discussion of higher education and the public good. Also, because an institution's mission is widely acknowledged to be the purview of the board, it is appropriate for the board both to promote and to oversee the institution's commitment to public service through the mission.

Where necessary, institutional missions can adapt and be made to reflect the evolving state and community needs. For instance, boards should look at proposals for the addition of programs or degree programs or schools and determine whether these additions respond to local or state needs or merely reflect faculty interest. Should a school of nursing be added, a department of education expanded, an engineering degree developed? Would these actions address the needs of the area? If so, do the proposed programs fit the institution's mission? If not, is it time to reexamine the mission and bring it into line with the community or state agenda? In a time of tight budgets, many schools are finding consortia helpful in addressing the educational needs of their communities without distorting their missions or undermining the budgets of mission-related programs. Conversations at the board level can make a significant difference in how institutions serve the public good by adhering to and fulfilling their missions or adapt their missions when appropriate.

For public institutions, it is particularly important that strategic planning carried out at the institutional or university system level be linked to the broader state agenda, as articulated in state higher education master plans or state strategic agendas established by elected leaders. Higher education institutions in Mississippi, Kentucky, South Carolina, and Texas have attempted to link more clearly the work of all institutions—public and private—to the future of the state as broadly defined in statewide public agendas. These agendas attempt to employ the expertise of institutions to address state problems, be they strengthening preK–12 education, enhancing economic development and workforce needs, or getting more students through the education pipeline. These states provide good examples of how setting statewide goals for higher education can ensure that service to the public is front and center for colleges and universities. It is critical that governing boards take an active part in such discussions where they can help articulate public needs as well as leverage the capacity of their colleges and universities to assist in addressing them. In support of this, MacTaggart and Mingle assert that, in the main, four primary objectives require trustee involvement in the fulfillment of their institution's public mission:

- Extending and sustaining prosperity to all of a state's citizens
- Expanding education systems to provide universal access to post-secondary education and lifelong learning
- Assuming more responsibility for improving the quality of life in the states and locales where institutions exist
- Partnering with social and educational organizations to achieve collaborative goals (2002, p. 4)

Hiring, Assessing, and Supporting the President

One of the most important responsibilities of governing boards is to hire the president. Done well, and followed with effective assessment of and support for the president, this activity has the potential to affect an institution for years into the future. Boards committed to ensuring that their institutions contribute to the public good can take an essential step toward this by hiring a president with experience and commitment to public service. In the search process, they can craft the position statement and list of qualifications to highlight the importance of community engagement for both the institution and the president. In doing so, they emphasize the value the board places on the institution's engagement with the community and the expectation they have for the new president to lead such efforts. Through annual assessments of the president, now a fairly standard activity in the board's calendar, trustees can reinforce the institution's commitment to public service by holding the president accountable for progress in this area. By assessing against such a mutually agreed upon strategic priority, the board can emphasize the importance it places on the institution's contributions to the public good. Similarly, board support for the president as he or she leads such efforts can be critical in making civic engagement an institutional priority. That support can take various forms, ranging from public expressions of praise or congratulations for the president and institution on accomplishments in this area to continued emphasis on community engagement as a strategic priority.

Addressing Enrollment, Tuition, and Financial Aid Concerns

Governing boards are broadly engaged in issues related to enrollment. For some institutions, that engagement takes the form of approving strategic plans identifying enrollment goals—total numbers as well as targets for the racial and ethnic diversity and the academic ability of the student body. Some boards monitor closely the composition of the incoming class and the retention rate of classes and groups of students, while others simply receive updates on numbers and demographics. As part of their focus on higher education and the public good, trustees may want to ask strategic questions about enrollment. For instance, how do enrollment patterns at our institution reflect access to higher education within our state? Do we have in place the support mechanisms required to ensure success for admitted students? Related to enrollment are matters of tuition and financial aid. Boards approve tuition annually, and while they do not typically get involved with financial aid, they should be aware of broad policies such as tuition discounting and the uses of need and merit aid. Commitment to the public good at the board level might encourage trustees to examine the effect of tuition and financial aid on access to education, and certainly a discussion of the institution's use of aid to support need or to reward merit would be appropriate for a board. Conversations about enrollment, tuition, and financial aid can be driven by competition for students and the pursuit of higher external rankings of quality, but a board committed to the public good can be guided by other priorities to address larger social needs.

Aligning Budgets with Priorities for Service

A close look at a budget can reveal a lot about an institution's priorities. This is especially true for institutions using a strategic budgeting process, with a multiyear budget linked to a strategic plan. Because boards are responsible for approving institutional budgets, they are in essence approving not only a financial plan but also a set of priorities. As suggested above, boards interested in addressing the public good can determine that financial aid and tuition are appropriate to address issues of access. They can ask questions concerning the underlying assumptions about enrollment patterns used to determine tuition revenues. Boards can ensure that their budgets contain adequate funding for initiatives in the community identified by the president and faculty in consultation with state and local representatives. For instance, a number of institutions located in urban settings budget institutional resources to address pressing social needs in collaboration with local governments and agencies. Likewise, institutions in smaller communities, where higher education might represent the largest "industry" in the area, allocate resources to work with the community on initiatives to build economic capacity, strengthen K–12 education, and a host of other needs.

Following from missions that emphasize institutional commitment to the public good, colleges and universities are also devoting financial resources to ensure that their campuses include space for public gathering to discuss community issues. While this may not mean constructing a special building, it might mean foregoing rental revenues from auditoriums and other large spaces and devoting more funding to make these gathering spaces accessible and inviting to the public.

The University of Pennsylvania provides an excellent example of the capacity of a board to put civic engagement at the center of an institution's planning and work, with the appointment of the right president, the development of a strategic vision for the institution, and the commitment of appropriate resources. In *Fulfilling the Promise of Civic Engagement,* Chambers and Burkhardt detail the ways in which President Judith Rodin and the board of trustees led Penn in initiatives to link the institution with the community through developments in academic programs and the dedication of institutional resources to address community needs (2004, pp. 4–5).

The Association of Governing Boards of Universities and Colleges' urban university project in 1995 identified other such examples of presidential and board leadership at the University of Louisville, the University of Illinois at Chicago, and Yale University.

One of the difficulties of community service and public outreach is the costs incurred by colleges and universities. Revenues are rarely generated from such activities that nonetheless require resources, financial and otherwise. As President James Votruba of Northern Kentucky University notes, public engagement activities are more often administered through "cost centers" and are very different from institutional activities that generate dollars and are considered "revenue centers" (2003). Even though there may be an implicit portion of dollars in state operating revenues for public service activities, without explicit external financial support, incentives for such important work can dissipate. Government and private support can underwrite the university's involvement, but such funding will be unlikely to sustain activities beyond the first few years or expand them to other needed areas. Sustainable commitments can come from governing board allocations of resources, a conscious decision to align dollars with public needs identified through deliberations with the board and representatives of the institution and the community or state.

Approving Faculty Policies That Support Civic Engagement

One of the greatest impediments to faculty involvement in the community is faculty policies that do not reward such activity. If faculty are asked to develop service-learning components for their courses, but they are required to have scholarly publications for tenure or promotion, service-learning is not likely to receive their attention. If faculty have expertise that could be used in addressing community problems, but they are criticized for not being on campus enough, the community may suffer. If faculty publish essays on what Ernest Boyer called "the scholarship of application," but their departments evaluate them primarily on "scholarship of discovery" (1990, p. 16), the tension may lead good faculty to seek employment elsewhere. Because trustees often approve faculty policies related to tenure and promotion, they should take a hard look at these policies to determine how effectively they support the institution's civic engagement efforts. If faculty policies and the institution's mission and strategic priorities are not aligned, the board should encourage a revision of the policies so that much needed social entrepreneurship by the faculty can be acknowledged and rewarded.

Monitoring the Assessment of Student Learning

Boards are responsible for securing the assets of their colleges and universities, and one of those assets is academic quality. Therefore, while trustees are not directly involved in academic assessment, they should expect to receive reports on assessment of student learning. For institutions committed to serving the public good, boards should look for assessment findings that gauge how well students are prepared to take their place in an educated citizenry and to engage in solving social problems. In addition to assessing student learning, boards could take a larger view of institutional assessment and seek data and qualitative information on how well the institution is fulfilling its civic responsibilities as a citizen of its community and state.

Boards can also monitor the curricular, co-curricular, and extracurricular experiences that engage students with the institution's communities. As discussed in *Stepping Forward as Stewards of Place: A Guide for Leading Public Engagement at State Colleges and Universities* (American Association of State Colleges and Universities, 2002), these experiences could include applied research, service-learning, and volunteer work. For instance, trustees can inquiry about the numbers of organizations, students, faculty, and staff engaged in volunteer work in the community. They can ask for reports on the numbers of students enrolled in classes that include service-learning and applied research. They could ask for assessments of these experiences and, if appropriate, engage academic leaders in a discussion of the appropriateness of adding requirements for such activities for all students. Even in the absence of such reporting requirements, governing boards should welcome an opportunity to discuss with staff, faculty, and students the importance of service to the community and the relation between that service and the institutional mission. In addition to contributing to a shared understanding of mission and the institution's role in its community, such discussions can reveal whether there is adequate support—financial or policy-related—to make community engagement effective and meaning-ful for all involved.

Bridging the Campus and the Community

One of the critical responsibilities of trustees is linking the campus and community; by doing so, trustees can help each to understand the values and needs of the other. By fulfilling this responsibility, board members can play an important role in an institution's at-tempts to engage with the community. Because board members are often citizens of the community or state in which their institutions are located, they are well positioned to assist the institutions in iden-tifying community needs. They can be particularly instrumental in obtaining public suggestions for appropriate institutional engage-ment. The board of trustees of the University of Tennessee, a multi-campus board of four universities, recently created a committee on outreach for the purposes of monitoring and understanding the myriad public service activities in which their institutions are en-gaged. In this structural way, a board can demonstrate that part of its responsibility to assure accountability to government and other stakeholders can encompass oversight of the activities of public pur-poses and civic engagement—and that such activities will be dis-cussed, evaluated, and valued as an essential part of the institution's mission. As Wellman notes, "Without some effort from within higher education to put its civic role into the accountability agenda, public and political measurement of higher education's 'results' will con-tinue to focus on performance measures that are much more utili-tarian" (1999, p. 10). Such board committees might seek ways to involve more of the campus and the community in its discussions; for instance, by inviting students and faculty to join their delibera-tions, discuss their community engagement and service-learning ex-periences, and assist in identifying additional opportunities.

Board members should see themselves as holding not only their own institutions in trust but also higher education as a whole. There-fore, in addition to seeking ways for individual institutions or systems to serve the public good, board members should be mindful of the responsibility of all of higher education to address important social issues such as access to high-quality education, preparation of students for meaningful contributions to society, and the effective application of academic might and institutional resources to social problems.

Trustees of colleges and universities are well positioned to lead their institutions in thoughtful examinations of higher education's obligation to serve the public good. From their responsibilities reasonably flow actions and inquiries that can result in meaningful institutional commitment to civic engagement. While trustees face a number of challenges in the execution of their responsibilities, resources are available to help them understand how they can effect change in their institutions so that the public good is intentionally addressed. Not only is it possible for trustees to do this, it is an obligation of their position. As board members, they hold higher education, the institution, and its resources in trust for society.

References

American Association of State Colleges and Universities. *Stepping forward as stewards of place: A guide for leading public engagement at state colleges and universities.* (2002). Washington, DC: Author.

Association of Governing Boards of Universities and Colleges (AGB). (2003). *AGB statement on institutional governance and governing in the public trust: External influences on colleges and universities.* Washington, DC: Author.

Boyer, E. (1990). *Scholarship reconsidered: Priorities of the professoriate.* Princeton, NJ: Carnegie Foundation for the Advancement of Teaching.

Breneman, D. W. (2004). *Are the states and public higher education striking a new bargain?* AGB Public Policy Paper Series, no. 04–02. Washington, DC: Association of Governing Boards of Universities and Colleges.

Chambers, T., & Burkhardt, J. (2004). *Fulfilling the promise of civic engagement.* AGB Priorities, no. 22. Washington, DC: Association of Governing Boards of Universities and Colleges.

Duderstadt, J. J., and Womack, F. W. (2003). *The future of the public university in America: Beyond the crossroads.* Baltimore: Johns Hopkins University Press.

Gumport, P. J. (2001). Built to serve: The enduring legacy of public higher education. In P. G. Altbach, P. J. Gumport, & D. B. Johnstone (Eds.), *In defense of American higher education.* Baltimore: Johns Hopkins University Press.

Kellogg Commission on the Future of State and Land-Grant Universities. (1999). *Returning to our roots: The engaged institution.* Washington, DC: National Association of State Universities and Land-Grant Colleges.

MacTaggart, T. J., & Mingle, J. R. (2002). *Pursuing the public's agenda: Trusteeship in partnership with state leaders.* Washington, DC: Association of Governing Boards of Universities and Colleges.

Votruba, J. (2003, September). Remarks at the Institute for Effective Governance 2003, Governor's Conference on Postsecondary Education Trusteeship, Hebron, KY.

Wellman, J. V. (1999). *Contributing to the civic good: Assessing and accounting for the civic contributions of higher education: Working Paper.* Washington, DC: The Institute for Higher Education Policy.

Wellman, J. V. (2002). *Weathering the double whammy: How governing boards can negotiate a volatile economy and shifting enrollments: Working paper.* Washington, DC: Association of Governing Boards of Universities and Colleges.

Chapter Seven

The Public Good and a Racially Diverse Democracy

Denise O'Neil Green, William T. Trent

Most educators would agree that diversity and democracy are universal principles that our higher education community and our publics hold dear. However, a diverse democracy, with an emphasis on race and ethnicity, requires substantial advocacy and leadership to promote it as a legitimate public good. Long-standing debates pertaining to inequitable educational opportunities, mortality rates, employment opportunities, affordable housing, income and wealth distribution, and voting behavior continue to shine the spotlight on persistent disparities that affect the ability of marginalized racial/ethnic populations to fully participate in our democratic society (U.S. Census Bureau, 2000). Furthermore, the protracted nature of such inequalities, combined with a false public perception that everyone essentially experiences the same democratic reality, adds more complexity to an already complicated situation. In light of these lingering tensions between racial/ethnic diversity and democratic participation, the discourse of a diverse democracy as a public good is unfortunately distorted by political and social entities that wish to ignore, discount, or vilify racial/ethnic influences in American life. Hence, understanding that there are many forms diversity takes in our society, this chapter focuses on racial/ethnic diversity because of the critical challenges racial/ethnic diversity poses to higher education institutions and the nation at large.

The challenge for higher education leadership today is to accept the responsibility of leadership and participation in the construction, development, and advancement of a new narrative and discourse that gives voice to diverse communities that have, for too long and too frequently, remained invisible. This essay explores the initial framing of how higher education leaders may redirect and anchor this discourse in the context of institutional mission, public engagement, and a participatory democracy. Starting with the premise that an engaged leadership serves the public good by understanding and operating from the perspective that our nation's legacy of racism, segregation, and civil rights abuses continues to hinder a diverse democracy and stifles the public good discourse, we argue that educational leaders can and should reshape the diverse democracy narrative.

We first explain why it is imperative that the issues of racial/ethnic diversity be placed in the forefront of the public good discourse. Second, under the guidance of this new diversity context, we reconceptualize aspects of the social contract to ensure that respect and consideration are given to groups that traditionally have been dismissed. Third, we address the need to confront challenges that undermine the importance of racial/ethnic diversity and allow leaders to wash their hands of these crucial public good issues. Lastly, we return to the notion of higher education leaders giving voice to a new narrative and describe several strategies to advance a new discourse.

Shifts in Racial and Ethnic Diversity: The Demographic Imperative

Most, if not all, leaders in higher education understand that our society is undergoing demographic shifts that were foreseen in the 1980s (Estrada, 1988; Hodgkinson, 1992; Hsia & Hirano-Nakanishi, 1989). Due to relatively higher birth rates and the steady immigration of nonwhites (Estrada, 1988; U.S. Census Bureau, 2000), the increasing diversification of the United States has enveloped our society, influencing the language, culture, education, economy, and racial discourse (Rodriguez, 2003). Although these shifts in racial/ethnic diversity have occurred, do they require a new paradigm or worldview? Is it safe for educational leaders to assume that they can proceed with business as usual or should they take stock in these shifts by developing strategies that recognize and capitalize on the changing social order? We would argue that these demographic shifts, in concert with remaining racial/ethnic disparities, give leaders legitimate reasons to pause and rethink the notions of leadership, diversity, democracy, and the public good.

Not surprisingly, some leaders would respond to this demographic shift with a litany of programs and initiatives on their respective campuses to enhance student diversity, campus climate, and possibly faculty and staff diversity. However, campus communities remain that have not embraced these demographic shifts and have done very little to transform their campuses, culture, and curriculum to reflect these changes. In these cases, student protest, political embarrassment, or litigation must often precede the installation of diversity efforts. On rare occasions do such diversity efforts gain support from executive leaders without the stimulus of adversarial conditions. Nevertheless, the divisive contexts from which these diversity programs emerge do not diminish their importance or contribution to campus, local, and statewide communities. In spite of such achievements, higher education leaders should no longer continue to operate under the assumption that conflict must first manifest itself before issues of diversity are substantively addressed. Taking proactive steps rather than instituting reactive measures begins with understanding that the demographic imperative has profoundly affected our higher education institutions on a number of dimensions, including our organizational missions, student enrollments, undergraduate curriculums, research, community outreach efforts, and levels of public engagement.

If leaders accept the premise that our country's racial/ethnic demographic shifts require a new perspective for leadership and public engagement, then issues of diversity and racial/ethnic sensitivity would not have second-class status or be delegated to a designee in the multicultural affairs or affirmative action office. The aim is not to reject, ignore, or remain unaware of forces of race and ethnicity but to recognize these forces as essential to decision making and integral to the maintenance and establishment of relationships with privileged as well as disadvantaged constituencies. Nevertheless, the natural course of history has demonstrated that educational leaders tend to retreat from racial/ethnic issues rather than offensively channel these forces to assist the greater good or public good. Only a few institutions, such as the University of Michigan-Ann Arbor, Heritage College (Washington), Mount St. Mary's College (California), Barry University (Florida), Bloomfield College (New Jersey), and the University of Maryland-College Park, have begun to articulate the link between the social contract, an emerging diverse democracy, and the public good. Therefore, before educational leaders can collectively begin to reshape the diverse democracy narrative, the first step is to reexamine the social contract in the context of the diversity paradigm.

A Revised Social Contract: Integration of the Diversity Paradigm

The ivory tower image of the academy has long been a part of the public's perception of higher education institutions. These organizations, which hold such great importance in our increasingly diverse society, have been granted deference to determine their educational missions and social roles. But, with the nation's changing faces, cultures, and values, the implicit social contract that public research institutions have with various sectors, including corporate America, K–12 school systems, government agencies, and, of course, the citizenry, must be revisited and reevaluated in light of these changing dynamics.

Reflecting upon the social contract provides a starting point in understanding how leaders may engage their institutions in diverse democracy work or advocacy. In particular, public research institutions function within our contemporary society in several important ways: (1) producing new knowledge, (2) validating knowledge, (3) educating citizens, and (4) certifying educational experiences for entry to professional careers (Lowenthal, 1975; Meyer, 1976). Though we can point out multiple ways in which higher education institutions have adequately served the public in these various capacities, more can be done to improve the advancement and acceptance of a diverse democracy that is increasingly more inclusive of racial/ethnic minorities. By filtering aspects of the social contract through a diversity frame, prior constituent groups that traditionally have gone unnoticed may be brought to the forefront to initiate a conversation and devise corrective measures that acknowledge and embrace their perspectives.

Producing New Knowledge

In the present knowledge economy and information age, the production of knowledge has a high premium and is greatly valued. Institutions of higher education play a vital role in producing new knowledge that has the potential to inform as well as transform thinking, attitudes, and behaviors. Research of this nature impacts the campus community and external constituencies, including corporate America, government agencies, and K–12 educational systems. However, irrespective of this great potential, the production of knowledge does not guarantee that all communities, especially racial/ethnic minority communities, will benefit. Though institutions of higher learning have contributed greatly to society through scientific discovery, the process of discovery in this country has also harmed communities of color, such as in the Tuskegee Syphilis Study and the Puerto Rico Birth Control Pill Trials. There are also many well-respected social science theories that were developed from studies that sampled only white male populations. Though we would assume the production of knowledge is an objective process, divorced of bias and subjectivity, cultural norms, attitudes, and values permeate the entire venture. Racial/ethnic diversity, values, and political contexts shape research in the social and human sciences (National Research Council, 2002). As such, research questions, subjects studied, qualitative and quantitative analyses, and reported results have contributed to the marginalization of minority communities, constructing them as pathological, uneducated, culturally deficient, violent, and essentially, un-American, rather than as American citizens who have been resilient in the face of oppressive social, economic, and political barriers. A process of discovery that perpetuates knowledge which objectifies and devalues the experiences of racially/ethnically diverse populations does not foster movement toward a diverse democracy but facilitates the status quo in that underrepresented minority groups continue to be seen as separate and not an integral part of the democratic citizenry. To counter the prevailing status quo, colleges and universities can provide legitimate spaces where competing research conceptions of minority communities can challenge one another, especially where the intellectual construction of a homogeneous societal context has been shown to be wrong and harmful.

Validating Knowledge

Closely linked to knowledge production is the validation of knowledge claims. Claims accepted as legitimate in the marketplace of ideas are given much weight in public policy, political, and legal debates, which impact the formation of laws, institutional policies, and governance structures. In conjunction with the responsibility of validating knowledge claims is the responsibility of accounting for the messages that knowledge claims purport. Messages and validated knowledge claims communicate to the campus and their respective constituencies which communities of color are affirmed or marginalized. The model minority myth of Asian Americans illustrates the point well. While there are those who attribute certain positive characteristics to Asian Americans, negative characteristics are attributed to African Americans, Native Americans, and Mexican Americans. However, all four groups continue to struggle for full participation within our democratic society. As institutions affirm or disconfirm knowledge claims and their corresponding messages, the public will readily accept the validation of concepts that either move us farther away from a pluralistic society or draw us closer to a democracy that embraces participation of all citizens. Given the vital responsibility of knowledge validation, higher education must begin to recognize its faults and shortcomings in perpetuating messages and knowledge claims that promote exclusion rather than inclusion of all citizens.

Educating Citizens

The role of educating the citizenry for a democratic society is critical to the perpetuation of values and norms that undergird the core principles of participation in that same democracy. In the not so distant past, the law of the land permitted the segregation of schools at the elementary, secondary, and postsecondary levels. Both *de facto* and *de jure* systems perpetuated disparities between school systems and institutions that primarily served majority versus minority students. Differences between resources, teacher salaries, facilities, and funding persisted. With the advent of the *Brown v. Board of Education* U.S. Supreme Court decision in 1954, the doctrine of "separate but equal" was struck down, giving hope to

African Americans, as well as other groups, who could finally reap the full benefits of a public education similar to their white counterparts and be recognized as truly American citizens. However, a half century later, many schools, colleges, and universities continue to be racially identifiable—either predominately white, black, or Latino/a. Though *Brown* paved the way for desegregating educational institutions, the integration of individuals from different racial/ethnic backgrounds remains a distant goal.

Today, postsecondary institutions continue to educate individuals in racially and ethnically homogeneous environments. Though there are benefits associated with homogeneity, diversity in the form of language, culture, worldview, political affiliation, religion, race, and ethnicity contribute to the advancement of free, pluralistic societies. Among institutions that have begun to generate an increasingly diverse student body, faculty, and administration, changing the curriculum to provide students ample opportunities to learn about citizenship and democracy from competing perspectives and experiences has been a difficult battle to win. Several institutions have made inroads in this arena (Musil, Garcia, Moses, & Smith, 1995); however, to educate citizens for a diverse democracy, the challenge not only entails attending to the racial/ethnic make-up of the college environment but also requires addressing the exclusionary nature of the curriculum that advances particular worldviews while denying historically marginalized groups their voice (Banks, 2002). Not attending to these issues hinders the advancement of a diverse democracy in which many worldviews are valued, enriching debate, democratic process, and the public good.

Certifying Educational Experiences

In the twenty-first century, educational institutions continue to stratify and maintain the hierarchical order of the haves and have-nots in our society. While there are institutions, namely community colleges, that facilitate open access for those who seek educational opportunities beyond high school, selective public institutions award credentials to those entering professional fields—law, business, medicine, and academia—to gain entrance into a higher stratum of society, a stratum which requires a unique collection of experiences that higher education institutions are expected to construct and validate (Bowen & Bok, 1998). As competition increases and professional fields continue to require advanced or terminal degrees, the importance of receiving credentials to certify that students were exposed to a particular set of diverse educational experiences will become even more salient as the nation's racial/ethnic demographics continue to shift. However, certification is not solely for the purpose of conferring credentials for personal gain but simultaneously serves the greater good of the community. Institutional leaders who understand the significance of this certification role recognize that both privileged and underserved communities ought to benefit from this process. Furthermore, certification of educational experiences that do not incorporate a diversity paradigm disadvantages both graduates and the communities they aim to serve, because these graduates have completed a certification program without experiences or competencies that are essential for working in a pluralistic society. Educational experiences that are constructed such that both minority and majority students learn multicultural competencies are likely to improve the status of the individual, their respective communities, and the public good. But, if competencies are ignored and certification is narrowly constructed to benefit only majority students and privileged communities, this exclusionary practice will continue to perpetuate the disparities between the haves and have-nots.

In summary, producing knowledge, validating knowledge, educating citizens, and certifying educational experiences are functions that public research universities contribute to the public good of society. Potentially, these functions can aid society in a greater way if only the demographic imperative was an integral, guiding component, used as a lens to assist in building a diverse democracy. As the above discussion illustrates, if these functions are divorced from a guiding diversity paradigm that acknowledges the country's demographic shifts and growing diversity of publics, the very institutions that are expected to lead the way will hinder rather than advocate for diversity and democracy. But for those institutions with clear missions to embrace racial/ethnic diversity with leaders who publicly validate diversity to their internal and external constituencies, they face opponents and mounting challenges that aim to diminish the importance of using a diversity paradigm.

Confronting Challenges That Impede Integration of a Diversity Paradigm

As higher education leaders begin to articulate the importance of accepting a racially and ethnically diverse democracy and characterize it as essential to the future well-being of the citizenry and democracy, leaders must be ready to face constituents who hold contrary paradigms and have competing interests that challenge the notion of consistently taking into account the factor of racial/ethnic diversity. The affirmative action debate of the 1990s demonstrates at least three worldviews that promote policies to address social justice issues, ensure racial/ethnic neutrality, or take into account the importance of racial diversity (Green, 2004). While the social justice and color-blindness camps anchor polarizing positions, the diversity camp takes the middle ground by arguing that racial/ethnic diversity should be taken into consideration because of its benefits (American Educational Research Association et al., 2003). Nevertheless, the diversity camp experienced resistance. As a result of legal and political resistance (such as the University of Michigan's *Gratz v. Bollinger,* University of Texas-Law School's *Hopwood v. Texas,* California's Proposition 209, and Washington's Initiative 200), educational leaders, who in theory agree with the diversity argument, advance diversity when it is convenient and retreat when it appears politically suicidal. Current examples of retreating are illustrated by institutions that have changed eligibility for various student services that traditionally targeted underrepresented students, and their efforts to truly affect minority recruitment and retention have been watered down due to threats of litigation (Schmidt, 2003). If leading educators of flagship institutions will not stand up for underserved minority students, then who will?

Various leaders, including government officials, corporate executives, and community advocates, have been withdrawing on the required investments needed to educate the country's underserved minority student population. Questions continue to mount regarding the significance of shifting demographics and how the public ought to be served in light of these changes. Nonetheless, higher education leaders are challenged to be engaged, responsive, and responsible toward all publics to which they are expected to serve. However, educational leaders allow myths of incompatibility between racial/ethnic diversity and traditional notions of educational excellence to dissuade them from practicing within the diversity paradigm. These are false dichotomies and artificial straw men that should be dismissed, but education's top leaders continue to operate from myths that have been debunked with empirical research (Chang, Witt, Jones, & Hakuta, 2003). To guard against these straw men, while striving to address the public good, three guiding principles will aid in keeping leaders centered and away from mythical traps: (1) inclusiveness emerges from change, (2) excellence thrives in a diverse environment, and (3) constituencies aid the development of a diverse democracy.

Inclusiveness Emerges from Change

As the discussion pertaining to a diverse democracy evolves, closer examinations of exclusive versus inclusive practices expose the tendencies of our higher education institutions to administer programs and enforce policies that continue to exclude or marginalize particular underrepresented racial/ethnic groups. For example, in difficult budgetary times, programs and services that support movement toward inclusiveness and diversity are often the first to go, except when political will is exerted to protect such programs and their funding. Furthermore, programs, funding, and policies that advance appreciation for a diverse democracy and inclusion in many cases exist in isolation, away from the mainstream priorities of the institution. They are simply afterthoughts. Though higher education institutions are increasingly giving lip service to the importance of diversity, these same organizations lack comprehensive plans to guide them in the right direction. While it is common for institutions to have strategic plans or financial plans, campuswide diversity plans are "missing in action" (community college administrators, personal communication, February 21, 2003). However, if a plan does exist, implementation requires change, challenging the status quo.

To challenge the status quo takes a great amount of political will and support from students, faculty, staff, alumni, and other constituents who view changing course as a challenge to their valued, exclusionary traditions. There is constantly a tug and pull between the old and new ways. Exclusionary practices are exhibited at all levels of the academy, including admissions criteria, curriculum offerings and requirements, faculty appointments, research on particular populations and social problems, and community ventures. Nonetheless, these challenges should not deter educational leaders from meeting their obligation to serve the public good through establishing a tradition of inclusion versus maintaining the status quo of exclusion. In particular, public institutions, whether they are community colleges, flagships, four-year colleges, or comprehensives, are required to recognize that they are not independent actors but rather dependent actors in critically important ways. Unlike private institutions, which are held accountable to very few external social entities, public institutions are expected to serve various constituencies. As such, external actors exert pressure for one agenda or another (such as social justice, racial/ethnic diversity, or color-blindness) for a plethora of reasons. What is important about the dependent status of public institutions is the potential for change due to pressure from external actors. Given the historical legacy and status quo of exclusion that permeates so many of our public institutions, challenges and institutional change to advance inclusion is expected.

Conversely, educational leaders of public institutions have the ability to challenge external actors to change in order to benefit the public good as well. This reciprocal relationship or codependency may keep leaders off balance but could ultimately serve as the impetus needed for change toward inclusion.

Excellence Thrives in a Diverse Environment

The debate of diversity versus excellence has long been a false dichotomy that aims to maintain inequities in educational opportunities, experiences, and outcomes. But, educational leaders must not continue to give life to this straw man and perpetuate the myth. The diversity versus excellence debate hinges upon the assumption that diversity and excellence are mutually exclusive. Much of this tension has been generated from the public's misperceptions of students, faculty, and administrators of racial/ethnic backgrounds. Unfortunately, prejudicial attitudes, stereotypical messages from the media, and blind ignorance help maintain the tension between institutional interests of promoting diversity and maintaining excellence in academic standards. Because many have bought into the idea that excellence is synonymous with grade-point averages or standardized test scores, it is assumed that merit is an objective goal that each individual achieves, irrespective of their environmental context or range of choices (Moses, 2002).

Merit is not an objective construct, divorced from one's range of opportunities and choices, even though the will to work and work hard is there (Moses, 2002). The *Castaneda v. Regents of the University of California* case filed in 1999 is an excellent example that illustrates this point. Over 750 students of color with 4.0 or better grade-point averages were denied admissions to the University of California at Berkeley because they could not compete with students who had access to advance placement courses, which inflate students' grade-point averages, making them more competitive for slots at highly selective universities (NAACP Legal Defense Fund, 2003). On the contrary, the myth would lead one to conclude that these minority students were rejected because they were not qualified. Because affirmative action opponents emphasize the gap between white and black test scores without addressing the gaps in environmental opportunities and choices, the image of minority students, especially African American students, has been hard hit (Perry, Steele, & Hilliard, 2003). In addition to students, minority faculty and administrators constantly confront the negative perceptions of their colleagues who view them as less qualified and incapable of excellent scholarship or leadership (Haro & Lara, 2003; Verdugo, 2003).

In spite of these perceptions, research that examines the benefits of racial diversity substantiates the claims that minority (such as African American, Native American, and Mexican American) students, faculty, and administrators add value to all facets of the academy, especially scholarship and teaching (Chang, Witt, Jones, & Hakuta, 2003; Orfield & Kurlaender, 2001). The evidence demonstrates that racial diversity is truly a "plus factor" for campus environments because it aids in the facilitation of critical thinking and viewing problems from different perspectives for both minority and nonminority students (Gurin, Dey, Hurtado, & Gurin, 2002; Gurin et al., 2004). Furthermore, diversity among faculty and staff also add value to the college environment in multiple ways (Orfield & Kurlaender, 2001). With solid evidence to refute this straw man, challenges to educational leaders who strongly support diversity are lessened and lose their credibility.

Constituencies Aid the Development of a Diverse Democracy

Educational institutions function in several ways to benefit individual students, faculty, and administrators, as well as their respective communities. Students receive important credentials in order to pursue their educational aspirations and advance their careers. Faculty members are free to engage in different forms of scholarship (Boyer, 1990) to advance their careers. In addition to their careers, administrators have opportunities to exercise their leadership skills and personal agendas. Each of these endeavors has a personal and individualistic orientation. Educational institutions by nature implement policies and practices that benefit individuals and their livelihood. But, increasingly voices from different corners of society challenge these organizations to embrace their public missions by attending to local communities, state concerns, and national issues. The tug of war that persists within public institutions that aim to foster both individual success and social responsibility continues to challenge our leaders in ways that force them to choose between these objectives when they ought to complement one another. Producing successful students, faculty, and administrators who have a strong commitment to developing and perfecting a diverse democracy demonstrates how the two goals can be achieved and embraced.

As these successful and committed individuals become members of external constituencies of public institutions, their respective organizations and affiliations are potential partners in developing a diverse democracy. Corporate America, state governments, and professional associations, as well as other external actors, can extend the university's reach and influence in addressing racial/ethnic diversity for the public good. First, corporations could greatly demonstrate the value of racial diversity and its public worth by giving a high priority to (1) minority hiring and promotion, (2) research and development, and (3) charitable giving and service. Second, government officials, rather than operate within a political paradigm, could make it standard practice to always consider the demographic imperative before making critical decisions. How will legislation, fiscal policies, and altering fundamental civil rights impact advancement of a diverse democracy? Lastly, professional associations, which set the standards for quality, could persistently express the message that diversity is necessary for quality. Some of these multiple constituencies have already proven to be allies in advancing a diverse democracy, but more can be done. Leadership that affirms and brings these voices together is the missing component. But, are higher education leaders ready to meet the challenge? Are they ready to give voice to a diverse democracy, or do they wish to remain silent and hope the issue of racial diversity goes away? Given the demographic imperative and the need for integration of a diversity paradigm, this issue will not go away. Hence, it is time for higher education leaders to direct the debate and give voice to a new narrative that speaks to racial/ethnic diversity.

Giving Voice to a New Diversity Narrative: Building a Tradition of Inclusion

As leaders of institutions that provide opportunities for those in the body politic to better their lives and their children's lives, educators' voices must be heard. They must challenge old traditions that are superficially fair and egalitarian but systematically exclude underrepresented racial and ethnic minority groups and devalue their contributions. In order to change these exclusionary practices, higher education leaders must (1) create a new diversity narrative, (2) advance a message of inclusion, and (3) lead the debate. Advocacy that incorporates this three-pronged communication strategy may pave the way for constituencies and all publics to eventually embrace the importance of a racially and ethnically diverse democracy.

Create a New Diversity Narrative

Although the demographic imperative provides a solid basis for the development and integration of a new diversity paradigm in order to reframe the social contract for the betterment of all publics in society, critical race theory (CRT) takes this argument a step further. According to CRT, there are master narratives or stories that support the status quo of domination by the white majority and disregard the voices and experiences of African Americans, Native Americans, Asian Americans, and Latino/a groups (Solorzana & Yosso, 2002). To counter these master narratives, CRT places issues of race and ethnicity front and center, allowing counternarratives to be heard and affirmed. Furthermore, the racialized experiences of these groups are not dismissed as pathological or uncommon but are considered worthy of merit. Though some would consider CRT an extreme way of examining the status of our diverse democracy, this lens could help in understanding the power and importance of narratives. Furthermore, CRT uncovers how hidden messages regarding race and ethnicity are embedded in these master narratives, perpetuating two extremes—either negative stereotypes or the assumption that an individual's racial/ethnic background does not affect one's educational, economic, or employment opportunities.

CRT can aid higher education leaders in rethinking the diversity narrative because it assumes the presence of multiple racial/ethnic realities and experiences. According to CRT, there is not one single reality, homogeneous experience, or one truth that we all share. Though we are all citizens of the same country, multiple realities, truths, and experiences exist among the publics, all of which are valid in their own right. In addition, the multiplicity of truths, realities, and experiences are influenced by a person's racial/ethnic background. Understanding and accepting that there are multiple realities and experiences dictated by an individual's or a community's race or ethnicity can help leaders to break from traditional thinking which assumes one truth, one American experience, and one reality that supersedes all others. The dominant "truth" is therefore embedded in narratives that do not allow different realities to surface or take center stage, leaving counternarratives on the periphery of the debate. For example, the claim that diversity is detrimental to educational excellence is a master narrative that benefits the white majority. However, there are counternarratives that speak from different vantage points and that give voice to the importance of racial/ethnic diversity for education and democracy. Therefore, to create a new diversity narrative, CRT directs leaders not only to acknowledge numerical shifts among racial/ethnic populations but to comprehend that these same citizens have stories and experiences that should be propelled from the margin to center stage in order to influence the debate.

Those who give voice to master narratives continue to perpetuate the tradition of exclusion that the country must overcome before a true diverse democracy can be realized. Over the years, many have voiced support for racial diversity, but unfortunately, higher education leaders cannot assume a consensus exists. Executive administrators who strongly support racial/ethnic diversity find themselves in an era of aggressive legal and political campaigns to eliminate policies (such as affirmative action) and programs (such as minority-targeted efforts) that have historically assisted educational institutions, businesses, and government in increasing minority participation and success. In light of these developments, leaders who understand that much can be lost if these campaigns succeed are needed to shape a new diversity narrative—a narrative of inclusion.

Build a Tradition of Inclusion

Building a tradition of inclusion in order to preserve democracy is a simple but potentially powerful task that can begin to counter the narratives that have for so long kept racial/ethnic minorities at the margins of society and the democratic process. Many of us can recall the line in the Pledge of Allegiance that states ". . . one nation under God, indivisible, with liberty and justice for all." Though many citizens believe this long-standing narrative, it does not reflect every citizen's reality. The United States of America continues to be a racially and ethnically divided country. This is reflected in our institutions of worship, education, and government. It has been said that Sunday morning is the time when we are the most segregated.

The second most segregated time is when school is in session, followed by election day. Segregation persists due to the many exclusionary practices and policies that higher education institutions sanction. However, this course can be altered by "building a tradition of inclusion" while pursuing educational excellence. Inclusion is ultimately the guiding narrative that ties together the demographic imperative, revised social contract, and guiding principles that protect against straw men who resist the integration of a robust diversity paradigm.

In light of how CRT frames concepts of multiple truths, at the heart of the new diversity narrative of building a tradition of racial/ethnic inclusion are three truths. First, racial/ethnic diversity still matters in American life. There is much research evidence to substantiate this. Furthermore, the fact that diversity matters speaks to the importance of attending to racial/ethnic diversity and allows concepts of "color-consciousness" rather than "color-blindness" to dominate the debate.

Second, all publics, especially racial/ethnic constituencies and communities, are valued by and add value to the campus community and democratic process. Higher education leaders, administrators, and faculty of public research institutions often start with a deficit model when accepting, hiring, or promoting any individual from a particular racial/ethnic minority group. The students who had 4.0 or higher grade-point averages and were rejected from Berkeley (such as those in *Castaneda v. Regents of the University of California*) did not receive the same media coverage as those in the *Gratz v. Bollinger* and *Grutter v. Bollinger* cases. Nor was there the same indignation in the press or declarations of support for these students. Deficit thinking and a legacy of exclusionary practices and policies maintain narratives that speak to the white majority's achievements and the racial/ethnic minority's limitations. In contrast, a valued-added model is more appropriate and helps to change the orientation that many predominantly white institutions have operated from for so long. Attributing value to all publics allows for dialogue to move toward a tradition of inclusiveness.

Third, difference is not a detriment but an asset. A revised social contract that has integrated a diversity paradigm recognizes that all publics are not homogeneous, and therefore, may need to be served differentially. However, heterogeneity between and among publics is not detrimental but is the basis of a diverse democracy. Too often educational leaders act based on narratives that assume unity and community equates with sameness. On the other hand, sameness works against inclusiveness because the process of including those who traditionally have not been marginalized naturally will lead to change and possibly conflict. As discussed above, inclusiveness emerges from change, and change enables institutions to accept differences that are reflected in their students, campus constituencies, and external publics. To welcome rather than retreat from the process of change because it concerns racial diversity may generate conflict in the short run, but in the long run change moves us closer to a tradition of inclusion.

Advance a CRT Narrative of Inclusion

In conjunction with creating a new diversity narrative, the message of inclusion should simultaneously be advanced in order for the public and constituencies to begin to understand its importance. How can such a task be accomplished? Organizational conflict or political models (Baldridge, 1971; Bolman & Deal, 1997; Katz & Kahn, 1978) provide guidance for message development and advancement in the realm of higher education policy. They underscore the importance of communication to the organization and its various constituencies. Nevertheless, increased communication does not always guarantee a reduction in conflicting views. Second, executive leaders must be involved in communicating the message of inclusion and need a supportive power base. Third, parties who have a stake in the issue need a place to voice their positions, and facilitation of this process aids policy development and decision making.

However, traditional models of this nature do not underscore the necessary communication strategy that is inevitably needed to advance one's message in the present media age. Recognition of the media and its power to teach the public and pertinent constituencies regarding racial diversity (Cortés, 2002) and its connection to democracy is an important lesson to learn if educators are to advance a message of inclusion. With multiple media outlets at the disposal of higher education leaders, particularly higher education associations, print media, e-mail, the Internet, film, and television are all possible venues to deliver the message that racial diversity is advantageous for society and important for democracy. Nevertheless, other narratives will counter these messages. Therefore the persistent communication of research findings to corporations, government, and K–12 school systems that demonstrate the positive effects of racial diversity is critical. Given the persistent negative coverage through television and newspapers, the public has been taught very little regarding the positive aspects of racial diversity (Cortés, 2002). The cycle can only be broken if countermessages and narratives begin to permeate the media. Of course, each college campus has its own history with respect to inclusive and exclusive policies and practices, as well as narratives regarding particular minority groups.

To break the cycle of negative messages that perpetuate the rejection of racial diversity and its benefits, three important steps are needed (Green, in press). First, develop a message that directly counters negative messages regarding racial/ethnic diversity. For example, excellence is a by-product of inclusion. Second, share this message frequently and publicly with the media, community members, constituencies, and all publics. Through op-ed pieces, press releases, speaking engagements, and radio and television appearances, the message can begin to resonate with the public. Because the publics are hearing it often and through different venues, this new narrative has a better chance at making a difference in the public discourse. Third, higher education leaders need allies outside of higher education to reiterate the same narrative or message. By having strong allies who voice the same message, the narrative gains ground and sustains the message when opposition attempts to regain the debate. Overall, changing narratives requires active leadership and dedicated advocacy to the issue.

Lead the Debate

Relying on government officials, corporate America, or other constituencies to dictate the terms of the debate regarding higher education's role in promoting a diverse democracy for the public good places education leaders at a disadvantage. By allowing others to determine the terms of discourse, higher education leaders are relegated to reactionary stances or, worse, dismissed. Nevertheless, the opportunity to take a substantial leadership role in the public good discourse is always at hand. Because the production, certification, and validation of knowledge, and the education of citizens are primary responsibilities of higher education institutions, engagement of these institutional leaders are essential to advance and elevate a discourse that recognizes a marriage between the goals of democracy, racial diversity, inclusion, and the public good. A debate devoid of this type of leadership inevitably leaves higher education vulnerable to political agendas that compromise the principles of a diverse democracy and the means of achieving an inclusive society.

References

American Educational Research Association, Association of American Colleges and Universities, & American Association for Higher Education. (2003). Brief of AERA et al. as *Amici Curiae* in support of respondents (02–241). Retrieved May 9, 2003 from http://www.umich.edu/~urel/admissions/legal/gru_amicus-ussc/um/AERA-gru.pdf.

Baldridge, J. V. (1971). *Power and conflict in the university: Research in the sociology of complex organizations.* Hoboken, NJ: Wiley.

Banks, J. (2002). Multicultural education: Historical development, dimensions, and practice. In C. Turner, A. L. Antonio, M. Garcia, B. V. Laden, A. Nora, & C. L. Presley (Eds.), *Racial and ethnic diversity in higher education* (2nd ed., pp. 427–457). Boston: Pearson Custom Publishing.

Bolman, L., & Deal, T. (1997). *Reframing organizations: Artistry, choice, and leadership* (2nd ed.). San Francisco: Jossey-Bass.

Bowen, W. G., & Bok, D. (1998). *The shape of the river: Long-term consequences of considering race in college and university admissions.* Princeton, NJ: Princeton University Press.

Boyer, E. (1990). *Scholarship reconsidered: Priorities of the professoriate.* Princeton, NJ: Carnegie Foundation for the Advancement of Teaching.

Chang, M., Witt, D., Jones, J., & Hakuta, K. (Eds.) (2003). *Compelling interest: Examining the evidence on racial dynamics in colleges and universities.* Stanford, CA: Stanford University Press.

Cortés, C. (2002). *The making and remaking of a multiculturalist.* New York: Teachers College Press.

Estrada, L. F. (1988). Anticipating the demographic future: Dramatic changes are on the way. *Change, 20*(3), 14–19.

Green, D. (2004). Justice and diversity: Michigan's response to *Gratz, Grutter,* and the affirmative action debate. *Urban Education, 39*(4), 374–393.

Green, D. (in press). Fighting the battle for racial diversity: A case study of Michigan's institutional responses to *Gratz* and *Grutter. Educational Policy.*

Gurin, P., Dey, E., Hurtado, S., & Gurin, G. (2002). Diversity and higher education: Theory and impact on educational outcomes. *Harvard Educational Review, 72*(3), 330–366. Available at: http://www.edreview.org/harvard02/2002/fa02/f02gurin.htm.

Gurin, P., Lehman, J., Lewis, E., Dey, E., Gurin, G., & Hurtado, S. (2004). *Defending diversity: Affirmative action at the University of Michigan.* Ann Arbor: University of Michigan Press.

Haro, R., & Lara, J. F. (2003). Latinos and administrative positions in American higher education. In J. Castellanos & L. Jones (Eds.), *The majority in the minority: Expanding the representation of Latina/o faculty, administrators and students in higher education* (pp. 153–167). Sterling, VA: Stylus.

Hodgkinson, H. (1992). *A demographic look at tomorrow.* Washington, DC: Institute for Educational Leadership/Center for Demographic Policy.

Hsia, J., & Hirano-Nakanishi, M. (1989). The demographics of diversity: Asian Americans and higher education. *Change 21*(6), 20–27.

Katz, D., & Kahn, R. (1978). The social psychology of organizations (2nd ed.). Hoboken, NJ: Wiley.

Lowenthal, R. (1975). The university's autonomy versus social priorities. In P. Seabury (Ed.), *Universities in the western world* (pp. 75–84). New York: Free Press.

Meyer, J. (Ed.). (1976). *Reflections on values education.* Waterloo, Ontario: Wilfrid Laurier University Press.

Moses, M. (2002). Affirmative action and the creation of more favorable contexts of choice. In C. Turner, A. L. Antonio, M. Garcia, B. V. Laden, A. Nora, & C. L. Presley (Eds.), *Racial and ethnic diversity in higher education* (2nd ed., pp. 704–725). Boston: Pearson Custom Publishing.

Musil, C., Garcia, M., Moses, Y., & Smith, D. (1995). *Diversity in higher education: A work in progress.* Washington, DC: Association of American Colleges and Universities.

National Association for the Advancement of Colored People (NAACP) Legal Defense Fund, Inc. (2003, June 17). *Settlement reached in suit over discriminatory admissions process at UC Berkeley.* Retrieved August 14, 2004 from http://www.naacpldf.org.

National Research Council. (2002). *Scientific research in education.* Committee on Scientific Principles for Education Research (R. J. Shavelson & L. Towne, Eds.). Center for Education. Division of Behavioral and Social Sciences and Education. Washington, DC: National Academy Press.

Orfield, G., & Kurlaender, M. (Eds.). (2001). *Diversity challenged: Evidence on the impact of affirmative action.* Cambridge, MA: Harvard Education Publishing Group.

Perry, T., Steele, C., & Hilliard, A. (2003). *Young, gifted, and black: Promoting high achievement among African American students.* Boston: Beacon Press Books.

Rodriguez, R. (2003). *Brown: The last discovery of America.* New York: Penguin Books.

Schmidt, P. (2003, March 7). Excluding some races from programs? Expect a letter from a lawyer. *Chronicle of Higher Education,* pp. A22–A23.

Solorzana, D. G., & Yosso, T. J. (2002). Critical race methodology: Counter-storytelling as an analytical framework for education research. *Qualitative Inquiry, 8*(1), 23–44.

U.S. Census Bureau. (2000). The population profile of the United States: 2000 (Internet release). Retrieved June 24, 2004, from http://www.census.gov/population/www/pop-profile/profile2000.html.

Verdugo, R. (2003). Discrimination and merit in higher education: The Hispanic professoriate. In J. Castellanos & L. Jones (Eds.), *The majority in the minority: Expanding the representation of Latina/o faculty, administrators and students in higher education* (pp. 153–167). Sterling, VA: Stylus.

Part Three

Cross-Sector Issues and the Public Good

Chapter Eight

Liberal Education and the Civic Engagement Gap

Carol Geary Schneider

Since the founding of the republic, Americans have seen a close and even necessary connection between education and the "public happiness." But for most of the twentieth century, higher education's role in fostering civic vitality was underexplored and underdeveloped. Civic education was assigned primarily to the schools, while the academy concerned itself with the advancement and dissemination of knowledge.

Today that missed connection between higher education and civic vitality is beginning to be addressed. A "new academy" ethos is growing up on the boundaries and, increasingly, within the departments, of American colleges and universities. The "new academy" is centrally concerned not just with knowledge but also with educating students who are both prepared and inspired to address society's difficult questions. This ethos places strong value on what it calls "engaged learning"—learning that emphasizes what students can do with their knowledge and that involves students, individually and collectively, in analyzing and working to solve significant problems in the larger world.

The orientation to engaged learning is especially prevalent in emergent fields such as ethic studies, women's studies, environmental studies, urban studies, policy studies, and the many other "bridging" fields where involvement with public questions is intrinsic, rather than ancillary, to the work of the discipline. But the same movement toward more engaged and collaborative learning also is bringing a new "civic turn" to longer established fields within the humanities, sciences, social sciences, and the professional fields. Many faculty members in these disciplines have developed courses that directly address "big problems" in the civic sphere, problems that range from gender equity to nuclear waste to cross-cultural power dynamics to the biology of HIV/AIDS.

Collectively, this movement toward new forms of civic learning in undergraduate education has the potential both to revitalize the core meanings of liberal education in the twenty-first century academy and to enrich its practices. But it remains an open question whether or not this "civic turn" will fulfill its potential. The growing national movement to make civic engagement an explicit goal for liberal education has many influential proponents, including campus presidents, distinguished scholars, and some major foundations and national educational associations. But the civic engagement momentum has not yet persuaded the majority of faculty, or students themselves.

There are, in short, two challenges confronting the civic engagement movement. The first is to change the practices of undergraduate education so that civic engagement and learning become central rather than elective. The second is to work to broaden students' own perception of what matters in college, so that students will come to view civic learning and engagement as important values in their own lives.

This chapter addresses both issues. In the first two sections, I provide an overview of the historical and contemporary relationships between civic engagement and liberal education. This overview locates the emerging focus on civic engagement as part of a larger effort to re-form liberal education in ways that make it more purposeful, more pragmatic, more public-spirited, and better attuned to the realities of contemporary society.

In the third section of the paper, I report disturbing findings about students' perception of civic engagement as a goal for their own education. And finally, I propose ways of connecting civic engagement with other educational agendas so that it can be embedded more solidly in the expected curriculum.

Liberal Education and the Civic Limits of Universalism

Liberal or liberal arts education has always been this nation's signature educational philosophy. But liberal education has altered dramatically over the centuries, in its subject matter, practices, and overarching rationales. As I suggest in these pages, liberal education is again in the midst of one of its transitional cycles, although the outcomes of that change remain uncertain. To understand the possibilities of the emergent "civic turn" in liberal education, we need to better understand what this movement is reacting against.

Notwithstanding the diversity of approaches to liberal education in the American academy, for most of the twentieth century there was a basic consistency to the visions of liberal education articulated both to students and to the public. Liberal education was described in that era as a way of engaging the "enduring questions" of mankind, as an orientation to disciplines concerned with "basic" research, and as a form of study "worthy in itself," without reference to any potential applications. Many proponents made the absence of practical application a defining feature of liberal education, the characteristic that differentiated it from preprofessional education (Kimball, 1995). The highest forms of education and scholarship, students and the public were told, probed universal questions, fundamental principles, constitutive elements, and basic processes. Knowledge ought to be pursued as an end in itself, and the most important knowledge would have implications for humanity as a whole, not just for particular communities.

The University of Chicago's Robert M. Hutchins distilled this Enlightenment-shaped preference for the enduring over the immediate with his pithy pronouncement: "Education implies teaching. Teaching implies knowledge. Knowledge is truth. The truth is everywhere the same. Hence education should be everywhere the same" (Kimball, 1995, p. 179).

This twentieth-century vision of a universalizing and transcendent approach to liberal learning nicely complemented the research thrust of the twentieth-century academy. Over time, liberal education helped build confidence among well-educated citizens both about the work of basic scholarship and about the long-term benefits— scientific, economic, and sociocultural—that scholarly research yields.

Simultaneously, as the disciplinary major became a focal point of twentieth-century liberal education, study in the liberal arts disciplines served the wider society successfully by honing graduates' analytical skills, cultivating their ability to think in context, and fostering intellectual resilience and adaptability. As many economists have pointed out, these capabilities became increasingly significant as the United States moved decisively toward a knowledge-based economy.

Buoyed by these strengths, liberal education consolidated its standing as the educational philosophy of choice at the nation's most sought-after colleges and universities, both public and private. Yet by the final years of the twentieth century, this vision, both for liberal education, and more broadly, for liberal democracies, had become the subject of severe and penetrating critiques.

As critics from many quarters pointed out, Western universalism—both as a social philosophy and as a framework for liberal education—had too often built from premises that proved both myopic and exclusionary. Because it had rushed too boldly to envision what "humanity" holds in common, Western universalism frustrated and frequently alienated many of those people—women, religious and ethnic minorities, persons of color—to whom its vision theoretically applied, but who had little or no part in the articulation of that vision. Where twentieth-century liberal education valued unity and commonalities, the critics argued for pluralism, for diverse viewpoints, and for far more attention to the relations between social position and perceptions of reality.

Yet despite the criticism, central aspects of Western universalism remain important for those who want to foster civic engagement and democratic empowerment in this new century. Thoughtful people in all parts of the world continue to find strong appeal in an encompassing vision that includes such basic rights as universal education, human dignity, equitable justice, liberty, and self-determination. Americans—citizens of the world's most powerful democracy—can scarcely afford to treat these topics as matters important only in established democracies. With struggles for self-determination continuing all over the world, the principles and premises that can guide just societies ought to be a central topic for study and debate in all college students' education. There is no need to approach such issues monolithically or through a single set of cultural lenses. Especially in an academy newly attentive to civic engagement and democratic vitality, democratic premises and principles—and the tensions between such principles as liberty and equality—ought to be probed and examined from multiple points of view: historical, cross-cultural, philosophical, and socioeconomic.

With this said, however, it is also true that the universalizing tendencies in the twentieth-century approach to liberal education proved problematic rather than generative when it came to the task of fostering active civic engagement in college students' own immediate communities. Both as premise and as practice, the twentieth-century conception of liberal education did not provide a rich sense of the public sphere, or of public work to change society.

As philosopher John Searle explains, the Western values driving liberal education in the twentieth century combined "what one might call extreme universalism and extreme individualism. This tends to be tacit and is seldom made explicit. The idea is that the most precious thing in the universe is the human individual, but. . . . one achieves one's maximum intellectual *individual* potential by coming to see oneself as part of a *universal* human species with a universal human culture" (Association of American Colleges and Universities [AAC&U], 1995, p. 11).

More by default than design, this orientation to the human community had the practical effect of pulling students away from the immediate public or civic questions confronting their own communities. Instead, college studies focused on an envisioned sphere defined as "the West" and on humanistic values rather than democratic challenges.

Following World War I, for example, many colleges and universities adopted variants of Columbia University's course on contemporary civilization, which was itself designed in 1919 to illuminate the values and institutions that had been at stake in the recent war. But tellingly, these new courses in "Western civilization," although established with civic education in mind, focused on overarching themes such as the relationship between religion and reason, or the scientific revolution, rather than on the more immediate challenges of U.S. democracy. Accordingly, students enrolled in Western civilization courses studied the ideas debated during the French Revolution in some detail but typically did not explore the several civil rights revolutions that were even then emerging, across the twentieth century, in their own backyards.

Moreover, as the disciplines became increasingly sophisticated and concerned with the refinement of their own scholarly methods, their educational goals focused intensively on teaching students how to use the analytical tools of their disciplines but only vaguely on the civic outcomes of liberal education. A 1990 report on the political science major from the American Political Science Association (APSA) illustrates this development of an avowed preference for the analytical over the civic.

The authors began by noting an earlier 1951 report on "Goals for Political Science":

> The purposes of political study set forth in that [1951] report all serve the primary goal once called "civic education." They include, principally, "education for citizenship," "education for public service," and [correction of "woeful public ignorance" of] international relations.
>
> Although we think sound political study is invaluable for American citizens, our emphasis is on its utility to citizens of any country in their social roles more broadly conceived. We think the goal for study in a political science major is to maximize students' capacity to analyze and interpret the dynamics of political events and governmental processes and their significance. (AAC&U, 1990, p. 133)

The authors went on to explain that "particularistic" learning about political problems, structures, and processes would prove insufficient to the goals of political science study. It was more important for students to develop broad general knowledge and analytical skills since these would enable graduates to apply their knowledge to problems in any place or time.

In a nod toward the trend of community-based learning that was already emerging in the early 1990s, the APSA report does recommend that each student have the opportunity to participate in "real-life political situations off-campus." But the reason given for this recommendation was to keep students' "conceptions realistic." No mention was made of the potential civic value of getting students involved in the real work of politics.

Other disciplines viewed their educational roles in much the same way. The APSA report was one of twelve reports on arts and sciences majors prepared by the relevant learned societies in conjunction with an Association of American Colleges and Universities (AAC&U) study of the major's contribution to liberal education.

Of these twelve learned society reports on the educational goals of their respective majors, only those from the American Sociological Association and the National Women's Studies Association included well-developed conceptions of the major's role in addressing social challenges and fostering civic capacity. The other nine reports—covering history, philosophy, religion, economics, psychology, biology, physics, mathematics, and interdisciplinary studies—were largely silent on the connections between study in their field and the development of civic capacities (AAC&U, 1990).

This same orientation to analysis over engagement also influenced the training of young scholars and future faculty members. As a budding historian in the 1960s and 1970s, for example, I was taught that undue "present-mindedness"—that is, an interest in tracing the connections between past and present—would lead to a misreading of the historical sources, and, ultimately, to shoddy scholarship. My advisors firmly warned me against the distracting temptations of "relevance."

Later I came to see that this aversion to making history relevant reflected a deeply held hierarchy of values in the twentieth-century academy. The discovery of new knowledge and underlying principles took pride of place. "Applied" knowledge held a much lower standing, both in scholarship and in the curriculum. And civic engagement was a form of applied knowledge.

I do not mean to imply that disciplinary scholars dismissed the civic value of liberal education out of hand. They expected and frequently promised that the intellectual training provided by college learning would contribute to good thinking and thereby to good citizenship. But as the APSA report cited above suggests, disciplinary scholars did not see it as part of their role to help students actually practice the arts of citizenship. Instead, liberal arts faculty left decisions about civic involvement almost entirely to each student's own private time and enterprise.

Moreover, as Searle's insights into the Western tradition suggest, the thrust of the twentieth-century approach to liberal education was highly individualistic, both in principle and in practice. Conceptually, liberal education in the twentieth century sought to help each student maximize his or her individual potential through the cultivation of intellect and knowledge. For most students, the curriculum provided such a wealth of choices that each college student's course of study was, for all practical purposes, highly individualized. The result was that liberal education came to be seen as individual enhancement—an investment in self-authorship with benefits to be realized across the lifespan.

As critics observed, the twentieth-century curriculum implicitly envisioned each learner as a separate and unencumbered self. Social and interpersonal development, like civic engagement, was delegated to the co-curriculum and to each student's private time.

Rethinking Liberal Education for a World Lived with Others

If the twentieth century emphasized the transcendent qualities of liberal education, the twenty-first century is beginning to promulgate quite a different conception. AAC&U is a national association concerned with the quality, vitality, and standing of liberal education. The organization provides resources and support for campuses that are working to rethink and reinvigorate their educational practices, both curricular and pedagogical. As a result, my colleagues and I have had access to literally hundreds of campuses' internal discussions and reports as they go through the periodic exercise of asking what they want their students to achieve from a college education and what new directions might be adopted to strengthen the quality of student learning in general and liberal education in particular.

From this vantage point, we are starting to see the emergence of an alternative vision for liberal education that places new emphasis on its benefits not just to individual learners but to society—to civil society, to a diverse democracy, to the global community, and to a creative economy.

Little is said these days about the academy as an ivory tower where students can withdraw, at least for a while, from the distractions of society. Instead, there is a new understanding, gaining ground both in scholarship and in pedagogy, that important conceptual breakthroughs can emerge from the intersection of theory and application.

In this context, engagement with "real-world" questions is coming to be viewed as an asset both to creative scholarship and to strong teaching and learning. As a result, campuses actively promote their involvement with global and local communities while turning a spotlight on programs that connect scholarship with identifiable public questions and challenges. Campuses across the country now feature their commitment to collaborative learning, community-based learning, diversity and cross-cultural initiatives, and myriad forms of experiential learning, including service, internships, and other forms of fieldwork.

Here are some of the indicators that suggest the scope of this civic momentum. Nearly three hundred colleges and universities have recently applied to take part in one or another of AAC&U's various initiatives on civic engagement and the "arts of democracy." Another two hundred colleges and universities are active participants in the American Association of State Colleges and Universities' American Democracy Project.

Campus Compact, which first initiated the movement to promote civic engagement and public service in undergraduate education some twenty years ago, now has over nine hundred institutional members. AAC&U and Campus Compact have each issued official statements in recent years that identify civic engagement as a core element in college education. Some eight hundred college and university presidents—from every part of higher education—signed one or both of these two statements (AAC&U, 2002a).

And in another harbinger of the times, the American Political Science Association released in 2004 a ringing call for new civic action to take responsibility for the future of democracy. Titled *American Democracy in an Age of Rising Inequality,* the report concludes: "Our Task Force has discovered disturbing deficits and trends that undermine the promise of American democracy in an era of persistent and rising social inequalities. We challenge our fellow citizens to join with us in a vigorous campaign to expand [civic] participation and make our government responsive to the many, rather than just the privileged few" (APSA, 2004, p. 20).

The sources of this "civic turn" in the academy and in undergraduate liberal education are diverse. Many proponents assume that the primary driver behind the new civic energy has been the rise of the service-learning movement, now some twenty years in the making. Indeed, campus faculty and academic leaders often use "service," "engaged learning," and "civic engagement" as though they were mutually synonymous and interchangeable terms.

If we look across the entire educational landscape, however, it becomes clear that there are many additional tributaries feeding into the new interest in engaged learning and community-oriented work. The service-learning movement certainly has been generative and strongly influential in making civic engagement an issue of central concern. But the following developments in educational reform also have contributed significantly to the shift toward a more engaged and public-spirited conception of college learning and liberal education:

• *The rise of new fields, especially fields established to address significant social issues, such as gender, race and ethnicity, cultural identity and power, the environment, health challenges, urban studies, and the like.* Frequently, these newer fields make community-based learning an integral part of the required educational experience for undergraduates. Invariably, they see the community as an important source of scholarly questions and problems and not just as a site for the application of knowledge.

• *The growing interest in integrative or connected learning, in which social questions or problems—such as the rise of inequality—become a catalyst for helping students connect insights across disciplines.* The learning community movement—now launched on at least five hundred colleges and university campuses—is one important locus of integrative learning; so too is the emergence of topically organized and interdisciplinary capstone experiences in general education.

• *Influential research on cognition and intellectual development.* Scholars working on cognition have convincingly demonstrated that learning is more powerful and more likely to be retained when it includes direct experience, attention both to context and to applications, active engagement in problem solving, and learning in communities. These findings, and direct support from both public and private foundations, have encouraged scholars in many fields—including science, mathematics, and engineering—to find ways of connecting basic concepts in their fields with important social questions. The intended goal is to help students examine the connections between knowledge and action and, through those connections, to deepen their understanding and strengthen their abilities to put knowledge to use.

• *The emergence of diversity as an educational value and catalyst.* In a comparatively short period of time, diversity has moved from the margins to the center as both content and context for student learning in college. Initially conceived as the study of multiple and intersecting cultures, diversity has increasingly been owned as both a civic value and a democratic commitment in many college classes. Court contests over affirmative action in admissions have prompted myriad studies exploring the educational benefits of diversity—with diversity learning understood both as academic content and as direct experience with people from different backgrounds. These studies have demonstrated that students with more experience of diversity learning have better cognitive skills, are better able to take diverse perspectives into account, and are more likely both to want to solve racial problems and to live themselves in diverse communities. These diversity outcomes were successfully presented to the Supreme Court in the recent Michigan cases (*Gratz* v. *Bollinger,* 2000, and *Grutter v. Bollinger,* 2001) as "democracy outcomes." Increasingly, campuses also frame their diversity initiatives as ways to build democratic capacities and values appropriate to a diverse society.

• *The pressure from employers to teach students how to function and solve problems in teams.* As is widely known, today's students have a strong orientation to career preparation. Employers, in turn, have forcefully communicated to professional programs their expectation that students should develop collaborative problem-solving skills while in college. While students' team projects are rarely described as "civic," team projects do provide significant opportunities for students to work on such important civic skills as: active listening, engaging diverse perspectives, creative conflict, negotiation, evaluating results, and taking corrective actions. Such projects also engage students in working to create real solutions to real problems. At least potentially, these are civic as well as workplace capacities.

Taken together, these multiple and intersecting movements have begun to lead to a reframing of liberal education. Where the twentieth century emphasized intellectual skills and individual development primarily, twenty-first-century proponents of liberal education are placing new emphasis on what AAC&U has termed "preparing students for a world lived in common."

AAC&U's first articulation of liberal education as engaged or connected learning came over a decade ago, in a 1991 report titled *The Challenge of Connecting Learning. Challenge* was written in dialogue with the twelve learned societies that took part in the AAC&U study of liberal learning and arts and sciences majors. Engaging the twelve learned society reports prepared for this study, *Challenge*'s authors contended that the work of an arts and sciences major was only partly done when a student had learned the languages and methods of a particular academic field. Majors committed to liberal education, *Challenge* asserted, also had a responsibility to help students connect the learning with the world beyond the academy. "There are two ways, by no means unrelated, in which the term 'connected learning' may be employed. The first refers to the capacity for constructing relationships among various modes of knowledge. . . ., the capacity for applying learning from one context to another. The second refers to the capacity for relating academic learning to the wider world, to public issues and personal experience" (AAC&U, 1991, p. 14).

AAC&U's 2002 report on *Greater Expectations: A New Vision for Learning as a Nation Goes to College,* calls for intentional connections between knowledge and action in even stronger terms. "Liberal education in all fields will have the strongest impact when studies look beyond the classroom to the world's major questions, asking students to apply their developing analytical skills and ethical judgment to significant problems in the world around them. By valuing cooperative as well as individual performance, diversity as a resource for learning, real solutions to unscripted problems, and creativity as well as critical thinking, this newly pragmatic liberal education will both prepare students for a dynamic economy and build civic capacity at home and abroad" (AAC&U, 2002b, p. xii).

Taking the implications of this conceptualization still further, *Greater Expectations* calls for colleges and universities to move beyond the traditional territorial divisions between "liberal" and "professional" or practical studies. All fields should be taught as a form of liberal or liberating education, *Greater Expectations* contends (AAC&U, 2002b, pp. 25–26). A contemporary liberal education is not just concerned with analytical judgment; it should foster practical judgment and social responsibility as well.

Are Students Included in This Civic Momentum?

For all the energy around this "civic turn" in the conception and practice of liberal education, it is important to recognize that these developments are at best described as a work in progress. The manifestations of a new interest in connecting college education with society are all around us, as we have seen. Yet it is also true that pervasive, transformative change comes slowly in the academy.

Faculty advocates of civic engagement who want to promote new connections between the campus and society still find themselves fighting against the power of established twentieth-century practice. In scholarship, the reward system is still tightly bound to publication and to funded grants for basic research. In the curriculum, community-linked topics and courses are increasing in number, but they are still likely to be elective, rather than required. The new, community-oriented fields still enroll only a small fraction of the student population. In the campus as a whole, community service programs are still far more likely to be led by student affairs staff than by faculty. On most campuses, community service is elective, not required. Diversity studies are more likely to be required, but many campuses have settled for a smorgasbord approach that subverts rather than foregrounds the civic potential of well-designed diversity studies and experiences. While team and field-based projects are very common in professional majors, these generally are presented—and seen by students—as career preparation, not civic preparation.

As a result, students themselves may be largely unaware of the new interest in making civic engagement an integral element in their college studies. Indeed, there is troubling evidence that many students think civic engagement has nothing at all to do with their own goals for a college education.

In the summer of 2004, AAC&U convened groups of students from several parts of the country: three groups of college juniors and three additional groups of college-bound juniors in high school. These six groups were each given a list of sixteen educational outcomes and asked to pick the college outcomes they considered most important and the ones they considered least important.

In each of these six groups, "civic engagement and leadership" was selected by students as the *least* or second least important educational outcome from college. When pressed by the focus group leader on the reasons for the low ranking they assigned to civic engagement, students' comments showed that they defined "civic engagement" as "voting" and thought their families had already told them whatever they needed to know about voting.

Collectively, these students had no developed conception what-soever of the role their education might play in preparing them to work on significant social questions confronting their democracy or the larger world. Indeed, it was clear from the conversation that civic responsibility was not really a part of their vocabulary at all. These students overwhelmingly viewed college primarily as a time to prepare for a job and to strengthen their capacity to take re-sponsibility for themselves and their own obligations. Many also thought it important to get a broader "liberal" education or at least were open to that conversation. But students in these groups didn't seem to make any connections between liberal learning and con-tributing citizenship.

If we take at face value these students' equation of civic engage-ment with "voting," the University of California-Los Angeles's Higher Education Research Institute (HERI) studies of students' college pri-orities may shed some light on their assumptions. As Linda Sax re-ports, HERI studies show that students' interest in politics has dropped sharply over the past forty years. As she reports, the percent of incoming college students who consider it a priority to keep up with political affairs declined from 57.8 percent in 1966 to 32.9 per-cent in 2002. Fewer than 20 percent of recent freshmen say they fre-quently discuss politics. There has been a modest upturn in the past two years, but overall HERI studies show that college students do not view politics as a vehicle for social change (Sax, in press).

It is noteworthy that in our focus groups' discussion of civic en-gagement, the students did not bring up the subjects of commu-nity service, service-learning, or volunteerism. One student did struggle to articulate the word "philanthropic." But he could not pronounce it, and the topic was dropped. Sax's data show, in fact, that students' rates of participation in volunteer service drop dra-matically from high school to college, with only 35.7 percent of col-lege students taking part, by comparison with 72.1 percent of high school seniors (Sax, in press, p. 9).

Collectively, the students in the AAC&U focus groups seemed puzzled that anyone was asking them about college and civic in-volvement. Their puzzlement shows us how far the academy still needs to go if it is to forge clear and powerful connections between learning in college and graduates' self-understanding of their own role in a democratic society. Many of the campuses these students attend (or hope to attend) are active in one or another of the civic engagement initiatives sponsored by AAC&U and other national organizations. Some of their campuses have launched civic engagement initiatives of their own.

But campus promotion of civic engagement may in practice involve only a handful of faculty members. Or it may mean presidential endorsement but only co-curricular civic programs.

As my colleague, Caryn McTighe Musil has written, too many campuses have managed only a "helter-skelter approach to civic engagement. Rather than a cohesive educational strategy, happenstance and impulse more typically govern. . . . All too often, civic engagement is not rooted in the very heart of the academy: its courses, its research, its faculty work. Institutions thus inadvertently model a mode of civic engagement that occurs offstage" (Musil, 2003, p. 4).

What Can Be Done?

The students' honest puzzlement over the meaning or educational significance of the term *civic engagement* shows us the decided limits of the current civic engagement movement. Much of the civic engagement energy is coming from a small group of faculty members who change their own courses to connect academic and public questions. Or it comes from student affairs, where, again, it reaches only students who volunteer their participation.

A more comprehensive approach would have to begin with a fundamental, campuswide consideration of the overarching goals for students' education. Hundreds of campuses have held such discussions. A subset of these campuses have already made civic engagement an explicit outcome for college learning. If the civic engagement movement is to gain real traction with students, the majority of institutions would need to recognize civic or democratic engagement as a core goal for all students' learning.

One way to build interest in this discussion would be to survey students on the campus about their own views of important college outcomes. College catalogs and mission statements routinely proclaim that educating students for citizenship is an important part of the mission. If the disconnect between campus intention and student perception is as wide as the AAC&U student focus groups suggest, then this in itself could create occasions for faculty and administrators to explore the root question: How do we close the civic engagement gap?

Frequently, when a campus identifies its graduation expectations for students, it then proceeds to revamp its general education program, to better align general education course requirements with its newly articulated goals for student learning. This is a desirable step but not sufficient.

Imagine the following scenario. A student enrolls in Green Valley State University. Following consultation with her advisor, she takes a required first-year learning community that meets several general education requirements. The learning community is organized around an important civic question, "Environmental Damage: Whose Responsibility?" Through two linked courses, one in environmental chemistry and one on grassroots politics, the learning community involves our student in exploring connections between science, government, and social activism. Taking part in the learning community—which includes a field component—the student discovers the way different groups perceive environmental problems and solutions. She also gains a new sense of her own potential agency in helping to prevent environmental degradation. And she fulfills, in the first semester of her first year the college's general education requirement that students take at least two courses that include a strong civic focus.

But after her initial year of college, our student never again takes another course that explores civic challenges and responsibilities. She majors in business, and she remembers that her first-year learning community explored the role of local businesses both in generating the environmental waste problems and in helping to solve them. But such civic topics are not part of the business major, and, taking her cues from her department, she does not pursue them either. She further completes a minor in psychology, but the courses she takes for the minor also have no civic or community focus.

What is the overall educational message to our student? It is reasonable to speculate that the civic outcome for her is the opposite of what faculty expected when they made civic engagement a theme in their general education program. What this student's educational experience teaches her over time is that civic engagement is peripheral to the core concerns of the academic fields with which she is most strongly identified. Much as she enjoyed her first-year learning community, in the end civic engagement was something to "get out of the way" before she moved on to her major and minor and to the serious work of preparing for a career.

Now envision an alternative scenario. Suppose that the faculty at Green Valley State had decided that civic engagement and learning ought to be core themes in every college major, as well as in general education. And suppose they had further concluded that, in a diverse democracy, civic engagement should include intercultural learning as well.

With this expanded focus, our student's first-year experience in a civically engaged learning community would have been a true beginning not just a detour from the "real" work of college. Our student completes the first-year learning community on the environment with the same enthusiasm she initially experienced. But now, as she moves into her advanced studies, she finds that civic and diversity questions remain on the table. They are embedded in several of her courses, both for her business major and for her psychology minor.

She is expected to complete a field placement in business, and the placement gets her involved in studying the environmental impacts of a local business's plans for expansion. Her studies raise questions about race and political power, as well as about business planning and environmental analysis. The student's psychology minor also includes a civic focus. To meet this expectation, she becomes involved in community-based research on ethnic stereotyping.

Because Green Valley State is assessing the outcomes of its collegewide requirements, each of our student's departments expects her to demonstrate her ability to analyze and address civic questions in the context of her advanced studies. Eventually, she completes a portfolio documenting that she has developed strong knowledge in both her fields and the ability to think through civic questions and to negotiate diverse perspectives on them.

It is perhaps worth noting that, in twentieth-century terms, our student had "chosen" a preprofessional rather than a liberal arts education, because her primary field—business—was not one of the liberal arts. Yet at least in scenario two, her studies have actively challenged her to look at her specialties in civic contexts, to encounter and make sense of diverse perspectives, and to become actively involved in connecting her learning with larger social challenges. Isn't this a fuller and more contemporary understanding of what liberal education for citizenship should include?

At the outset of this chapter, I observed that it remains uncertain whether the emerging "civic turn" in liberal education will fulfill its potential. The great weakness in the movement, I am persuaded, is the failure to fully engage either students or faculty. There are many islands of innovation on our campuses and in our curricula where civic engagement is already a lively concern. But, overall, these islands have only a comparatively small number of visitors.

If civic engagement is to become a core theme in most students' education, then it will need to become a core concern in every academic field. If civic engagement is not centrally addressed—and, yes, required—in the fields that students and faculty choose as their sources of identity and focus, then, for all practical purposes, civic engagement remains a marginalized concern.

Lee Shulman, president of the Carnegie Foundation for the Advancement of Teaching, has proposed that liberal arts and sciences fields would gain a great deal if they consciously adopted such features of a profession as its commitment to service, its engagement with the realities of practice, and its cultivation of judgment in context of application and collaborative reflection.

We might modify his useful insight to recommend that both liberal arts and sciences *and* professional fields would benefit immensely if they all made such forms of civic engagement a clear and central educational theme in ways appropriate to their particular subject matters. The commitment to service, engagement with practice and with diverse perspectives, and cultivation of judgment in the context of application and collaborative reflection—these are at one and the same time civic arts, professional arts, and liberal arts.

If we want to succeed with the "civic turn" in undergraduate education, the next step, I propose, is to move toward a unified vision for liberal education and civic responsibility in *every* field of academic study, whatever its subject matter. And that would be a clear gain both for the quality of student learning and for a civically engaged democracy.

References

American Political Science Association (APSA). (2004). *American democracy in an age of rising inequality.* Washington, DC: Author.

Association of American Colleges and Universities (AAC&U). (1990). *Liberal learning and the arts and sciences major* (vol. 2): *Reports from the field.* Washington, DC: Author.

Association of American Colleges and Universities (AAC&U). (1991). *The challenge of connecting learning.* Washington, DC: Author.

Association of American Colleges and Universities (AAC&U). (1995). *American pluralism and the college curriculum: Higher education in a diverse democracy.* Washington, DC: Author.

Association of American Colleges and Universities (AAC&U). (2002a). *Wingspread declaration on the civic responsibilities of research universities.* Available at: http://www.compact.org/civic/Wingspread/Wingspread.html.

Association of American Colleges and Universities (AAC&U). (2002b). *Greater expectations: A new vision for learning as a nation goes to college.* Washington, DC: Author.

Gratz v. Bollinger, 122 F. Supp. 2d 811 (E.D. Mich. 2000), *rev'd.* 539 U.S. 244 (2003), *on remand* to 80 Fed. Appx. 417 (6th Cir. Mich.).

Grutter v. Bollinger, 137 F. Supp. 2d 821 (E.D. Mich. 2001), *stay granted,* 247 F.3d 631 (6th Cir. 2001), *hr'g. en banc ordered,* 277 F.3d 803 (6th Cir. 2001), *rev'd.* 288 F.3d 732 (6th Cir. 2002), *aff'd.* 539 U.S. 306 (2003).

Kimball, B. A. (1995). *Orators and philosophers: A history of the idea of liberal education.* New York: College Board.

Musil, C. M. (Spring 2003). Educating for citizenship. *Peer Review,* 5(3), 4–8.

Sax, L. J. (in press.) *Citizenship development and the American college student.* New Directions for Institutional Research, no. 122. San Francisco: Jossey-Bass.

Chapter Nine

The Disciplines and the Public Good

Edward Zlotkowski

Were one to ask most faculty about forces threatening the future of the academic enterprise, one would, in all likelihood, hear a lot about inadequate funding, public misconceptions, vocationalism, and insufficiently prepared students. But the significance of these external threats may be in some ways misleading. While they are real, they do not account for a less discussed but more pervasive problem at the very heart of the contemporary academy. As Thomas Bender (1993) writes in the concluding essay of his book *Intellect and Public Life: Essays on the Social History of Academic Intellectuals in the United States,* "The integrity of academic intellect is not endangered by competing discourses of social inquiry [that is, nonacademic modes of analysis and assessment]. The risk now is precisely the opposite. Academe is threatened by the twin dangers of fossilization and scholasticism. . . . The agenda for the next decade, at least as I see it, ought to be the opening up of the disciplines, the ventilating of professional communities that have come to share too much and that have become to self-referential" (p. 143).

In other words, if one is concerned about the health of the academy, one would be well advised to focus less on threats from without and more on the danger of solipsism within. And such solipsism—"fossilization," "scholasticism," "self-referential[ity]"—perforce implies a critical examination of the role of the disciplines.

The importance of recognizing the disciplines as strategic leverage points in any discussion of the academy and the public good would be hard to overestimate. Their influence—through their organization into academic departments—is immediately apparent to anyone who looks at the structure of the modern college or university. On an institutional level, it is the department rather than the administration that determines *how*, if not actually *what*, policy decisions are implemented; on a cultural level, the agenda of a faculty member's discipline often takes precedence over her or his commitment to institutional priorities. In other words, as important as presidential leadership and institutional mission are with regard to issues of civic engagement, they cannot in most instances achieve even modest goals without paying careful attention to culture of discipline-based departments. (See, for example, Elison, 2002.)

In the Beginning

In the early years of the modern American university, linking the work of the disciplines to issues related to the public good would have been self-evident. In an essay entitled "Service-Learning, Academically Based Community Service, and the Historic Mission of the American Urban Research University," Ira Harkavy (2000), director of the University of Pennsylvania's Center for Community Partnerships and an historian by training, points out that a "tradition of problem-driven, problem-solving strategic academically based community service" (p. 30) is immediately evident in the histories of schools like Johns Hopkins University, the University of Chicago, Columbia University, and Penn State around the turn of the twentieth century. Thus, as Bender (1993) notes, "When the graduate school at Columbia, the Faculty of Political Science, was established in 1881, it was intended, as the name suggests, to reform our political life, our civic life, our politics" (p. 130).

But it was not only the faculties at the new universities that saw issues of the public good as central to their work. As many of those faculties began to be organized into professional associations, those associations themselves—especially in the new social sciences—clearly saw the public and its problems as germane to who they were and what they aspired to do. In an afterword to *Cultivating the Sociological Imagination: Concepts and Models for Service-Learning in Sociology* (1999), Carla Howery, deputy executive officer of the American Sociological Association, observes that "the very roots of American sociology dovetail with service-learning. In 1906, Lester Frank Ward helped found the Society to bring scientific attention to social problems, and became the first president of the American Sociological Association (then American Sociological Society). Our field has always espoused the interplay of theory, research, application, and reformulation, as an ongoing and iterative process" (p. 151).

Howery's linking of her discipline's, and its professional association's, "very roots" with the concept of public service would also hold true for many other contemporary disciplinary organizations.

Which is not to deny those roots are in need of serious stimulation. For as Howery goes on to remark, "Service-learning is the right topic to help sociologists to rediscover their disciplinary roots" (p. 155). Whether the "right topic" is service-learning, public problem solving, participatory action research, applied research, professional service, or the public intellectual, clearly most contemporary disciplines—working through both their national and their regional associations as well as through individual academic departments—have for many years now prioritized interests, values, and standards identified exclusively by their members over more public concerns. They have, in the terminology of William Sullivan (1995), sacrificed "civic professionalism" to "technical professionalism," creating in the process an ethos in which "public service can only appear as an admirable but accidental feature" (p. 11) of the main work at hand.

Recent Developments

There is, however, some reason to believe that questions of the public good may once again be returning to a position of importance—even within the traditional academic disciplines. Ernest Boyer (1990), who did so much to open up the idea of what counts as scholarly work within the academy, also provided much of the intellectual scaffolding needed to create new ties between the academy and society in general. Indeed, toward the very end of his life he formulated what has come to be seen as a classic description of what such a rapprochement might look like. He called it "the scholarship of engagement" (1990):

> At one level, the scholarship of engagement means connecting the rich resources of the university to our most pressing social, civic,

and ethical problems. . . . Campuses would be viewed by both students and professors not as isolated islands but as staging grounds for action.

But at a deeper level. I have this growing conviction that what's also needed is not just more programs, but a larger purpose, a larger sense of mission. . . . Increasingly, I'm convinced that ultimately, the scholarship of engagement also means creating a special climate in which the academic and civic cultures communicate more continuously and more creatively with each other, helping to enlarge what anthropologist Clifford Geertz describes as the universe of human discourse and enriching the quality of life for all of us. (pp. 19–20)

Scattered across the academic landscape, one can now identify many specific developments that resonate with Boyer's idea of a scholarship of engagement—both as program and as cultural ethos.

To be sure, not all these developments enthusiastically identify themselves with efforts to address the public good. Take, for example, a statement by the Association of American Geographers (AAG) included in the first volume of Diamond and Adam's *The Disciplines Speak: Rewarding the Scholarly, Professional, and Creative Work of Faculty* (1995). At the end of a section on "outreach," the association suggests that "the ability and propensity of geographers to grapple with real problems is a disciplinary strength. . . . Geography departments should ensure that their departmental and institutional reward systems weigh such contributions accordingly" (p. 40). However, in the statement's next section on "citizenship," the association not only embeds that concept in service first and foremost to the department and the discipline but also makes an explicit distinction between "professional citizenship" and the "fulfillment of *civic* responsibilities" [original emphasis, p. 41]. While faculty should be recognized and rewarded for activities—including outreach activities—"grounded in disciplinary knowledge," more generic forms of citizenship have "no place in faculty reward evaluations" (p. 41).

In the same volume we also find the "Report of the American Chemical Society Taskforce on the Definition of Scholarship in Chemistry." The report's introductory section explicitly recognizes that "forces at work in higher education . . . are calling for institutions of higher education to be more responsive to their roles of teaching students and providing various kinds of community service" (Diamond & Adam, 1995, p. 48) and that these forces provide the context within which the following report must be read. Drawing directly on the work of Boyer, the report goes on to assert that "although research is only scholarship, not all scholarship is research" (p. 52). Indeed, the health of the discipline itself demands that much more attention henceforth be paid to "a new area that we refer to as the scholarship of outreach" (p. 53). Recognizing the degree to which this new area diverges from what has come to be the accepted norm for scholarship within chemistry departments, the report concedes that interest in outreach is both "of vital importance" and "relatively new and undeveloped" (p. 53).

While the Diamond and Adam volume focuses on changing approaches to what constitutes acceptable scholarship, a volume compiled five years earlier by the Association of American Colleges and Universities (then the Association of American Colleges) consists of disciplinary statements dealing with the undergraduate major. But *Reports from the Field* (1990), despite its different focus, yields many analogous statements of public interest. For example, one of the recommendations made in a report sanctioned by the American Psychological Association reads as follows: "We recommend an additional component for all undergraduate majors in psychology. An interpersonal skills and group-process laboratory is included in all of our proposed models in order to develop students' abilities to work in groups. Whenever possible, we recommend that this laboratory (or the senior year applied project) be combined with a community-service component. . . . Supervised community service can instill a sense of responsibility that is critical for informed citizenship while addressing a broad range of human needs" (pp. 163–164).

Here, on the undergraduate level, the line between "professional" and "civic" is much less sharply drawn. Study of the discipline goes hand in hand with "informed citizenship."

In the case of the statement made by the task force of the American Institute of Biological Sciences, study of the discipline goes hand in hand with "an understanding of how science can make major contributions to a free society" (p. 11). This is especially true because "most of the critical problems society faces have a biological component" (p. 19).

Indeed, the task force goes so far as to suggest that "If biologists are unable or uninterested in acquainting themselves and the millions of undergraduate students with the natural world that con-

trols the destiny of all life on Earth, the value of biology departments to education in the liberal arts stands in question" (p. 16).

Environmental education and environmental awareness are
disciplinary imperatives.

Concrete Resources

But if it is increasingly easy to find signs of public awareness in the
more programmatic statements of many disciplinary groups, there
remains a great distance between the statements of those groups and
the actual practice of their members. For many faculty, indeed, for
most faculty at four-year institutions, disciplinary and institutional
recognition remains securely tied to traditional research. At the
same time, the challenge they face in their teaching is not how to integrate into their courses a broader societal perspective but how to
achieve sufficient "coverage." If faculty are to come to embrace some
consequential commitment to the public good, they will need more
than general pronouncements to help them on their way.

At least two major initiatives of the last decade have attempted
to provide just such concrete assistance. Early in 1995, a new faculty-
based organization under the aegis of Campus Compact called for
the development of a series of volumes on service-learning in individual academic areas. Responsibility for funding and organizing the series quickly passed to the American Association for
Higher Education (AAHE), largely due to the leadership of then
vice president Lou Albert. By 2000, the project as originally conceived had reached completion. AAHE's eighteen-volume series
on service-learning in the academic disciplines was the largest publication project the association had ever undertaken (http://www.
aahe.org/publications.htm).

Drawing upon the talents of four hundred contributors from
every sector of higher education, the series explored both theoretical, contextual, and practical issues involved in linking academically rigorous course work with projects involving the public good.
English instructors explored a variety of literacy-related initiatives
in community-based organizations. Biologists described not only
course-based environmental research but also the creation of sup-
plemental science resources for public schools. Accountants discussed the many ways in which participation in the Volunteer

Income Tax Assistance program (VITA) could provide both a teaching resource and a public service. The medical education volume took the idea of service-learning to the professional school level. Volumes in peace studies and women's studies demonstrated the relative ease with which new interdisciplinary areas could frame syllabi organized around public issues. Since completion of the original set, new volumes in religious studies and hospitality management have been added to the series.

However, far more important than the volumes themselves are the many ways in which these publications have either contributed to or, in some cases, actually precipitated related undertakings in and through the disciplines. Thus, the political science volume, *Experiencing Citizenship: Concepts and Models for Service-Learning in Political Science* (Battistoni & Hudson, 1997), added timely momentum to the American Political Science Association's (APSA) renewed interest in civic education—an interest perhaps most strikingly concretized in the appointment of a special Task Force on Civic Education for the Next Century (1996).

Meanwhile, the teacher education volume, *Learning with the Community: Concepts and Models for Service-Learning in Teacher Education* (Erickson & Anderson, 1997), quickly led to a follow-up volume, *Service-Learning in Teacher Education: Enhancing the Growth of New Teachers, Their Students, and Communities* (Anderson, Swick, & Yff, 2001) while the Spanish volume, *Construyendo Puentes (Building Bridges): Concepts and Models for Service-Learning in Spanish* (Hellebrandt & Verona, 1999) just as quickly led to *Juntos: Community Partnerships in Spanish and Portuguese* (Hellebrandt, Arries, & Verona, 2004). A new professional journal in composition and rhetoric (*Reflections: A Journal of Writing, Service-Learning, and Community Literacy*), an independently published volume in economics (*Putting the Invisible Hand to Work: Concepts and Models for Service-Learning in Economics* [McGoldrick & Ziegert, 2002]), a service-learning faculty fellows program in management studies, and countless sessions at national and regional disciplinary conferences can also be linked to the AAHE project.

A second important resource also owed its conception to Campus Compact. Thanks to a grant from the Pew Charitable Trusts, the Compact in 1999 launched an initiative to explore systematically what it called the "pyramid of service-learning." As the Compact conceived of this pyramid, colleges and universities can be seen as embodying one of three stages of civic engagement. At the beginning stage, engagement efforts are loosely organized and have little bearing on the institution's academic mission. At the advanced stage, an institution can be identified as an "engaged campus," that is, a campus that has embraced service-learning and civic engagement as essential to who it is. In between, there exists a broad intermediate stage at which many of the key structures that make possible an engaged campus are put into place. One such structure is the "engaged department."

Since the summer of 2000, the Compact has run a series of Engaged Department Institutes in a variety of forms—at the national level via a competitive application process, at the state level for the California State University System, and for individual institutions (for example, Portland State University and Miami-Dade College). However, regardless of level, the purpose, structure, and format of the institute have remained the same. Over a two- or three-day period, depending on the time available, departmental teams consisting of the chair, several faculty members, and a community partner of the department's choosing come together to create a profile of and action plan for civic engagement on the departmental level. Over the course of the institute each team tackles four key issues:

1. Unit responsibility for engagement-related initiatives
2. Departmental agreement on the concepts and the terminology that will allow faculty most effectively to explore the dimensions of engaged work
3. Departmental agreement on how best to document, evaluate, and recognize the significance of engaged work
4. Strategies for deepening the department's community partnerships

Unlike the AAHE series on service-learning in the disciplines, the Engaged Department Institute is not focused exclusively on service-learning—although, very often, service-learning turns out to be the engagement tool of choice. Instead, teams also explore a combination of internships, capstone projects, applied research, participatory action research, professional service, and other campus-community ventures that accord most naturally with the department's interests and skills, on the one hand, and, on the other hand, with the community's interests and priorities.

The approximately one hundred departmental action plans that the institute has thus far facilitated represent perhaps one of the best examples to date of how the kinds of general disciplinary statements referred to above can be operationalized on the department level. Like the AAHE series on service-learning in the disciplines, the *Engaged Department Toolkit* (Battistoni, Gelmon, Saltmarsh, Wergin, & Zlotkowski, 2003, available at http://www.compact.org/publica tions/)—a strategic development tool any department can use on its own—constitutes a resource essential for every higher education institution seeking to promote the scholarship of engagement. For as Deborah DeZure (1996), director of faculty development at Michigan State, has noted, even strictly academic initiatives—such as traditional faculty development programs—need to take the self-referentiality of disciplinary cultures explicitly into account. Centralized efforts "while useful in many ways . . . are often underused by faculty, rejected by many as too remote from their disciplinary teaching concerns. For many faculty, *teaching* means *teaching history* or *teaching music* or *teaching biology*. For them, instructional development should become more disciplinary, engaging these faculty by exploring issues of teaching in the context of their departmental expectations and their disciplinary values and modes of discourse" (original italics, p. 9).

In short, colleges and universities seeking to renew their social contract with the larger community need to create "resource units" deliberately targeted to specific departments and disciplines or interdisciplinary areas. These resource units should include

- Models of successful courses, programs, and projects from other comparable institutions
- Texts that explore an academic area's historic and contemporary commitment to civic engagement
- Contact information for engaged colleagues at the local, regional, and national levels
- Information on discipline-specific opportunities to present on and to publish engaged work

- Information about funding opportunities for engaged work
- Opportunities to bring relevant presenters to campus

No doubt, assembling such resource units for every academic department represents a serious investment of time and energy. However, the alternative may well be a more or less permanent state of stasis whereby only the "usual suspects" actively participate in engagement efforts, while the vast majority of the faculty continue with business as usual.

One of the few university presidents to recognize the importance of developing an ethos of civic engagement in and through mainstream faculty work *and* to succeed in crafting a strategy to make that happen is Judith Ramaley, former president of Portland State University. In an article entitled "Embracing Civic Responsibility" (2000), Ramaley shares some of what she has learned about the process of winning faculty support for "activities that promote civic responsibility and sustain campus-community engagement" (p. 12).

She begins by noting that, in her experience, "10 to 15 percent of the faculty or staff on campus already have a broad repertoire of interests . . . consistent with the full realization of engagement." A second group, roughly double in size, has "a genuine interest in new ways of doing things but want clear signals [of support] . . . if they venture into new territory, in this case, literally, into the community." Group three, approximately the same size as group two, sees the new agenda as a fad or institutional whim, "certain [to] disappear when the new president/provost/dean moves on to greener pastures." Finally, there is "a small number (maybe 10 percent) of the faculty or staff . . . certain that the new agenda or the new modes are not legitimate faculty work" (p. 12).

According to Ramaley, each of the last three groups has its own distinctive barrier to participation. What is most relevant to the present discussion is the barrier holding back group two: "The boundary between the committed [group one] and the cautious [group two] is defined by a *disciplinary barrier* and discipline-based definitions of research and scholarship" (original emphasis, p. 12). If Ramaley is correct in her analysis, the single most important step any institution can take to move beyond the "usual suspects" to a genuinely healthy base of 30 to 45 percent participating faculty is to lower the disciplinary barrier. In the pages that follow we will look briefly at three disciplinary areas where especially effective resources have been created to help institutions in this task.

Outstanding Disciplinary Resources

The Engaged Discipline

Perhaps no national disciplinary association has more effectively or enthusiastically embraced the idea of a scholarship of engagement than the National Communication Association (NCA). Beginning with its co-publication of the communication studies volume in the AAHE series, NCA staff and elected officers have demonstrated how vision, commitment, and organizational know-how can enable a discipline to appropriate and contribute to the national conversation on "creating a new [academic-civic] compact for the next millennium. . . . a compact [that] could energize and reorganize the talent and power we possess for the common good and for maintaining the support of our constituencies" (Applegate & Morreale, 1999, p. ix).

NCA's strategy for helping its members appreciate the importance of such a compact has had at least three broad dimensions. First, at the level of national and regional programming, the association's leaders have skillfully created forums that allow communication scholars to define engagement in a way that derives from and conforms to their own disciplinary culture. Luckily for NCA, communication studies and engagement do indeed exist in a "reflexive relationship" (Applegate & Morreale, 1999, p. xi) that sees theory and *praxis,* the study of communication and efforts to improve it, as complementary aspects of a single whole. Still, one should not underestimate the effort it takes to put this "reflexive relationship" squarely in front of influential individuals and to transform a rhetorical commonplace into a principal of action. Meetings with "divisional leaders . . . elected association leadership, and journal editors" (Applegate & Morreale, 2001, p. 9) require of engagement advocates more than logistical skills. They also require a willingness to invest political capital.

A second key aspect of NCA's strategy has involved the creation of concrete resources to help its members succeed in their engaged teaching and research. Particularly noteworthy in this respect is the "Disciplinary Toolkit" (Conville & Weintraub, n.d.) the association commissioned and disseminated to support service-learning in communication studies. Complementing the AAHE communication studies volume, the toolkit includes units on such practical items as managing risk, understanding terms, getting started, reflection, assessment, and frequently asked questions. It also includes a bibliography, a list of helpful Web sites, and summaries of model courses from across the communication studies spectrum, together with relevant contact information. The product of a special subcommittee, the toolkit is only one of several special initiatives launched to help ensure that engaged work in communication studies really exemplifies quality scholarship, in Boyer's expanded understanding of the term.

The third dimension of the association's engagement strategy also can be considered a resource, but a resource of a very different nature. In 2000, NCA entered into a formal partnership with the Teaching Tolerance project of the Southern Poverty Law Center (SPLC). The partnership, which is called Creating Common Ground (CCG), calls for communication studies scholars to utilize Teaching Tolerance curricular materials in designing service-learning partnerships with K–12 classrooms and nonprofit organizations across the country. Thus, it brings together two highly complementary sets of interests and strengths. On the NCA side, it offers a ready-made platform for the practice and study of diversity-related communication issues. Participating scholars gain access to a potentially rich professional opportunity through their national disciplinary organization. On the SPLC side, it provides an opportunity to increase the impact of the Teaching Tolerance project by enlisting a whole new group of teacher-facilitators. Schools and organizations that might otherwise lack the personnel or the expertise to sponsor a diversity program now can do so. From a broad, structural perspective, the NCA-SPLC partnership pioneers a whole new kind of disciplinary outreach, one that combines the advantages of centralized organizing and training with unit flexibility and sensitivity to local needs and considerations.

Sector Focus

A complementary but very different kind of disciplinary resource can be found in Community-Campus Partnerships for Health (CCPH), located at the University of California, San Francisco. Founded in

1996, CCPH "promotes health through partnerships between communities and higher educational institutions." The fact that "community" precedes "campus" in the organization's name is no accident. Partnerships, more specifically partnerships in which the community has a powerful voice, are the "tools" CCPH focuses on in its efforts to improve "health professional education, civic responsibility and the overall health of communities" (http://www.futurehealth.ucsf.edu/ccph.html).

At the same time, CCPH has been both vigorous and creative in attending to the needs of its academic constituencies. Fully committed to the value of service-learning, community-based research, and community service, it has helped to provide a wide range of discipline-specific as well as interdisciplinary resources for those working in health-related disciplines. It was, for example, CCPH that co-sponsored both the nursing and the medical education volumes in the AAHE series. It has also reached out to over thirty discipline-related associations in the health area, seeking to collaborate with professionals not just in nursing and medicine but in dentistry and dental hygiene, pharmacy, public health, allied health, physical and occupational therapy, and other related fields. Through its national and regional conferences, its publications, and its links to health-related programs and agencies of every kind, it has promoted the scholarship of engagement more extensively than almost any other organization of its kind.

In many ways similar to CCPH, Imagining America (IA) represents a "national consortium of colleges, universities, and cultural institutions dedicated to supporting the civic work of university artists, humanists, and designers" (http://www.ia.umich.edu/whoweare/whoweare.html). Located at the University of Michigan, IA provides members with a variety of resources to facilitate engaged arts and humanities programming. These include networking opportunities (such as conferences), publications, site visits, and public advocacy. The University of Washington's recent public humanities institute for graduate students, the University of California-Irvine's Humanities Out There program, the Arts of Citizenship Program at the University of Michigan, and other similar initiatives at universities and colleges from coast to coast document IA's success in building a coalition of schools committed to innovative civic programming. As IA director Julie Elison notes in a recent newsletter (Fall 2003), the kinds of projects IA features and facilitates change higher education by testing the ability of a campus to sustain major partnerships and pushing it to adapt to the realities of innovative practice. Such examples offer rallying points for artists and humanists who are eager to learn from one another across nations and continents and also are resolutely committed to local alliances. Integrating these two aims—local engagement and global engagement—is the trick. Since, for the most part, the humanities (as opposed to the arts) have not been leaders in exploring how higher education can more effectively and directly serve the public good, IA's efforts help address a special need in the overall engagement movement.

Another academic sector less than well represented, at least until recently, in the contemporary engagement movement is the natural sciences. Despite the kinds of statements by organizations like the American Chemical Society and the American Institute of Biological Sciences cited earlier in this essay, faculty in disciplines like chemistry, biology, and physics have not, for the most part, seen the call to reexamine the academic-social contract as relevant to them. Not only do many feel locked into course sequences and research agendas that seem to leave little room for "nonessentials"; they also have to deal with an engagement movement whose language and social issues frequently fail to resonate with their own disciplinary traditions.

Hence, the importance of Science Education for New Civic Engagements and Responsibilities (SENCER) launched by the Association of American Colleges and Universities with funding from the National Science Foundation (NSF). According to David Burns (2002), principal investigator for the program, "SENCER is a national dissemination program seeking to improve learning and stimulate civic engagement by teaching science through a growing collection of complex, capacious, largely unsolved, civic issues, issues that interest large numbers of students" (p. 20).

Unlike Community-Campus Partnerships for Health and Imagining America, SENCER focuses less on academy-community partnerships and more on the kind of problem- or inquiry-based learning that science and math reformers have favored for years. In this case, however, the problems to be addressed necessarily include a public or civic dimension that helps students move, to return to a distinction made above, in the direction of "civic" as well as "technical" professionalism (Sullivan, 1995).

SENCER also lacks the kind of fiscal and organizational self-sufficiency CCPH and IA have achieved. Nevertheless, its NSF funding lends it considerable disciplinary legitimacy, and its web-based formatting argues for potentially widespread impact. During 2001–2003, the program has featured courses focused on topics ranging from HIV, tuberculosis, and human genetics to environmental issues (such as energy use, global warming, toxic brownfields) to the application of statistical probability to civic issues (http://www.aacu.org/SENCER/). Each in its own way, CCPH, IA, and SENCER demonstrate the kind of sensitivity to disciplinary cultures and practices that is essential if the larger engagement movement is to succeed.

Institutional Program Model

Still another kind of special disciplinary resource can be found in the Engineering Projects in Community Service (EPICS) program created by faculty in the College of Engineering at Purdue University. Although the creation of a single institution, EPICS has become a national resource both through its own replication program and through the lead role it has played in a series of regional workshops on service-learning in engineering. Through both these outreach efforts, the concept of community-based projects in engineering has been brought to institutions from the Massachusetts Institute of Technology to the University of Texas-El Paso, from Georgia Tech to the University of Washington.

Organized around interdisciplinary technology-based projects (both within engineering and between engineering and other disciplines), EPICS fields student teams that work to address specific public needs until those needs have been adequately met. In other words, EPICS projects need not be limited to a single semester or term. Instead, they are passed from one student cohort to the next until they reach genuine closure. Completed projects include:

- Creation of a web-based program of standardized housing plans that allows future Habitat for Humanity homeowners to choose their own building design.
- Construction of a "life-sized camera" for Happy Hollow Elementary School.

- Creation of various "Imagination Stations" for a local children's museum. The stations help children understand such things as principles of magnetism, electromagnetism, speed, and mechanical gearing.
- Design and construction of a variety of devices to help disabled children at the Wabash Center Children's Clinic, such as devices to improve body posture and develop motor skills.

(For a summary of all completed projects, see http://128.46.121.174/delivered_projects/.)

Apart from both the intrinsic educational and community value of projects like these, what has made the EPICS program so successful is the way in which it has capitalized on a reform movement within the engineering education community. In 1998, the Accreditation Board for Engineering and Technology (ABET), the accrediting body for schools of engineering and technology, issued *Engineering Criteria 2000*, which calls for a far more inclusive, broad-based set of competencies for those graduating from engineering programs than has traditionally been the case. Among the competencies ABET now calls for are such things as "an ability to function on multidisciplinary teams; an understanding of professional and ethical responsibility; an ability to communicate effectively; the broad education necessary to understand the impact of engineering solutions in a global and societal context; and a knowledge of contemporary issues" (Tsang, 2000, p. 2).

It is to criteria like these that EPICS can respond far more effectively than most standard engineering curricula. Communication skills, teamwork, professional ethics, and community awareness are as essential to the success of EPICS projects as is technical engineering know-how (http://128.46.121.174/about/overview.htm).

Hence, it might be more accurate to identify Purdue's EPICS program *and* ABET's *Engineering Criteria 2000* as together constituting a special disciplinary resource. For although they can function independently, in tandem they provide engineering educators with both a discipline-specific motive and a discipline-specific means to reformulate the relationship between their field and the public good. It is, indeed, hard to see how one could make a stronger case for civic engagement in and through a discipline's own culture.

But, of course, not all engineering programs are rushing to emulate EPICS—or to meet ABET's new criteria in a socially responsible manner. Many engineering educators still see such nontechnical demands as irrelevant to or even subversive of the discipline's core work. What hope is there, then, for other disciplines where no accrediting body calls for reform and no extra-academic interest group—such as engineering firms—exist to demand a less parochial course of study? Are the disciplines, and the disciplinary associations that represent them, capable of rising to the challenge of rethinking and rewriting the academic-civic compact, or must we instead resign ourselves to strategies that seek to bypass them?

Conclusion

The gap between the traditional academic disciplines and an engaged academy has been well described. Elizabeth Minnich (1996) contrasts the "professionalized" disciplines at the heart of the campus with a "new academy"—consisting largely of interdisciplinary and area studies—establishing itself at the campus's edge, where the nonacademic community begins. Julie Elison (2002) makes an analogous distinction when she speaks of the "two professional cultures for liberal arts faculty in American research universities: the dominant departmental culture and the culture of engagement" (p. 1). Despite variations in the specific players assigned to each of the two sides, the fundamental point of tension always remains more or less the same: relatively self-contained disciplinary pursuits and reciprocal academy-community partnerships.

As the present essay may serve to illustrate, the disciplinary camp is hardly monolithic. Not only do professional societies like the National Communication Association, the American Studies Association, and the Conference on College Composition and Communication housed within the National Council of Teachers of English actively support the engaged scholarship of their members, but many faculty in traditional disciplines—especially those not teaching at research-intensive institutions—have embraced the idea of engagement and made it a part of their own disciplinary culture. While the culture of research universities is certainly very visible and very influential, it does not dictate much of what happens at community colleges, minority-serving institutions, faith-based colleges, and even some regional universities. Indeed, many of the faculty teaching at these schools have long since let their national disciplinary membships lapse precisely because the agenda of their national societies reflects too narrowly the culture of research universities and comports so poorly with their own interests and priorities.

Still, there can be little doubt that the dichotomy Minnich, Elison, and others refer to represents a significant barrier to renewing American higher education's compact with civil society. What then is one to do? However much one might wish it were otherwise, the fact remains that the traditional academic department continues to be central to the vast majority of our colleges and universities. At the very least, we must recognize the relevance of an observation the historian Howard Zinn (1996) once made of sociopolitical reform in general that usually change does not happen quickly. It takes time for people to enlarge their perspective, and often if something doesn't happen in the near future, people give up. But this attitude is just what prevents change.

But we can do more than grit our teeth and persevere. If this essay has any practical lesson for leaders both inside and outside higher education, it could probably be summarized in a single, simple observation: since the disciplines, and the intellectual power they embody, are not going to go away anytime soon, our efforts to build an engaged academy will have to include them. This means we will need to make much more of a serious investment in working with them than we have up until now. Many of the initiatives described in this essay represent both useful starting points and invaluable resources. However, many of them also struggle for the kind of funding that would significantly increase the effectiveness of their work. This is something national funders—public and private—should take to heart.

But perhaps even more important, the colleges and universities that could benefit so much from the increased efficacy of these initiatives need to be much savvier, much more deliberate in how they press reform. They need to develop and implement the kind of change strategies and political skills we tend to associate with industrial and community organizing. They need to make the kinds of resources identified in this essay part of a carefully formulated plan to move beyond centralized engagement efforts. For many institutions, such a plan would probably yield significant results much sooner than one might expect.

References

Accreditation Board for Engineering and Technology. (1998). *Engineering criteria 2000.* ABET Web site: www.abet.org.

American Political Science Association Task Force on Civic Education for the Next Century. (1996). Expanded articulation statement: A call for reactions and contributions. *PS: Politics and Political Science, 31*(3), 636.

Anderson, J. B., Swick, K. J., & Yff, J. (Eds.). (2001). *Service-learning in teacher education: Enhancing the growth of new teachers, their students, and communities.* New York: AACTE Publications.

Applegate, J. L., & Morreale, S. P. (1999). Service-learning in communication: A natural partnership. In D. Droge & B. O. Murphy (Eds.), *Voices of strong democracy: Concepts and models for service-learning in communication studies* (pp. ix–xiv). Washington, DC: American Association for Higher Education.

Applegate, J. L., & Morreale, S. P. (2001). Creating engaged disciplines. *AAHE Bulletin, 53*(9), 7–10.

Association of American Colleges. (1990). *Reports from the field.* Washington, DC: Author.

Battistoni, R. M., Gelmon, S. B., Saltmarsh, J., Wergin, J., & Zlotkowski, E. (Eds.). (2003). *The engaged department toolkit.* Providence, RI: Campus Compact.

Battistoni, R. M., & Hudson, W. E. (Eds.). (1997). *Experiencing citizenship: Concepts and models for service-learning in political science.* Washington, DC: American Association for Higher Education.

Bender, T. (1993). *Intellect and public life: Essays on the social history of academic intellectuals in the United States.* Baltimore: Johns Hopkins University Press.

Boyer, E. L. (1990). *Scholarship reconsidered: Priorities of the professoriate.* Princeton, NJ: Carnegie Foundation for the Advancement of Teaching.

Burns, W.M.D. (2002). Knowledge to make our democracy. *Liberal Education, 88*(4), 20–27.

Conville, R. L., & Weintraub, S. C. (Eds.). (n.d.). *Service-learning and communication: A disciplinary toolkit.* Washington, DC: National Communication Association.

DeZure, D. (1996). Closer to the disciplines: A model for improving teaching within departments. *AAHE Bulletin, 48*(6), 9–12.

Diamond, R. M., & Adam, B. E. (Eds.). (1995). *The disciplines speak: Rewarding the scholarly, professional, and creative work of faculty.* Washington, DC: American Association for Higher Education.

Elison, J. (2002). *The two cultures problem.* Paper presented at the Research University as Local Citizen Conference, October 6–7.

Elison, J. (2003). "Let's do it": Local and global engagement. *Imagining America Newsletter, 4* (Fall), 1–2.

Erickson, J. A., & Anderson, J. B. (Eds.). (1997). *Learning with the community: Concepts and models for service-learning in teacher education.* Washington, DC: American Association for Higher Education.

Harkavy, I. (2000). Service-learning, academically based community service, and the historic mission of the American urban research university." In I. Harkavy & B. M. Donovan (Eds.), *Connecting past and present: Concepts and models for service-learning in history* (pp. 27–41). Washington, DC: American Association for Higher Education.

Hellebrandt, J., Arries J., & Verona, L. T. (Eds.). (2004). *Juntos: Community partnerships in Spanish and Portuguese.* (AATSP Professional Development Series Handbook, Vol. 5.). Boston: Heinle.

Hellebrandt, J., & Verona, L. T. (Eds.). (1999). *Construyendo puentes (Building bridges): Concepts and models for service-learning in Spanish.* Washington, DC: American Association for Higher Education.

Howery, C. B. (1999). Sociology, service, and learning, for a stronger discipline. In J. Ostrow, G. Hesser, & S. Enos (Eds.), *Cultivating the sociological imagination: Concepts and models for service-learning in sociology* (pp. 151–155). Washington, DC: American Association for Higher Education.

McGoldrick, K., & Ziegert, A. L. (Eds.). (2002). *Putting the invisible hand to work: Concepts and models for service-learning in economics.* Ann Arbor: University of Michigan Press.

Minnich, E. (1996). *Liberal learning and arts of connection for a new academy.* Washington, DC: American Association of Colleges and Universities.

Ramaley, J. A. (2000). Embracing civic responsibility. *AAHE Bulletin, 52*(7), 9–13.

Sullivan, W. M. (1995). *Work and integrity: The crisis and promise of professionalism in America.* New York: Harper Business.

Tsang, E. (2000). Introduction. In E. Tsang (Ed.), *Projects that matter: Concepts and models for service-learning in engineering* (pp. 1–12). Washington, DC: American Association for Higher Education.

Zinn, H. (1996, October 16). An interview with Howard Zinn. *Spare Change,* p. 1.

Chapter Ten

Scholarship for the Public Good

Living in Pasteur's Quadrant

Judith A. Ramaley

The major challenge facing contemporary higher education is to enhance its relevance and connectedness to the issues and problems faced by the broader society—as these problems are defined by community members and not by academics acting independently of the views of others (Kenny, Simon, Kiley-Brabeck, & Lerner, 2002).

Education has been our means to instruct our youth in the values and accomplishments of our civilization and to prepare them for adult life. We have been arguing for centuries about what an education means and how to distinguish an educated person from an uneducated one. Our answers have been built upon contemporary beliefs about the public good and the role of education in preparing students for various learned roles in society.

Two views have contended for our allegiance since the time of the ancient Greeks (Marrou, 1956). One perspective is the rational and humane vision of the Sophists and later the philosopher-teacher Isocrates, for whom the test of an education was its ability to prepare a citizen to engage in public affairs. The other view is that of Plato and Socrates, who taught that education must guide the student toward an uncovering of the Truth and Beauty that underlies our human experience, the universal themes and natural laws that a well-schooled mind can discern beneath the surface confusion of life, the awakening of the spirit within that allows us to care intensely about life and learning.

In my view, an ideal education lies between these two poles of experience and purpose, thought and action, self-realization and social responsibility. When asked whether an education is meaningful because it liberates the spirit and feeds the soul or because it prepares us to make good decisions, contribute to public life, and live as a responsible citizen of our democracy, my answer is always *yes*. Education can and must accomplish all of these things. This is the basis for my intense interest in civic engagement and social responsibility and my growing commitment in recent years to the challenge of rethinking the societal role of higher education and how this role can best be expressed in an age where almost all citizens, not just a small elite, must now obtain a significantly higher level of education.

This essay will explore institutional, educational, and scholarly models that can support the expression of a full range of intellectual interests, define and advance individual and shared goals that are coherent and articulated with each other, and generate knowledge that is both intellectually stimulating and clearly practical. The purpose of this piece is to show that it is possible to advance the interests of individual faculty, staff, and students while also serving the public good through the development of appropriate goals for research, through the design of the curriculum, and through the relationships that an institution develops with the broader society. My premise is that it is possible to advance our understanding and explore theoretical and analytic conceptions, while at the same time addressing very practical problems for which new knowledge or the integration of knowledge is needed. In so doing, we can engage our students in these efforts and thus prepare them for citizenship and for the professional responsibilities that they will later assume.

New Approaches to Scholarship and the Curriculum: Pasteur's Quadrant

Roger Geiger (1993) has pointed out that academics tend to picture themselves as scholars whose primary aim is to enable students to learn through innovative pedagogical strategies. According to Geiger, in these intellectual spheres we produce increasingly specialized knowledge, rather than broad, critical thinking skills. We do not forge a meaningful link between learning and life. Yet some of our forebears had a very different concept of knowledge and the role of learning in forming and preserving our way of life. For many early educators, "theory and utility" could be combined to create an appropriate education for our young people. The Reverend Daniel Clark Sanders, the first president of the University of Vermont, wrote about the purposes of a collegiate education. "It teaches the young where are the sources of knowledge, the means by which it is attained, where truth may be found without error, and where wisdom has chosen her place of residence. To become a real scholar is to be a student for life" (quoted in Daniels, 1991, p. 94).

The relationship between basic research and its applications in both the curriculum and in the development of new technologies is not always linear or derivative. It is both possible, and often desirable, to conduct research while also advancing educational and societal goals. The concept that brings these elements together was articulated by Donald Stokes in his book *Pasteur's Quadrant* (1997).

How might scholarship change in order to link theory and utility? It has been customary to distinguish basic from applied research and research from education. By keeping these vital functions apart, we limit the productive relationship between basic research and technological innovation. Stokes (1997) sought a "more realistic view of the relationship between basic research and technology policies" (p. 2) and hence between private interests (those of the researcher) and the public good (the advance of technology and its effects on society and the economy).

According to Stokes (1997), we must connect the goals of science (to develop theory and advance understanding) and technology (to solve practical problems and develop new useful products). To pave the way toward this kind of integration, Stokes developed the concept of intellectual spaces that he calls *quadrants* defined by the balance of theory and practical use pursued. No one wants to be in the first quadrant framed by low theoretical or practical interest, and we trust that few projects reside there. Thomas Alva Edison's work would nicely describe the second quadrant framed by high interest in use and low interest in advancing understanding. He was "the applied investigator wholly uninterested in the deeper scientific implication of his discoveries." As Stokes puts it, "Edison gave five years to creating his utility empire, but no time at all to the basic physical phenomena underlying his emerging technology" (Stokes, 1997, p. 24).

In the third quadrant, Niels Bohr represents the classic researcher engaged in a search for pure understanding as he explored the structure of the atom (Stokes, 1997, p. 24). For him, any possible practical use of his modeling was not even a consideration. Occupying the fourth quadrant is Louis Pasteur who had a strong commitment to understanding the underlying microbiological processes that he had discovered and, simultaneously, a motivation to use that knowledge to understand and control food spoilage and microbial-based disease. He occupies his own intellectual space where basic research is inspired by considerations of its potential use and where research advances both theoretical (basic) knowledge and applied (practical) knowledge. Here we have Pasteur's Quadrant. It has been my goal over the years to encourage more work in this quadrant, while never losing sight of the value and importance of basic research and knowledge for its own sake.

The Value of Working in Pasteur's Quadrant

Why would we want to work in Pasteur's Quadrant? There are a number of reasons to invent new approaches to our institutional models and to rethink how we approach the classic functions of research, teaching, and service (Ramaley, 2001.) By doing so, we can integrate a number of related, but often distinctive, aspirations and goals espoused by higher education or advanced on behalf of higher education by its many constituencies.

1. To prepare students to be good citizens by providing them ways to help the institution itself be a good citizen
2. To foster and renew bonds of trust in the community, that is, "social capital," and to use the neutrality of the campus to provide a common ground where differences of opinion and advocacy for particular points of view can be addressed in an open and constructive way and where people with similar goals can come together and create ways to work together
3. To create leadership development opportunities for students and to foster a commitment to social and civic responsibility

4. To enhance the employability of graduates by providing opportunities to build a strong résumé and to explore career goals
5. To promote learning both for students and for community members
6. To play a role in creating capacity in the community to work on complex societal problems
7. To design a more effective way for the campus to contribute to economic and community development
8. To build support for public investment in higher education, to provide both access and opportunity for students of all backgrounds to pursue an education and to generate knowledge that will address critical societal needs
9. To accomplish a campus mission of service

But how to go about this? I have tried over the years to understand and then reinterpret the conception of a university to shape it to both public and private ends and to broaden the working definition of what constitutes scholarship so that both advancement of theoretical knowledge and investigations that address practical problems will be supported and encouraged. The concept of the "engaged university" captures this integration in very concrete terms. Within an engaged institution, as we shall see, the classic traditions of research, teaching, and service will be changed, with significant implications for faculty scholarship, the design and intentions of the curriculum, and the mechanisms by which knowledge is generated, interpreted, and used. These changes are essential in order to support the kind of work that can take place in Pasteur's Quadrant. To get to that idea, we need first to explore some of the earlier ideas about what a university should be.

Conceptions of the University and Its Purposes: Disengaged or Engaged?

In his review of *The Uses of the University*, Clark Kerr (2001), traces the more recent debates about the purpose of the university and concludes with his interpretation of the contemporary American university, which he dubs the "multiversity." After dwelling a bit on the medieval origins of our current academy, he dwells on "the academic cloister of Cardinal Newman" and the "research organism" of Abraham Flexner (p. 1), which represent the ancestral types from which our contemporary interpretations of the university derive. What are these forebears of our modern institution? In exploring these ideas, I will assume that the "university" represents an ideal against which other institutional types are frequently compared, often inappropriately. I will not attempt to derive the history of each differentiated institutional type now flourishing in the United States.

Cardinal Newman derived his vision from the Platonic ideal. He insisted on "the cultivation of the intellect, as an end which may reasonably be pursued for its own sake. . . . Truth of whatever kind is the proper object of the intellect" (Newman, 1960, p. 114). As he put it, "A university may be considered with reference either to its Students or its Studies" (p. 74).

If the purpose of education is to cultivate the intellect, what is the purpose of "Studies," or as we might say today, the disciplines or scholarship or research? For Cardinal Newman, all branches of knowledge are connected together and "complete, correct, balance each other" (1960, p. 75). He argued that the university was the "high protecting power of all knowledge and science, of fact and principle, of inquiry and discovery, of experimentation and speculation; it maps out the terrain of the intellect" (quoted in Kerr, 2001, p. 2). As far as he was concerned, useful knowledge was trash and had no place in the academy. The special purview of the university was to raise the intellectual tone of society, cultivate the public mind, and give "enlargement and sobriety to the ideas of the age" (quoted in Kerr, 2001, p. 3).

Knowledge for its own sake and the concept of education as a means to enrich and improve the public mind were soon eclipsed by the concept of the research university where, as Clark Kerr put it, "Science was beginning to take the place of moral philosophy, research the place of teaching" (p. 3). The modern university, as envisioned by Abraham Flexner in 1930 was an entity "not outside, but inside the general social fabric of a given era. . . . It is not something apart, something historic, something that yields as little as possible to forces and influences that are more or less new. It is on the contrary . . . an expression of the age, as well as an influence operating upon both present and future" (quoted in Kerr, 2001, p. 3).

Yet even as Flexner wrote, the "modern university" he envisioned was being replaced by a uniquely American form that Kerr called the *multiversity.* The hegemony of research as the ideal form and function of a university would soon by solidified as the federal government called upon university researchers to conduct studies that would contribute to the war effort during World War II. Soon after the war, Vannevar Bush presented to President Truman a prospectus for a continued investment in scientific research that was already widely believed to be "absolutely essential to national security" (Bush, 1980, p. 17). As he put it, "The bitter and dangerous battle against the U-boat was a battle of scientific techniques—and our margin of success was dangerously small" (p. 17). Beyond the demands of national security, there was also the connection between science and jobs, jobs created by the technology that will arise from scientific discovery.

For Bush, "Basic research is performed without thought of practical ends. It results in general knowledge and an understanding of nature and its laws" (p. 18). It was to be someone else's task to translate these discoveries into practical use. Basic science was to be conducted in universities and research institutes where "scientists may work in an atmosphere which is relatively free from the adverse pressure of convention, prejudice or commercial necessity" (p. 19). Government laboratories and private industry would translate this work into something practical. In the perfect model envisioned by Bush, research was kept relatively separate from teaching. The university was still viewed as an ivory tower, whose function was to look out upon society and elevate its taste and values through the generation of basic research.

New Institutional Designs: The Engaged University

Pasteur's Quadrant will not be found in the Platonic institutions of Cardinal Newman or Abraham Flexner. It is also not altogether clear where such an environment might develop in Clark Kerr's multiversity. The model most receptive to the concepts of Pasteur can be found in the "engaged university." *Engagement* can be distinguished from *outreach,* a model developed in the early days of the land-grant mission and originally supported by a series of cooperative extension offices and agents. In the extension model, experts apply their knowledge to problems brought to them by people in the community. The patterns of these questions and concerns provide input to a research agenda, originally maintained by agricultural field stations. Outreach is primarily the transfer of knowledge from a university agent to a client. Although the infrastructure needed to sustain outreach has evolved beyond cooperative extension, and, indeed, cooperative extension itself has evolved to include programs that address the needs of children and families as well as small business, it is still primarily a one-way rather than a shared enterprise that provides research-based answers to clearly defined questions.

Higher education institutions will usually elect to use outreach for fairly straightforward questions and problems and will initiate engagement activities to address more complex issues that lack clarity (such as problems where either the question or the solutions are unclear) or issues that must be explored with the use of leveraged funding from multiple parties. An excellent example of the kind of problem for which an engagement strategy is ideally suited is the issue of K–12 reform and, in particular, the improvement of teaching and learning in science and mathematics. Another good example is the call for scientific research in education and evidence-based practice in education in the No Child Left Behind Act that addresses the federal interest in K–12 education.

The engaged institution takes many forms ranging from state and land-grant universities to regional comprehensive institutions, urban universities, community colleges, and liberal arts colleges. Institutions that take on the mantle of engagement are committed to direct interaction with external constituencies and communities through mutually beneficial exchange, exploration, and application of knowledge, expertise, resources, and information. These interactions enrich and expand the learning and discovery functions of the academic institution while also enhancing community capacity. The work of the engaged institution is responsive to (and respectful of) community-identified needs, opportunities, and goals in ways that are appropriate to the campus's mission and academic strengths.

For this approach to work, the other organizations with which a university is affiliated must also have the capacity for engagement including strong leadership, some appropriate infrastructure, and the time and means to participate in collaborative ventures. In fact, in many ways, the barriers to engagement that are often identified by faculty are problems for K–12, government agencies, and the business community as well. Obstacles often mentioned by faculty who have been considering becoming involved in engaged scholarship and teaching are "the time it takes to create new activities, cultivate partnerships, organize the logistics of service activities, and recruit students or other participants" (Holland, 1999, p. 38)). They also express apprehension about the lack of support for this kind of work, which generally does not "count" for professional advancement and, increasingly, they describe an "overflowing plate" of demands upon their time that is overwhelming.

Engaged institutions, no matter what the foci of their interests or the pathways by which they arrive at substantial engagement, share the following common characteristics, adapted from Bringle and Hatcher (2001), Holland (2001), and Ramaley (2000).

1. Civic engagement is articulated in the institutional mission and strategies. Public perspectives and needs consistently influence campus priorities.
2. The campus involves the community in continuous, purposeful, and authentic ways and listens carefully to what community members have to say.
3. The curriculum contains a variety of ways for students to learn in ways that engage them in community concerns.
4. The campus thinks carefully about the consequences of all of its decisions on its relationship with the community and its capacity to collaborate with the community.
5. The institution has a policy environment and appropriate infrastructure and investment to promote, support, and reward engagement.
6. Individuals throughout the campus community play leadership roles in fostering engagement. This is especially important in order to ensure that a commitment to engagement will survive leadership transitions at presidential, provost, and decanal levels.
7. The campus approach to scholarship includes support of interdisciplinary work, since societal issues do not come in "disciplinary form."
8. The campus honors and makes visible its engagement work, both internally and externally.
9. Engagement activities are held to high standards of excellence and are rigorously evaluated.

To undertake genuine engagement, an institution must be willing to open itself up to the possibility that it, too, will change and will learn from the experience. The element of an engaged partnership that is especially hard to achieve is the experience of genuine mutuality. The experience of engagement, however, may result in a different conception of an engaged college or university. In the next section, we will explore how this might come about.

New Approaches to Research in Pasteur's Quadrant: Engaged Scholarship

In my opinion, the experience of engagement will become the pathway to a fresh interpretation of the role of higher education in the twenty-first century. This conception rests on a rethinking of the core of the academy—namely, the nature of scholarship itself and our expectations for the undergraduate experience. The goal of engaged scholarship is not to define and serve the public good directly on behalf of society but to create conditions for the public good to be interpreted and pursued in a collaborative mode with the community. In contemporary society, the exercise of citizenship requires constant learning and the thoughtful and ethical application of knowledge. By including our students in engaged scholarship, we introduce them to basic concepts and, at the same time, offer them a chance to explore the application and consequences of ideas in the company of mature scholars and practitioners.

During its examination of the future of this nation's state and land-grant institutions in the mid 1990s, the Kellogg Commission on the Future of State and Land-Grant Universities reframed the classic triad of research, teaching, and service into a new framework of discovery, learning, and engagement. The reason for doing this was that the new terms describe shared activities, usually, but not always, led by faculty, that have shared consequences for the academy as well as the community. The older terms tend to connote a one-way activity, generally conducted by experts, like the outreach and extension model of the earlier land-grant movement. The new triad works well for describing the range of ways in which a college or university can incorporate good citizenship into its traditional work and move from an expert-centered model to an engagement model of partnership with the community. As a design, this framework sits comfortably in the intellectual domain established by Stokes (1997) in *Pasteur's Quadrant* where rigorous basic research and questions inspired by use meet and become a new form of engaged scholarship.

Discovery can encompass community-based scholarship and the development of new knowledge through collaborations with community participants. Learning can be done in a way that links educational goals with the challenges of life. Common forms of engaged learning are service-learning and problem-based learning, both utilizing community issues as a starting point for accomplishing educational goals. Engagement can be achieved through community-university alliances and partnerships and can support any combination of scholarly activity including discovery, integration, interpretation, and application.

It is not easy to work in a collaborative way, but the rewards are well worth the effort. No other model affords the same rich context for exercising the habits of good citizenship or for exposing our students to the realities of the complexity of a democratic way of life or for showing graphically that knowledge really can have consequences.

The Consequences of Engagement: What Will It Mean to Be Educated in the Twenty-First Century?

An essential education in the twenty-first century will be a practical liberal education that captures the strengths of Pasteur's Quadrant. The report entitled *Greater Expectations: A New Vision for Learning as a Nation Goes to College* (Association of American Colleges and Universities [AACU], 2002) calls for "A philosophy of education that empowers individuals, liberates the mind, and cultivates social responsibility. Characterized by challenging encounters with important issues, and more a way of learning than specific content, liberal education can occur in all disciplines. This concept is different from the term *liberal arts* which refers to specific disciplines in the humanities, social sciences and sciences" (AACU, 2002, p. x).

The *Greater Expectations* report called for all students to become "intentional learners who can adapt to new environments, integrate knowledge from different sources, and continue to learn throughout their lives (AACU, 2002, p. xi). The report goes on to explain how a student might exhibit these basic traits of an educated person and prepare to lead a responsible, productive, and creative life. There is increasingly strong evidence that educational experiences that engage students in discovery, interpretation of knowledge, and the responsible application of knowledge to meaningful problems can provide the means by which students can become intentional, empowered, informed, and responsible.

To engage students in this way, we can introduce into the undergraduate curriculum the intellectual challenges encountered in Pasteur's Quadrant and draw students into the full spectrum of scholarship as originally described by Boyer (1990) and later developed by others (for example, see Rice, 2003). This broader conception arises from the belief that "at no time in our history has the need been greater for connecting the work of the academy to the social and environmental challenges beyond the campus" (Boyer, 1990, p. xii). Boyer's intention was to explore the obligation of our nation's colleges and universities "to break out of the tired old teaching versus research debate and define, in more creative ways, what it means to be a scholar"(1990, p. xii). Engaged learning is the curricular manifestation of the creative ways he sought, applied to learning that has consequences for students, faculty, and society-at-large.

In Boyer's hands, scholarship has four facets: discovery, integration, application, and teaching. Of these, discovery is the closest to the conceptions of Plato, Cardinal Newman, and Vannevar Bush since it "contributes not only to the stock of human knowledge but also to the intellectual climate of a college or university" (Boyer, 1990, p. 17). Central to the scholarship of today is the *scholarship of integration* which to Boyer means "making connections across the disciplines, placing the specialties in larger context, illuminating data in a revealing way, often educating non-specialists, too" (p. 18). In this expanded idea, the scholar is both integrator and interpreter. Most essential to the modern interpretation of the scholar is the *scholarship of application,* which moves toward engagement as the scholar asks, "How can knowledge be responsibly applied to consequential problems? How can it be helpful to individuals as well as institutions? Can social problems themselves define an agenda for scholarly investigation?" (1990, p. 21).

My basic argument is that we can consistently contribute to the public good only if research and education is conducted within institutions that have embraced the habits of engagement and if researchers care about the educational and societal implications of their work and involve students in work of genuine scholarship, all facets of it. In the course of their undergraduate experience, all students should pursue discovery, integration and interpretation, and application of knowledge to real-world problems. If possible, some of this work should take place in modes common to Pasteur's Quadrant so they can acquire habits of lifelong learning now essential for the exercise of good citizenship as well as advancement in the workplace.

Becoming a Student for Life

Continuing education divisions still offer valuable programming for professionals and, no doubt, will continue to do so, but it is now becoming clear that lifelong learning is an essential condition for the sustaining of our democratic way of life as well as for solving practical problems while contributing to our fund of knowledge and theory at the same time—the defining qualities of Pasteur's Quadrant. We need to capture the importance of an enlightened and capable citizenry to the democratic way of life and the maintenance of our sense of community through the generation of greater social capital as well as human capital. The challenges of this kind of learning must be accepted by the entire university community.

The changing societal conditions that will reshape our approach to lifelong learning and the role that universities will play in the generation of community capacity as well as the promotion of individual "personal enrichment and occupational growth" are complex. We must consider a number of issues that are only now beginning to enter our thinking or even our sense of our own responsibilities as scholars and educators. A learning organization has a number of features that require a new approach to shared as well as individual lifelong learning. According to David Garvin (1995), "A learning organization is an organization skilled at creating, acquiring, interpreting, retaining and transferring knowledge; and at purposefully modifying its behavior based on new knowledge and insights" (p. 80).

Among the societal functions that now require the formation of communities of learning or learning organizations are (1) the changing role of learning within larger organizations as a mechanism for better product quality and customer service; (2) the movement toward community-based decision making in school systems, healthcare delivery, social service delivery, and economic and community development and the need to provide support for the continuous learning that community decision-making groups must undertake if they are to make wise choices; (3) the expansion of integrative models that blend preservice and inservice training (such as professional development) and community-based research in community settings such as schools and school systems, social service agencies, healthcare environments, and so on; and (4) new options for undertaking college-level work in alternative settings such as high schools and new forms of educational articulation that provide better access and opportunity for additional education that involve more complex pathways and more effective educational and career planning.

All of these models represent examples of collaborative learning within groups and organizations. Most of them begin to blur the edges of our traditional categories of teaching, research, and service and represent variations of "engagement" in which knowledge is generated, applied, and interpreted in a collaborative mode. *Learning* is becoming a more complex concept that includes all aspects of scholarly work (discovery, integration, interpretation, and application) conducted by different groups of people in a variety of settings. It is no longer simply the effective absorption and faithful application of knowledge transmitted by an expert. Many of these approaches depend upon interinstitutional alliances as well and institutional support structures that must be designed and used effectively to blend discovery, learning, and innovation in new and productive ways.

In this conception, lifelong learning must be both an avenue for sustaining individual skills and competence as well as the shared competencies of groups and organizations. In addition, lifelong learning will increasingly include a component of discovery and application, rather than the absorption of knowledge recently generated by others. It will mean an integration of research and continuing professional development that advances theoretical knowledge in the same process that addresses practical problems, while advancing the skill and knowledge of all of the participants at the same time.

Conclusion

The challenge of engagement is really to bring life and work together—in the lives of our students and faculty, in the collective work of our institutions, and in our working relationships with the broader community. All of our discussions about the conditions required for engagement have at their heart the problem of achieving coherence and integrity—to allow personal meaning and intellectual work to come together for us, for our disciplines, for our departments, and for our institutions.

True engagement offers the opportunity to experience learning in the company of others in a situation where learning has consequences and where individuals are respected and given voice. It is in this process of mutual inquiry where contributions can be made to the public good while, at the same time, advancing the personal and private interests of the participants. It is this blending of the personal and the public that will help us resolve the tensions that now exist between the expectations of society and its elected representatives, on the one hand, and the higher education community, on the other, about the appropriate roles and responsibilities of higher education in contemporary society.

In an engaged institution, an ideal education lies between the two poles of experience and purpose, thought and action, self-realization and social responsibility. An education is meaningful when it liberates the spirit and feeds the soul *and,* at the same time, prepares us to make good decisions, contribute to public life, and live as responsible citizens of our democracy. To foster a society in which learning has consequences, our colleges and universities must direct themselves to bringing public purposes and private benefits together. The basic premise of this essay is that individual aspirations and personal goals can be most productively advanced when research and education are inspired by *both* a thirst for knowledge and a desire for practical outcomes. This should be the defining feature of all kinds of postsecondary institutions, whatever their mission.

References

Association of American Colleges and Universities (AAC&U). (2002). *Greater expectations: A new vision for learning as a nation goes to college.* Washington, DC: Association of American Colleges and Universities.

Boyer, E. L. (1990). *Scholarship reconsidered: Priorities of the professoriate.* Princeton, NJ: Carnegie Foundation for the Advancement of Teaching.

Bringle, R. G., & Hatcher, J. (2001). *Assessing and planning campus/community engagement.* Paper presented at the University as Citizen: Engaging Universities and Communities Conference, University of South Florida.

Bush, V. (1980). *Science—The endless frontier.* A Report to the President on a Program for Postwar Scientific Research. National Science Foundation. (Original work published in 1945.)

Daniels, R. V. (1991). *The University of Vermont. The first two hundred years.* Hanover, VT: University Press of New England.

Garvin, D. A. (1995). Barriers and gateways to learning. In C. R. Christianson, D.A. Garvin, & A. Sweer (Eds.), *Education for judgment.* Boston: Harvard Business School Press.

Geiger, R. L. (1993). *Research and relevant knowledge: American research universities since World War II.* New York: Oxford University Press.

Holland, B. (1999). Factors and strategies that influence faculty involvement in public service. *Journal of Public Service and Outreach, 4*(1), 37–43.

Holland, B. (2001). Toward a definition and characterization of the engaged campus: Six cases. *Metropolitan Universities, 12*(3), 20–29.

Kenny, M., Simon, L.A.K., Kiley-Brabeck, K., & Lerner, R. M. (2002). *Learning to service. Promoting civil society through service learning.* Boston: Kluwer.

Kerr, C. (2001). *The uses of the university* (5th ed.). Cambridge, MA: Harvard University Press.

Marrou, H. I. (1956). *A history of education in antiquity.* Madison: University of Wisconsin Press.

Newman, J. H. (1960). *The idea of a university* (Introduction and Notes by M. J. Svaglic). Notre Dame, IN: University of Notre Dame Press.

Ramaley, J. A. (2000). Embracing civic responsibility. *AAHE Bulletin, 52*(7), 9–13, 20.

Ramaley, J. A. (2001). Why do we engage in engagement? *Metropolitan Universities, 12*(3), 13–19.

Rice, R. E. (2003). Rethinking scholarship and engagement: The struggle for new meanings. *Campus Compact Reader,* Fall 2003, pp. 1–9.

Stokes, D. E. (1997). *Pasteur's quadrant. Basic science and technological innovation.* Washington, DC: Brookings Institution Press.

Part Four

Institutional Governance and Leadership for the Public Good

Chapter Eleven

Integrating a Commitment to the Public Good into the Institutional Fabric

Lee Benson, Ira Harkavy, Matthew Hartley

> *It is not possible to run a course aright when the*
> *goal itself is not rightly placed.*
> FRANCIS BACON, *NOVUM ORGANUM* (1620)

> *The philosophers have only interpreted the world,*
> *in various ways; the point is to* change *it.*
> KARL MARX, *THESES ON FEUERBACH* (1845–1846)

> *In conception, at least, democracy approaches most*
> *nearly the ideal of all social organization; that in which*
> *the individual and the society are organic to each other.*
> JOHN DEWEY, *THE ETHICS OF DEMOCRACY* (1888/1969)

> *Democracy has been given a mission to the world,*
> *and it is of no uncertain character. I wish to show that*
> *the university is the prophet of this democracy, as well*
> *as its priest and its philosopher; that in other words,*
> *the university is the Messiah of the democracy, its*
> *to-be-expected deliverer.*
> WILLIAM RAINEY HARPER, *THE UNIVERSITY*
> *AND DEMOCRACY* (1905)

What constitutes a good American university in our democracy and how should it function? To answer these questions most convincingly, we think it necessary to first respond to the fundamental question raised in the first part of this book: What are American universities good for?

In a recent essay, "The Idea of a University," the president of Columbia University, Lee Bollinger (2003), answered that question in the following way:

> There are many reasons why [American] universities have endured the test of time, but a few are fundamental. Foremost is the purpose they serve. Universities remain meaningful because they respond to the deepest of human needs, to the desire to understand and to explain that understanding to others. A spirited curiosity, coupled with a caring about others (the essence of what we call humanism) is a simple and unquenchable human drive, certainly as profound an element of human nature as the more often cited interests in property and power, around which we organize the economic and political systems.

We respectfully disagree with President Bollinger's essentially idealist theory of the function of universities. Rather than primarily satisfying "a spirited curiosity," we argue for the real-world problem-solving, action-oriented proposition Karl Marx (1970) asserted in his eleventh thesis on Feuerbach (quoted above). In effect, for Marx the most profound, unquenchable "human drive" is not *curiosity* about the world but the innate materialist *need*—and therefore drive—to change it for the better; to create, maintain, and continually develop the Good Society that would enable human beings to lead long, healthy, active, virtuous, happy lives. Although this chapter focuses on research universities—and particularly on our experience at the University of Pennsylvania—we contend that liberal arts institutions, state colleges, and community colleges alike share this noble purpose. To accept our version of Marx's general proposition, and apply it to institutions of higher learning, poses two basic problems: What is the Good Society and what is the primary agency that can bring it into existence? To help solve those problems, we follow leads provided by John Dewey and the first president of the University of Chicago, William Rainey Harper.

In 1888, directly challenging the antidemocratic political philosophy expounded in "Sir Henry Maine's remarkable book on *Popular Government*," Dewey (1969) claimed that:

In conception, at least, democracy approaches most nearly the
ideal of all social organization, that in which the individual and
society are organic to each other. For this reason democracy, so far
as it is really democracy, is the most stable, not the most insecure
of governments. In every other form of government there are individuals who are not organs of the common will, who are outside of
the political society in which they live, and are in effect, aliens to
that which should be their own commonwealth. Not participating
in the formation or expression of the common will, they do not
embody it in themselves. Having no share in society, society has
none in them. (pp. 237–238)

A decade after Dewey identified participatory democracy as the
Good Society, William Rainey Harper (1905) passionately identified
the new urban university as the strategic agency to bring it about.

The university, I contend, is this prophet of democracy—*the agency
established by heaven itself to proclaim the principles of democracy* [empha-
sis added]. It is in the university that the best opportunity is afforded
to investigate the movements of the past and to present the facts
and principles involved before the public. It is the university that,
as the center of thought, is to maintain for democracy the unity so
essential for its success. *The university is the prophetic school out of which
come the teachers who are to lead democracy in the true path* [emphasis
added]. It is the university that must guide democracy into the new
fields of arts and literature and science. It is the university that fights
the battles of democracy, its war-cry being: "Come, let us reason together." It is the university that, in these latter days, goes forth with
buoyant spirit to comfort and give help to those who are downcast,
taking up its dwelling in the very midst of squalor and distress [emphasis
added]. It is the university that, with impartial judgment, condemns
in democracy the spirit of corruption, which now and again lifts up
its head, and brings scandal upon democracy's fair name. . . . The
university, I maintain, is the prophetic interpreter of democracy;
the prophet of her past, in all its vicissitudes; the prophet of her
present, in all its complexity; *the prophet of her future, in all its possibilities* [emphasis added]. (pp. 19–20)

As the quotation demonstrates, long before Clark Kerr hailed the
post–World War II American "multiversity" as the most important institutional innovation of the mid-twentieth century, Harper, in effect,
viewed the new type of urban Great University (his term) which he

struggled to develop in Chicago as theoretically the strategic organizational innovation of modern society. Given that theory, he understandably placed great importance upon his university's active engagement with the severe problems confronting its dynamically growing city, particularly its public school system. Moreover, by taking an active role in grappling with the city's problems, among numerous other benefits, Harper hoped to gain enthusiastic support for his new university from wealthy Chicago elites, especially those highly interested in improving the city's public schools. What might be called Harper's institutional pragmatism, therefore, was highly compatible with, indeed powerfully reinforced, his theoretical conviction that collaborative, action-oriented, real-world problem solving was by far the best strategy to advance knowledge and learning.

According to Harper's theory of democracy in industrial societies, the schooling system functions as the leading societal subsystem. Its continuing development *and effective integration at all levels* (elementary to university) is mandatory to produce significant democratic progress. Given his messianic philosophy, activist temperament, extraordinary organizational skills and experience, given his societal theory and the strategic location of the city of Chicago in the Midwestern communication system and economy, Harper worked tirelessly to make the university of that "central city" function as the dynamic hub of a highly integrated network of Midwestern schools, academies, and colleges dedicated to fulfilling democracy's "mission to the world" (Benson & Harkavy, 2000).

For example, when criticized by a university trustee for sponsoring a journal focused on pedagogy in precollegiate schools, Harper passionately defended such engagement. Harper's devotion to pedagogy logically derived from two propositions central to his vision for the University of Chicago in particular and American universities in general.

1. "Education is the basis of all democratic progress. The problems of education are, therefore, the problems of democracy" (Benson & Harkavy, 2000, p. 32).
2. More than any other institution, the university determines the character of the overall schooling system.

To quote rather than paraphrase Harper (1905): "Through the school system, the character of which, in spite of itself, the university determines and in a large measure controls . . . through the school system every family in this entire broad land of ours is brought into touch with the university; for from it proceeds the teachers, or the teacher's teachers" (pp. 19–20).

Given those two propositions and the role Harper assigned the American University as the Messiah, the "to-be-expected deliverer" of American democracy, he theorized that the major responsibility of American universities was the performance of the overall American schooling system. If the schooling system does not powerfully accelerate democratic progress, then American universities must be performing poorly—no matter whatever else they are doing successfully. "By their [democratic] fruits shall ye know them" (Bacon, 1972, p. xi) was the pragmatic, Francis Baconian, *performance test* which Harper prescribed for the American university system.

Though Harper theorized that the major responsibility of American universities was to improve the performance of the overall American schooling system, except in very general terms, he failed to specify how universities might fulfill that responsibility—how they could concretely advance the public good. As our chapter title suggests, we believe that among the different ways that American universities can respond to this challenge, service-learning holds tremendous promise as a means for the development of democratic schools, democratic universities, and the Democratic Good Society.

The Promise of Service-Learning for American Society

Is service-learning merely a technique, a method, one way of teaching and studying society? Or is service-learning much more than that? More precisely, *can* service-learning have a much higher, much more significant, purpose? In the *Encyclopedia of Community*, two of us (Benson & Harkavy, 2003a) defined service-learning as "an active, creative [pedagogy] that integrates community service with academic study in order to enhance a student's capacity to think critically, solve problems practically, and function as a lifelong moral, democratic, citizen in a democratic society. In most cases, service-learning takes place within an academic course. . . . service-learning also involves student reflection on the service experience, an emphasis on providing genuine service to the community, and the development of democratic, mutually beneficial, mutually respectful, relationships between the students and the community members with whom they work" (pp. 1223–1224).

For us, moreover, service-learning best accomplishes its goal by engaging students in collaborative, community-based, community action-oriented, reflective, real-world problem solving designed to develop the knowledge and related practice necessary for an optimally democratic society capable of continually advancing the public good.

Given this definition of service-learning, it follows that for us service-learning should work to develop strategies and actions to help fulfill the democratic promise of America's colleges and universities in particular and the democratic promise of American society in general. We should, in our judgment, therefore, evaluate service-learning by the extent to which it actually advances democracy in our classrooms, communities, and society. To be more specific: The impact of service-learning on student learning should be one component, not the primary focus, of any evaluation of its utility. Similarly, increased acceptance of service-learning in the disciplines, while important, is not an indication that anything like serious, substantial, significant change in higher education is occurring. To be even more direct, if research on service-learning conceptualizes learning outcomes and acceptance by disciplines as *ends,* rather than as *means* to larger educational and societal ends, the service-learning movement will lose its way and result in the inevitable reduction of service-learning to just another technique, method, or field.

The reduction of service-learning would, we believe, be even more devastating than the reduction of disciplines (such as history, political science, economics, sociology) that occurred in the early decades of the twentieth century. Founded for the purpose of advancing "scientific . . . study" and "practical reform," the disciplines, largely in reaction to the horrors of World War I, turned inward, focusing on themselves rather than the contributions they could make to "the relief of man's estate" (Bacon, 1972; DuBois, 1899). Why will the reduction of service-learning have even more negative consequences than the post–World War I taming of the disciplines? Simply put, because service-learning should not be conceived of as a discipline, but as a systematic, democratic, collaborative, experimental approach to learning, personal and civic development, knowledge production, and societal change. Even more important, service-learning can, and has, served as the driving force and center of an intellectual movement to create democratic schooling from pre-K through higher education. It has been the leading edge of an academic "glasnost" to create democratic, engaged, civic universities after nearly a century (to mix metaphors) of the narrowing and hardening of academic arteries. In short, the reduction of service-learning would be particularly devastating because it would result in dashing hope that significant schooling and societal change can occur, creating a perception and feeling that no matter how promising the strategy, in the end it will be "the same old same old."

In effect, we are calling for a Baconian-inspired strategy for the development and advancement of a comprehensive approach to service-learning. To Bacon, the first principle for progress is "know thy goals." As Bacon (Benson, 1978) wrote in 1620: "It is not possible to run a course aright when the goal itself is not rightly placed." The goal for service-learning, we believe, should be to contribute *significantly* to developing and sustaining democratic schools, colleges, universities, communities, and society. By working to realize that goal, service-learning will powerfully help American higher education in particular, and American schooling in general, return to their core mission—educating students for a democratic society.

Given the position outlined above, we have to do three things to give credence to our argument:

1. Demonstrate that a democratic mission is the core mission of American higher education.
2. Identify the obstacles that have helped prevent higher education from realizing its democratic mission.
3. Propose a practical strategy by which service-learning can help reduce those obstacles and help higher education realize its democratic mission to advance the public good.

Democratic Mission as Core Mission

If we are to fulfill the democratic promise of America for all Americans, we need to be a nation comprised of individuals with an "inclination joined with an ability to serve." We take the phrase "inclination joined with an ability to serve" from that extraordinary patriot, statesman, scientist, educator, scholar, and activist—Benjamin Franklin. In 1749, Franklin (Best, 1962) published a pamphlet entitled "Proposals

Relating to the Education of Youth in Pennsilvania *[sic]*" to describe the purposes and curriculum of the "Academy of Philadelphia," later named the University of Pennsylvania. To quote him more fully: "The idea of what is *true merit,* should also be often presented to youth, ex-plain'd and impress'd on their minds, as consisting in an *Inclination* join'd with an *Ability* to serve Mankind, one's Country, Friends and Family . . . which Ability should be the great *Aim* and *End* of all Learn-ing" (pp. 150–151).

An inclination joined with an ability to serve was the original rationale for public schools, which were to educate youth for citizenship. Moreover, colonial colleges were founded with service as a central aim. While Franklin founded the University of Pennsylvania as a secular institution to educate students in a variety of fields, the other colonial colleges were largely created to educate ministers and religiously orthodox men capable of creating good communities built on religious denominational principles. Specifically, Harvard (Congregationalist), William and Mary (Anglican), Yale (Congregationalist), Princeton (Presbyterian), Columbia (Anglican), Brown (Baptist), Rutgers (Dutch Reformed), and Dartmouth (Congregationalist) were all created with religiously based service as a central purpose.

As Judith Ramaley underscores in her chapter, service to society, fulfilling America's democratic mission, was the founding purpose of the land-grant universities. Established by the Morrill Act of 1862, land-grant colleges and universities were designed to spread education, advance democracy, and improve the mechanical, agricultural, and military sciences. The spirit of the Morrill Act was perhaps best expressed at the University of Wisconsin, which at the turn of the century designed programs around the educational needs of adult citizens across the state.

In 1912, Charles McCarthy, a graduate of the University of Wisconsin and the first legislative reference librarian in the United States, coined the phrase "the Wisconsin Idea" to describe a concept that had been in practice for a number of years. The Wisconsin Idea began its "take off phase" in 1903 when Charles Van Hise became president of the University of Wisconsin and joined forces with his former classmate, Governor Robert La Follette, to make "the boundaries of the university . . . the boundaries of the state." When asked what accounted for the great progressive reforms that spread across the Midwest in the first two decades of the twentieth century, Charles McCarthy (1912) replied, "a combination of soil and seminar" (Stark, n.d., pp. 2–3). McCarthy's answer captures the essence of the Wisconsin Idea—focusing academic resources on improving the life of the farmer and the lives of citizens across the entire state.

The urban research universities founded in the late nineteenth century also made service their central goal. In 1876, Daniel Coit Gilman (Long, 1992), in his inaugural address as the first president of Johns Hopkins, America's first modern research university, expressed the hope that universities should "make for less misery among the poor, less ignorance in the schools, less bigotry in the temple, less suffering in the hospitals, less fraud in business, less folly in politics" (p. 119). Following Gilman's lead, the abiding belief in the democratic purposes of the American research university echoed throughout higher education at the turn of the twentieth century. As we noted above, in 1899 the University of Chicago's first president, William Rainey Harper (Long, 1992), characterized the university as the "prophet of democracy" and its "to-be-expected deliverer" (p. 119). And in 1908, Charles W. Eliot (Long, 1992), the president of Harvard, proclaimed: "At bottom most of the American institutions of higher education are filled with the democratic spirit of serviceableness. Teachers and students alike are profoundly moved by the desire to serve the democratic community" (p. 119).

Simply put, the democratic mission served as *the* central mission for the development of the American research university, including both land-grant institutions *and* urban universities, such as Johns Hopkins, Chicago, Columbia, and Penn. As political scientist Charles Anderson (1993) observed in *Prescribing the Life of the Mind*:

> With deliberate defiance, those who created the American university (particularly the public university, though the commitment soon spread throughout the system) simply stood this [essentially aristocratic] idea of reason on its head. Now it was assumed that the widespread exercise of self-conscious, critical reason was essential to *democracy* [original emphasis]. *The truly remarkable belief arose that this system of government would flourish best if citizens would generally adopt the habits of thought hitherto supposed appropriate mainly for scholars and scientist* [emphasis added]. We vastly expanded access

to higher education. We presumed it a general good, like transport, or power, part of the infrastructure of the civilization. (pp. 7–8)

History is not the only useful guide to help us determine whether the democratic mission should be the primary mission of American higher education. Alexander Astin's discussion of the "public pronouncements that U.S. colleges and universities make in their catalogues and mission statements" is also helpful. Astin (1997) observed that:

In many ways, these sometimes lofty statements come as close as anything to Dewey's conception of the proper role of education in society. If we were to study the mission statements of a randomly selected group of U.S. higher education institutions, we would seldom, if ever, find any mention of private economic benefits, international competitiveness, or filling slots in the labor market. On the contrary, when it comes to describing its educational mission, the typical college or university will use language such as "preparing students for responsible citizenship," "developing character," "developing future leaders," "preparing students to serve society," and so forth. In other words, if we are to believe our own rhetoric, those of us who work in the academy see ourselves as *serving the society and promoting and strengthening our particular form of democratic self-government* [emphasis added]. (pp. 210–211)

American higher education in general, however, has, in our judgment, very far to go before it actually fulfills its historic public purposes. In her 2001 study for the Grantmaker Forum on National and Community Service, Cynthia Gibson noted that when it comes to civic engagement, higher education's rhetoric far exceeds its performance. Weaving together her own words, with those of Barry Checkoway and Kevin Mattson, Gibson (2001) observed:

Other higher education leaders have echoed Derek Bok's concern that universities are disassociated with the civic missions on which they were founded—missions that assumed responsibility for preparing students for active participation in a democratic society and developing students' knowledge for the improvement of communities. Currently, it is "hard to find top administrators with consistent commitment to this mission; few faculty members consider it central to their role, and community groups that approach the

university for assistance often find it difficult to get what they need."
In short, the university has primarily become "a place for professors
to get tenured and students to get credentialed." (p. 11)

How far higher education *is* from where it *should* be is also evident in the parlous state of democracy on campus (exemplified by
the hierarchical, elitist, competitive culture that pervades the academy), the state of the communities in which our institutions are located, and the state of American democracy itself.

Obstacles to the Realization of Higher Education's Democratic Mission

Why has American higher education failed to realize its democratic
mission? In an earlier chapter, Adrianna Kezar points to one powerful force thwarting such efforts—the abrogation of the social
contract between higher education and society. The obstacles facing research universities are distinct. Summarily stated, the forces
of Platonization, commodification, and disciplinary ethnocentrism,
tribalism, and guildism prevent them from translating democratic
mission into democratic practice.

Platonization

Plato's elitist, idealist theory of schooling has incalculable day-to-
day impacts on education and society. In part, the extraordinary
impact of Plato's antidemocratic, idealist theory on American democracy can be explained by John Dewey's failure to translate his
own ideas into practical action.

Plato was the philosopher Dewey most liked to read. Though he
admired Plato, their worldviews differed radically. Plato's worldview
was aristocratic and contemplative; Dewey's was democratic and activist. Despite their many differences, in certain crucial respects Dewey
shared Plato's views about the relationships between education and
society. Like the ancient Greek philosopher, Dewey theorized that education and society were dynamically interactive and interdependent.
Plato's philosophy of education aimed to achieve aristocratic order;
Dewey's to achieve democratic community. For Dewey it followed,

then, that if human beings hope to develop and maintain a participatory democratic society, they must develop and maintain a participatory democratic schooling system.

Ironically, in direct contrast to Plato who pragmatically created
a remarkably influential Academy to implement his aristocratic philosophy of education and society, the philosophical activist Dewey
failed to work to institutionalize his democratic philosophy of education and society, except by "lay preaching." That is, despite the
powerful example of Plato's Academy—an academy whose elitist,
idealist, philosophy *continues to dominate Western schooling systems to this
day*—Dewey flagrantly violated his own general theory of thinking
and action. Oversimply stated, Plato's idealist theory of education,
his corollary theory of knowledge, for example, the great superior-
ity of elegant "pure theory" and "pure science" compared to "infe-
rior" real-world practice, as well as his elitist theory of governance,
are deeply embedded in the culture and structure of American colleges and universities.

The dead hand of Plato continues to shape American higher education, and through American higher education it shapes the entire
schooling system. Broadly viewed, we contend that service-learning
can be conceptualized as a strategy to release the vise-like grip of
Plato's dead hand. "Overthrowing" Plato, however, would only
achieve a partial victory. A clear and present danger to the democratic
mission of higher education and to American democracy in general
also comes from the forces of commodification (education for profit,
students as customers, syllabi as content, academics as superstars). It
is worth emphasizing that these forces, although particularly perni-
cious at this time, were alive and well at the very birth of the colonial
college.

Commodification

More than an ethic of religious-inspired service shaped the colonial
colleges. They also constituted a significant form of community competition. Colleges, it was anticipated, would bring more than religious
and educational benefits to a local community; they would bring economic (and a wide variety of other) benefits. The Brown brothers of
Providence, Rhode Island, provide a particularly clear statement
of anticipated economic benefits. Appealing for support to "busi-

nessmen of Providence and . . . surrounding towns," they promised
that: "Building the college here will be the means of bringing great
quantities of money into the place, and thereby greatly increasing the
markets for all kinds of the country's produce, and consequently increasing the value of estates to which this town is a market" (Cochran,
1972, p. 35). Succinctly stated, contradictory capitalist market motives, not simply traditional medieval Christian motives, inspired and
shaped the contradictory origins and increasingly contradictory development of the American higher educational system.

To systematically discuss the history of commodification in American higher education would require many more pages than we have
been allotted. We merely note, therefore, that it was the Cold War
and its extraordinarily complex consequences, direct and indirect,
short-term and long-term, that "redefined American science" and
accelerated and deepened the commodification of American universities in powerful and, in our judgment, deeply disturbing ways.

To place that highly complex development in historical perspective, we cite Stuart Leslie's (1993) analysis that, during World War II,
to a far greater extent than during World War I, universities had "won
a substantial share of the funds [going into wartime mobilization],
with research and development contracts that actually dwarfed those
of the largest industrial contractors. . . . Vannevar Bush, the chief ar-
chitect of wartime science policy and a strong advocate of university
research, was the man behind the change" (p. 6).

Bush engineered that change as director of the powerful wartime
Office of Scientific Research and Development. Late in 1944, President Roosevelt, highly impressed by its accomplishments, asked Bush
to draft a long-term plan for postwar science. Bush delivered his famous report, *Science, the Endless Frontier,* in 1945. General agreement
exists that, since 1945, it has profoundly influenced America's science
policy. For our purposes, the chief importance of Bush's "Basic Science Manifesto" (our term for it) is that it rapidly produced what
Benson and Harkavy (2002) have previously characterized as the Big
Science, Cold War, Entrepreneurial, Commodified, American Research University System. Derek Bok (2003) brilliantly stigmatized
this development in his recent book *Universities in the Marketplace,* as
the "commercialization of higher education."

Perhaps the most important consequence of the commercialization of higher education is the devastating impact that it has on the

values and ambitions of college students. When universities openly and increasingly pursue commercialization, it powerfully legitimizes and reinforces the pursuit of economic self-interest by students and contributes to the widespread sense among them that they are in college solely to gain career skills and credentials. It would only belabor the argument to comment further on how student idealism is even more sharply diminished, student disengagement is even more sharply increased, when students see their universities abandon academic values and scholarly pursuits to openly, enthusiastically function as entrepreneurial, ferociously competitive, profit-making corporations.

Disciplinary Ethnocentrism, Tribalism, and Guildism

Disciplinary ethnocentrism, tribalism, and guildism (Benson & Harkavy, 2003b) strongly dominate American universities today and strongly work against their actually doing what they rhetorically promise to do. The famous postmodern literary theorist Stanley Fish pontifically provides us with a marvelous case in point. In his monthly column in the *Chronicle of Higher Education* (May 16, 2003), Fish caustically attacked "the authors of a recent book [Anne Colby and Thomas Ehrlich et al.], *Educating Citizens: Preparing America's Undergraduates for Lives of Moral and Civic Responsibility* (Jossey-Bass 2003). A product of the Carnegie Foundation for the Advancement of Teaching, the volume reports on *a failure that I find heartening*" [emphasis added] (p. C5).

What precisely is the failure? The failure is that, according to the authors of *Educating Citizens,* undergraduate education now does not provide "the kind of learning [college] graduates need to be involved and responsible citizens." Why is that failure "heartening" to the former dean of Liberal Arts and Sciences at the University of Illinois at Chicago? Because, he insists unequivocally, professors cannot possibly provide that kind of learning nor should they attempt it. Their job is simply to teach what their discipline calls for them to teach and to try to make their students into good disciplinary researchers. Professors can't make their students "*into good people and . . . shouldn't try.*" Indeed, for Fish (2003), "emphasis on broader goals and especially on the therapeutic goal of 'personal development' can make it difficult to interest students in *the disciplinary training it is our job to provide* [emphases added]" (p. C5).

In effect, Fish not only calls on American academics to repudiate John Dewey and his democratic adherents, but also calls on them to repudiate Plato and his antidemocratic elitist adherents. Since Plato's philosophy of education, like Dewey's, gives its highest priority to making good citizens, according to the Fish doctrine of professorial responsibility, they both were completely wrong. As teachers, the only duty of professors is to teach their discipline; it emphatically does not require or permit them to try to make their students "into good people."

In a perverse way, Fish's caustic attack on the authors of *Educating Citizens* actually performs a valuable function. It splendidly illuminates what might be called the *disciplinary fallacy* afflicting American universities, namely, the fallacy that professors are duty-bound only to serve the scholastic interests and preoccupations of their disciplines and have neither the responsibility nor the capacity to help their universities keep their long-standing promises to prepare "America's Undergraduates for Lives of Moral and Civic Responsibility." In effect, Fish baldly asserted what most professors now believe and practice but strongly tend not to admit openly. This belief and practice also strongly tends to produce disciplinary isolation and what has been stigmatized as "siloization" (Organization for Economic Development, 1982), which strongly inhibits the interdisciplinary cooperation and integrated specialization necessary to solve significant, highly complex, real-world problems.

Toward a Strategy to Help Higher Education Practically Realize Its Democratic Mission

Having briefly—and perhaps oversimply—identified the obstacles that prevent higher education from realizing its democratic mission, we turn now to the really hard, really significant, question. What is to be done to release higher education from the dead hand of Plato and the live hands of commodification and the disciplinary fallacy? More specifically, what is a practical strategy that would enable service-learning to help American higher education overthrow Plato and institute Dewey, reject commodification and disciplinary guildism, and practically realize its democratic mission? In our view, the first step is to clarify and even redefine the purpose of undergraduate education.

Refocusing the Ends of Undergraduate Education

In the Foreword to *Educating Citizens,* Lee Shulman, President of the Carnegie Foundation for the Advancement of Teaching, emphasized the critically important role colleges play in the development of the virtues and understanding vital for democratic citizenship. Observing that a democratic society required an "educated citizenry blessed with virtue as well as wisdom," Shulman (2003) hailed the book's demonstration that achieving the requisite "combination of moral and civic virtue accompanied by the development of understanding occurs best when fostered by our institutions of higher education. It does not occur by accident, or strictly through early experience. Indeed, I argue that there may well be a critical period for the development of these virtues, and that period could be the college years. During this developmental period, defined as much by educational opportunity as by age, students of all ages *develop the resources needed for their continuing journeys through adult life"* [emphasis added] (p. viii).

Shulman's astute observation helps us see the critically important role that, in a wide variety of ways, colleges play in the lifelong, all-encompassing development of all the different types of personnel who, *directly and indirectly,* control and operate the American schooling system. If their critically formative years at college neither contribute to their own development as democratic citizens nor concretely demonstrate to them how schools can function to produce democratic citizens, *they will necessarily reproduce what they have learned*—more precisely, failed to learn in college. As a result of that disastrously flawed reproductive process, the schooling system will be incapable of developing an effective program for democratic citizenship. Put another way, we agree with Lee Shulman that American colleges constitute the strategically important component of American universities when the goal is to help develop an American schooling system capable of producing students who possess the set of attributes they must possess to function as democratic citizens. But what might impel our universities to embrace this goal actively as well as rhetorically?

Shame and Cognitive Dissonance

For many years we have argued that the immoral state of America's cities and the enlightened self-interest of colleges and universities would lead higher education to embrace significant service-learning partnerships with their communities. More significantly, we argued that the increasingly obvious, increasingly immoral, contradiction between the growing status, wealth, and power of American universities—particularly elite research universities—and the increasingly pathological state of a great many American cities would *shame* universities into taking action to reduce the contradiction. In addition, we argued that universities would not only be pressured by external agencies (such as federal and state governments) to work hard to improve the quality of their local schools and communities but would increasingly recognize that it was in their own enlightened self-interest to do that. It has recently become clear to us, however, that we seriously underestimated the ability of universities to effectively resist making substantive changes of the kind many academics have been advocating since the 1980s. Probably the main form of resistance has been for universities to make eloquent rhetorical pledges of support for "community engagement" and service-learning and then fail to put "their money (and other necessary resources) where their mouth is."

Aside from deploring it, what can practically be done to overcome or reduce that hypocritical form of university resistance to change? Part of the solution, we believe, is to follow Derek Bok's lead in *Universities in the Marketplace* and apply the powerful social psychological theory of *cognitive dissonance*. Bok (2003) did not explicitly cite that theory. But he *used* it with devastating effect in his book-length demonstration that "the commercialization of higher education" not only fundamentally contradicts traditional "academic standards and institutional integrity" but, in a "process [which] may be irreversible," threatens to sacrifice "essential values that are all but impossible to restore" (p. 208).

In *A Theory of Cognitive Dissonance* (1957), Leon Festinger described the theory that became one of the most influential in social psychology. Summarized in oversimplified form, the theory focuses on "the feeling of psychological discomfort produced by

the combined presence of two thoughts that do not follow from
one another" [e.g., smokers who agree that smoking is very un-
healthy but continue to smoke]. Festinger proposed that "the
greater the discomfort, the greater the desire to reduce the dissonance of the two cognitive elements" (book jacket).

In *Universities in the Marketplace,* Bok clearly wanted to produce
such great discomfort among university administrators and faculty
members who either engaged in commercial activities or tolerated
them that they would feel compelled to change their behavior. In
similar fashion, the egalitarian values proclaimed in the Declaration of Independence have long been invoked in American history
to produce the cognitive dissonance and great discomfort indispensable to "agitators" who wanted to abolish slavery, win equal
rights for women, overcome segregation, and achieve similar egalitarian goals.

Learning from history and following Bok's lead, this chapter is
designed to support the campaign he began—to shame universities
into translating their democratic rhetoric into practical action. Taking a leaf from Lincoln Steffens's (1957) famous muckraking work
The Shame of the Cities, as we see it, that campaign, in effect, tries to
overcome *the shame of the universities.* A highly effective way to conduct the campaign, we believe, would make use of Alexander Astin's
(1997) powerful essay "Liberal Education and Democracy: The Case
for Pragmatism."

In effect, like Bok, Astin skillfully used the theory of cognitive
dissonance to develop a devastating critique of the hypocrisy of universities which rhetorically proclaim that their mission is to help their
students become responsible democratic citizens and then do almost
nothing *positive* to realize that mission. In fact, as Astin (1997) observed, by their antidemocratic organization and functioning, "by
their obvious preoccupation with enhancing [their] resources and
reputations," and in a variety of other ways, universities strongly contribute to their students accepting the "values of materialism, competitiveness, and individualism" (p. 221). Guided by cognitive
dissonance theory and American history (and the history of other
countries' reforms and revolutions), we are convinced that a sustained, massive, many-sided campaign to expose and denounce university hypocrisy can produce sufficient "great discomfort" to *help*

change American university behavior for the better. But in itself such a campaign will not bring about the radical changes we support. A comprehensive strategy to bring those changes about needs additional prongs, two of which we briefly describe below.

Act Locally

In *Building Partnerships for Service-Learning,* Barbara Jacoby (2003) and her colleagues emphasize that creating effective, democratic, mutually beneficial, mutually respectful partnerships should be a primary, if not the primary, goal for service-learning in the first decades of the twenty-first century. Jacoby calls on colleges and universities to focus their attention on improving democracy and the quality of life in their local communities. Here Jacoby is echoing one of John Dewey's (1927) most significant propositions: "Democracy must begin at home, and its home is the neighborly community" (p. 213). Democracy, Dewey emphasized, has to be built on face-to-face interactions in which human beings work together cooperatively to solve the ongoing problems of life. In effect, Jacoby and colleagues have updated Dewey and advocated this proposition: *Democracy must begin at home, and its home is the engaged neighborly college or university and its local community partner.*

The benefits of a local community focus for college and university service-learning courses and programs are manifold. Ongoing, continuous interaction is facilitated through work in an easily accessible local setting. Relationships of trust, so essential for effective partnerships and effective learning, are also built through day-to-day work on problems and issues of mutual concern. In addition, the local community also provides a convenient setting in which a number of service-learning courses based in different disciplines can work together on a complex problem to produce substantive results. Work in a college or university's local community, since it facilitates interaction across schools and disciplines, can create interdisciplinary learning opportunities. And finally, the local community is a real-world site in which community members and academics can pragmatically determine whether the work is making a real difference, whether *both* the neighborhood and the institution are better as a result of common efforts.

Focus on Significant, Community-Based, Real-World Problems

To Dewey (1990), knowledge and learning are most effective when human beings work collaboratively to solve specific, strategic, real-world problems. "Thinking," he wrote, "begins in . . . a *forked road* situation, a situation which is ambiguous, which presents a dilemma, which poses alternatives" (p. 11). A focus on universal problems (such as poverty, unequal healthcare, substandard housing, hunger, and inadequate, unequal education) that manifest themselves locally are, in our judgment, the best way to apply Dewey's brilliant proposition in practice. To support the argument, we turn to the example we know best, the University of Pennsylvania's work with its local ecological community, West Philadelphia. The example reveals that not only is the act of learning transformed through such efforts but grappling with significant, local problems has the capacity to begin mending a fractured academic community because the very enterprise depends upon the participation of a multiplicity of faculty and administrators from across the university.

A University-Assisted Community School Based on Service-Learning

Since 1985, Benson and Harkavy have been engaged in an increasingly complex project to help develop university-assisted community schools in West Philadelphia, the section of Philadelphia in which the University of Pennsylvania is located. Committed to undergraduate teaching, convinced by their personal experiences during the 1960s that undergraduates might function as catalytic agents to help bring about university change, they designed an honors seminar that aimed to stimulate undergraduates to think critically about what Penn should do to remedy the rapid deterioration of West Philadelphia—a development that had devastating consequences for the university. The seminar's title suggests its general concerns: Urban University-Community Relationships: Penn-West Philadelphia, Past, Present and Future, As a Case Study.

As the seminar was originally conceived, its students would be given the general assignment of developing a research project focused on some problem that adversely affected the quality of life in West Philadelphia. In a relatively short time, however, after the seminar actually began operations, it became clear that the best strategy was to have students concentrate their work on helping to solve one highly critical problem—the problem of developing *university-assisted community schools.* In sharp contrast to traditional neighborhood schools, Benson and Harkavy conceived the idea that university-assisted community schools should be developed which would educate, engage, activate, and *serve all members of the community in which a school is located.* Put another way, in the course of the seminar's work, it developed a strategy based on this proposition: Universities can best help improve their local environment if they mobilize and integrate their great resources, particularly the "human capital" embodied in their students, to help develop and maintain *community schools* that function as focal points to help create healthy urban environments.

Somewhat more specifically, the strategy developed in the course of the seminar's work assumed that, like institutions of higher education, public schools can function as environment-changing institutions and can become the strategic centers of broad-based partnerships that genuinely engage a wide variety of community organizations and institutions. Public schools "belong" to all members of the community. They are particularly well suited, therefore, to function as neighborhood "hubs" or "nodes" or "centers" around which productive local partnerships can be generated and formed. When public schools play that role, they function as community institutions *par excellence*; they then provide a decentralized, democratic, community-based effective response to significant community problems and help develop the democratic, cosmopolitan, neighborly communities John Dewey envisioned.

The university-assisted community school, of course, essentially reinvents and updates an old American idea, namely that the neighborhood school can effectively serve as the core neighborhood institution—the core institution that provides comprehensive services and galvanizes other community institutions and groups. But by their very nature, community schools engage in far more activities and serve far wider constituencies than do traditional neighborhood schools. To do all that successfully, however, a community school serving a specific neighborhood requires far more resources (broadly conceived) than does a traditional school serving the same neighborhood. Where would those resources come from?

Once that problem was recognized, the service-learning that students had been performing in West Philadelphia schools helped Benson and Harkavy see that the solution was to really mobilize the great resource of universities like Penn to assist the transformation of traditional neighborhood schools into innovative community schools. And once that was seen, the concept of university-assisted community schools followed logically. From then on, their seminar concentrated on helping to develop and implement that concept in real-world practice. In effect, the highly complex problem that the seminar concentrated on solving became the problem of effectively mobilizing *and integrating* Penn's great resources to help transform the *traditional public schools* of West Philadelphia into *innovative community schools.*

Over time, as students continually worked to develop and implement the concept and theory of university-assisted community schools, the seminar increasingly developed and implemented an innovative service-learning program. Summarized succinctly, the program is based on collaborative, action-oriented, community problem-solving that provided both Penn students and students in West Philadelphia schools "with a real motive behind and a real outcome ahead," to quote John Dewey's powerful proposition about the conditions most likely to permit effective learning to take place (Dewey, 1991, p. 12).

Observing the work of their students and the students in West Philadelphia community schools over a number of years led Benson and Harkavy to develop a critically important principle that has guided their thinking and practice in a wide variety of ways and situations. That principle can be formulated as follows:

At all levels (K–16 and above), collaborative, community-based, community action-oriented, service-learning projects that innovatively and effectively depart from customary teacher-dominated school routines permit and stimulate both teachers and students to participate democratically in school and classroom governance and functioning. Put another way, the principle can be summarized as follows: Collaborative, action-oriented, community-based, effective, innovative, problem-solving projects create spaces in which school and classroom democracy can grow and flourish.

In our judgment, that general principle can powerfully help inspire and develop effective programs for democratic citizenship in a wide variety of schools (at all levels) and communities. It warrants careful consideration, we believe, by everyone engaged in trying to solve the complex problems inherent in education for democratic citizenship.

Space restrictions prevent us from giving a detailed account of how, over time, the seminar's increasingly successful work stimulated development of a number of "academically-based community services" courses in a wide range of Penn schools and departments. (For historical reasons peculiar to Penn, "academically-based community service" [ABCS] is the term it uses for what elsewhere is called "service-learning.") ABCS focuses on community problem-solving and the integration of research, teaching, learning, and service, as well as reflection on the service experience. For our present purposes, we need only note that, encouraged by the success of Penn's increasing engagement with West Philadelphia, in July 1992, the president of the university, Sheldon Hackney, created the Center for Community Partnerships. To highlight the importance he attached to the center, he located it in the Office of the President and appointed Ira Harkavy to be its director, while continuing to serve as director of the Penn Program for Public Service created in 1988.

Symbolically and practically, creation of the center constituted a major change in Penn's relationship to West Philadelphia and Philadelphia. The university as a corporate entity now formally committed itself to finding ways to use its truly enormous resources to help improve the quality of life in its local community—not only in respect to public schools but to economic and community development in general.

Very broadly conceived, the center is based on the assumption that one highly efficient way for Penn to carry out its traditional academic missions of advancing universal knowledge and effectively educating students is to function as what we now call an "engaged democratic cosmopolitan civic university." Penn's research and teaching would actively focus on solving universal problems, such as schooling, healthcare, economic development, as those universal problems *manifest themselves locally in West Philadelphia and Philadelphia.* By effectively and efficiently integrating general theory and concrete practice, as Ben Franklin had advocated in the eighteenth century, Penn would symbiotically improve both the quality of life in its local ecological community *and* the quality of its academic research and teaching. The center is based on the proposition that when Penn is creatively conceived as a community-engaged university, it constitutes in the best sense both a *universal* and a *local* institution of higher education.

The emphasis on partnerships in the center's name was deliberate; it acknowledged, in effect, that Penn could not try to go it alone, as it had long been (arrogantly) accustomed to do. The creation of the center was also significant internally. It meant that, at least in principle, the president of the university would now strive to achieve university alignment by strongly encouraging all components of the university to seriously consider the collaborative roles they could appropriately play in Penn's efforts to improve the quality of its off-campus environment. Implementation of that strategy accelerated after Judith Rodin became president of Penn in 1994. A native West Philadelphian and Penn graduate, Rodin was appointed in part because of her deeply felt commitment to improving Penn's local environment and to transforming Penn into the leading American urban university, and she has strongly supported the work of the center from the start of her administration.

Since its creation in 1992 to help solve the complex problems adversely affecting the quality of life in West Philadelphia, the center has tried to function as an integrating agency to effectively align Penn's numerous schools and departments and bring about their mutually-beneficial collaboration. Easier said than done, alas.

Particularly since 1945, Penn, like all American research universities, has increasingly developed an organizational culture and structure that makes competitive fragmentation the norm and interdisciplinary, interschool collaboration the exception. To reduce competitive fragmentation and increase collaborative alignment, the center has tried to make use of Muzafer Sherif's (1958) "superordinate goal" theory. Sherif defined "superordinate goals" as "goals which are compelling and highly appealing to members of two or more groups in conflict which cannot be attained by the resources and energies of the groups separately. In effect, they are goals attained only when groups pull together" (p. 349).

Developing solutions to critical, complex, West Philadelphia problems would, of course, directly and indirectly significantly benefit Penn as an institution and would be in the enlightened self-interest of everyone at the university. In principle, therefore, developing such solutions should logically constitute "goals which are compelling and highly appealing" to almost all members of Penn's multitudinous departments, centers, institutes, and schools. In practice, however, the long-standing competitive fragmentation built into Penn's organizational culture and structure has strongly trumped the logic of collaboration and enlightened self-interest. As a result, until recently, attempts to apply Sherif's superordinate goal theory have produced only very limited success.

Though the number and variety of academically-based community service courses at Penn has greatly increased since 1992, they have strongly tended to function independently of each other, even when linking them together would obviously be mutually beneficial. But a recent development has strengthened the conviction that the center, by focusing its efforts on complex problems that are both widely recognized as important and require the effective integration of specialized knowledge and skills, can successfully apply superordinate goal theory to reduce Penn's competitive fragmentation and increase its interdisciplinary, interschool collaboration.

Community Healthcare as a Complex Strategic Problem to Help Bring About "One University"

Penn is perhaps the only major university where all its schools and colleges are located on a contiguous urban campus. In the early 1970s, the newly appointed president of the university, Martin Meyerson, emphasized the extraordinary intellectual and social benefits that would result if the university took optimum advantage of the ease of interaction that a single campus location provides. To realize those benefits, he called for implementation of a "One University" organizational realignment—a realignment in which Penn would be characterized by an intellectual collaboration and synergy across departments, divisions, colleges, and schools that would result in powerful advances in knowledge and human welfare.

As we noted above, that kind of radical realignment is much easier said than done. In practice, overcoming Penn's long-standing disciplinary fragmentation and conflict, narrow specialization, bureaucratic barriers, and what Benjamin Franklin (Best, 1962) stigmatized in 1789 as "ancient Customs and Habitudes" (p. 173), proved enormously difficult to achieve; the One University idea essentially remained an idea, not an action program.

Given the recent recognition, however, that improving the health of urban communities is among the most significant problems confronting American society, it seemed possible to use it to resurrect the One University idea; solutions to the highly complex urban healthcare problem obviously require interschool and interdisciplinary collaboration. And that indeed proved to be the case when a school-based community healthcare project began at a West Philadelphia public school. To make the argument concretely, we describe the project and its wider implications in some detail.

Conceptualizing and Implementing the Sayre Community Healthcare Project

In recent years, it has been increasingly recognized that lack of accessible, effective healthcare is one of the most serious problems affecting poor urban communities. In fact, since Benson and Harkavy began work in 1985, community leaders have identified improving healthcare as a critical need. As a result, beginning in the late 1980s, Benson and Harkavy have been trying, largely unsuccessfully, to develop a sustainable, comprehensive, effective healthcare program at local public schools. In the spring and summer of 2002, however, a group of undergraduates in their academically-based community service seminar focused their research and service on helping to solve the healthcare crisis in West Philadelphia. The students' research and work with the community led them to propose establishment of a health promotion and disease prevention center at a public school in West Philadelphia, the Sayre Middle School.

From their research, the students were well aware that community-oriented primary care projects frequently flounder because of an inability to sustain adequate external funding. They concluded that for a school-based community healthcare project to be sustained and successful, it had to be built into the curriculum at both the university and the public school. Only then would it gain a degree of permanence and stability over time. They proposed, therefore, creation of a health promotion and disease prevention center at a local school that would serve as a teaching and learning focus for medical, dental, nursing, arts and sciences, social work, education, fine arts, and business students. Their proposal proved to be so compelling that it led to the development of a school-based Community Health Promotion and Disease Prevention Center at Sayre Middle School. It is worth noting that one of the undergraduates who developed the Sayre project, Mei Elansary, received the 2003 Howard R. Swearer Humanitarian Award given by Campus Compact to students for outstanding public service.

The school-based Community Health Promotion and Disease Prevention Center at Sayre Middle School was formally launched in January of 2003. It functions as the central component of a university-assisted community school designed both to advance student learning and democratic development and to help strengthen families and institutions within the community. A community school is an ideal location for healthcare programs; it is not only where children learn but also where community members gather and participate in a variety of activities. Moreover, the multidisciplinary character of the Sayre Health Promotion and Disease Prevention Center enables it to be integrated into the curriculum and co-curriculum of both the public school and the university, assuring an educational focus as well as sustainability for the Sayre Center. In fact, the core of the program is to integrate the activities of the Sayre Center with the educational programs and curricula at both Sayre Middle School and Penn. To that end, Penn faculty and students in medicine, nursing, dentistry, social work, arts and sciences, and fine arts, as well as other schools to a lesser extent, now work at Sayre through new and existing courses, internships, and research projects. Health promotion and service activities are also integrated into the Sayre students' curriculum. In effect, Sayre students serve as *agents* of healthcare change in the Sayre neighborhood.

The Health Promotion and Disease Prevention Center at Sayre is connected to a small learning community (SLC) that involves 350 students from grades six through eight. In that SLC, health promotion activities are integrated with core subject learning in science, social studies, math, language arts, and so on. Ultimately, every curriculum unit will have a community education or community problem-solving component (usually this will function as the organizing theme of the unit). Given this approach, Sayre students are not passive recipients of health information. *Instead, they are active deliverers of information and coordination and creative providers of service.*

A considerable number and variety of Penn academically-based community service courses provide the resources and support that make it possible to operate, sustain, and develop the Sayre Health Promotion and Disease Prevention Center. Literally hundreds of Penn students (professional, graduate, and undergraduate) and dozens of faculty members, from a wide range of Penn schools and departments, work at Sayre. Since they are performing community service while engaged in academic research, teaching, and learning, they are simultaneously practicing their specialized skills and developing, to some extent at least, their moral and civic consciousness and democratic character. And since they are engaged in a highly integrated common project, they are also learning how to communicate, interact, and collaborate with each other in wholly unprecedented ways that have measurably broadened their academic horizons and demonstrated to them the real value of working to overcome disciplinary ethnocentrism, tribalism, and guildism. Successful concrete real-world, problem-solving actions speak louder and more convincingly than abstract exhortation.

Conclusion

It is still early, of course, but we think that the successful creation and operation of the Sayre Health Promotion and Disease Prevention Center strongly supports the validity of this chapter's basic proposition, namely: Universities can significantly help overcome the terribly harmful effects of disciplinary fragmentation and conflict, narrow specialization, bureaucratic barriers, and "ancient Customs and Habitudes" by identifying and actively trying to solve a highly complex, highly significant, real-world, local community problem that, by its very nature, requires sustained interschool and interdisciplinary collaboration.

Although we have focused on the efforts at one research university, we believe this strategy holds promise for all institutions of higher learning. Indeed, many already have made significant commitments to serving their local communities. Campus Compact, an association of college and university presidents that provides training and technical assistance about service-learning and civic engagement to students, faculty, and administrators, now has more than nine hundred institutional members and supports thirty state offices nationwide. The organization's Website (www.compact.org) highlights a variety of civic engagement efforts now underway, some of them quite substantial. Consider these two examples. Macalester College (St. Paul, Minnesota) is a selective, private liberal arts college with 1,800 undergraduates and 146 full-time faculty members. The college has become an active participant in the revitalization effort of nearby East St. Paul, and faculty members from across the institution are involved. Andrew A. Latham (2003), associate professor of political science, describes the effort: "The college is collaborating with the University of Minnesota's Center for Urban and Regional Affairs (CURA) and Metropolitan State University (under a $400,000 grant from HUD) on 'action research' projects in the economically and racially diverse neighborhood of East St. Paul. These projects involve inter-disciplinary student-faculty teams conducting research requested by local nonprofit, governmental or neighborhood organizations" (p. 5).

Such an initiative is consonant with Macalester's mission as a liberal arts college, which prides itself on providing students with opportunities for close collaboration with faculty members and sees helping students develop leadership skills as central to its work (students are leading many of the community-based projects). Raritan Valley Community College (North Branch, New Jersey) is another example. RVCC has made a significant institutional commitment to providing free training and assistance to local nonprofit organizations. These efforts involve more than seventy faculty members who have incorporated service-learning into eighty-seven courses: accounting students help nonprofit organizations refine their record keeping; criminal justice students serve as auxiliary staff members at the local courthouse, prosecutor's office, and probation department; and nursing students are involved in programs that aid the elderly and the disabled. Here too the effort also has enabled faculty members from various departments to participate in a common effort and is consistent with RVCC's institutional mission. The service-learning projects allow students to apply the professional skills they are learning in the classroom. The program is an expression of the college's commitment to the local area and a useful strategy to help students build competencies that will help launch new careers. Such examples express the tremendous diversity of the American system of higher education. However, they underscore that any institution, regardless of location, type, or mission, can find local issues significant enough to engage the entire institution in meaningful work.

When institutions of higher learning give very high priority to actively solving strategic, real-world problems in their local community, a much greater likelihood exists that they will significantly advance the public good. More specifically, they will be able to translate the theoretical advantages of the One University idea into practical action and help create the university-assisted community schools based on service-learning which, this chapter concludes, is one of the best ways to help develop democratic students, K–16, and thereby significantly contribute to the development of democratic schools, democratic universities, and a democratic American Good Society in the twenty-first century.

References

Anderson, C. W. (1993). *Prescribing the life of the mind.* Madison: University of Wisconsin.

Astin, A. W. (1997). Liberal education and democracy: The case for pragmatism. In R. Orrill (Ed.), *Education and democracy: Re-imagining liberal learning in America* (pp. 210–211). New York: College Entrance Examination Board.

Bacon, F. (1972). Novum organum. In L. Benson (Ed.), *Toward the scientific study of history* (p. xi). Philadelphia: J. B. Lippincott.

Benson, L. (1978). Changing social science to change the world: A discussion paper. *Social Science History, 2,* 427–441.

Benson, L., & Harkavy, I. (2000). Integrating the American system of higher, secondary, and primary education to develop civic responsibility. In T. Ehrlich (Ed.), *Civic responsibility in higher education* (pp. 174–196). Phoenix: Oryx Press.

Benson, L., & Harkavy, I. (2002). Saving the soul of the university: What is to be done? In K. Robins & F. Webster (Eds.), *The virtual university? Information, markets, and management* (pp. 169–209). Oxford: Oxford University Press.

Benson, L., & Harkavy, I. (2003a). Service-learning. In K. Christian & D. Levinson (Eds.), *Encyclopedia of community: From the village to the virtual world* (pp. 1223–1224). Thousand Oaks, CA: Sage.

Benson, L., & Harkavy, I. (2003b, July). *Informal citizenship education: A neo-Platonic, neoDeweyan, radical program to develop democratic students, K–16.* Paper presented at University of Pennsylvania, Philadelphia.

Best, J. H. (Ed.) (1962). *Benjamin Franklin on education.* New York: Teachers College Press.

Bok, D. (2003). *Universities in the marketplace: The commercialization of higher education*. Princeton, NJ: Princeton University Press.

Bollinger, L. C. (2003). *The idea of a university*. Retrieved October 11, 2004, from Columbia University, Office of the President Web site: http://www.columbia.edu/cu/president/communications%20files/wall-streetoped.html.

Cochran, T. C. (1972). *Business in American life: A history*. New York: McGraw Hill.

Dewey, J. (1927). *The public and its problems*. Denver: Alan Swallow.

Dewey, J. (1969). The ethics of democracy. In L. E. Hahn (Ed.), *The early works of John Dewey, 1882-1898* (pp. 237–238). Carbondale: Southern Illinois University Press.

Dewey, J. (1990). *How we think*. Boston: Heath.

Dewey, J. (1991). *The school and society*. Chicago: University of Chicago Press.

DuBois, W.E.B. (1899). *Philadelphia Negro: A social study*. Philadelphia: University of Pennsylvania Press.

Festinger, L. (1957). *A theory of cognitive dissonance*. Stanford, CA: Stanford University Press.

Fish, S. (2003, May 16). Aim low. *Chronicle of Higher Education*, p. C5.

Gibson, C. (2001). *From inspiration to participation: A review of perspectives on youth civic engagement*. Berkeley, CA: The Grantmaker Forum on Community and National Service.

Harper, W. R. (1905). The university and democracy. In W. R. Harper (Ed.), *The trend in higher education* (pp. 19–20). Chicago: University of Chicago Press.

Jacoby, B. (Ed.) (2003). *Building partnerships for service-learning*. San Francisco: Jossey-Bass.

Latham, A. A. (2003). *Liberal education for global citizenship: Renewing Macalester's traditions of public scholarship and civic learning*. Retrieved October 11, 2004, from Macalester College, Project Pericles Web site: http://www.macalester.edu/pericles/discussionpaper.pdf.

Leslie, S. W. (1993). *The cold war and American science: The military-industrial-academic complex at MIT and Stanford*. New York: Columbia University Press.

Long, E. L., Jr. (1992). *Higher education as a moral enterprise*. Washington, DC: Georgetown University Press.

Marx, K. (1970). Theses on Feuerbach. In C. J. Arthur (Ed.), *The German ideology* (p. 123). New York: International Publishers.

McCarthy, C. (1912). *The Wisconsin idea*. New York: MacMillan.

Organization for Economic Development. (1982). *The university and the community*. Paris: Organization for Economic Development.

Sherif, M. (1958). Superordinate goals in the reduction of intergroup conflict. *American Journal of Sociology, 63*, 349.

Shulman, L. S. (2003). Foreword. In A. Colby, T. Ehrlich, E. Beaumont, & J. Stephens (Eds.), *Educating citizens: Preparing America's undergraduates for lives of moral and civic responsibility* (p. viii). San Francisco: Jossey-Bass.

Stark, J. (n.d.). *The Wisconsin idea: The university's service to the state.* Reprinted from the 1995–1996 Wisconsin Blue Book, 2–3. Retrieved December 26, 2003, from www.legis.state.wi.us/lrb/pubs/feature/wisidea.pdf.

Steffens, L. (1957). *The shame of the cities.* New York: Hill and Wang.

Chapter Twelve

Rethinking Faculty Roles and Rewards for the Public Good

Kelly Ward

What role do faculty play in meeting higher education's call of the public good? What faculty roles support the public good? How are faculty rewarded for such work? If higher education wants to serve the public good in direct ways, these and other questions need to be addressed. Faculty members, in their roles as arbiters of the curriculum, teachers, knowledge producers, and citizens, hold a prominent role in realizing the goal of making higher education more responsive to community and public welfare. For faculty to claim, own, and foster institutional efforts to connect the campus more meaningfully with society calls for reward structures that clearly define and reward this type of work.

Faculty roles are typically thought of in terms of teaching, research, and service with the service role most closely aligned with community outreach and the public good. Yet this conception of service is too narrow. Faculty at work supporting the public good can do so through their teaching, research, *and* service. The purpose of this chapter is to first define faculty work and its relationship to the public good; second, to talk about a view of scholarship that encompasses teaching, research, and service in ways that support the public good with particular emphasis on the scholarship of engagement; and finally to address the need for reward structures and how they can be conceptualized and practiced to promote faculty involvement in activities that promote institutional priorities for community involvement.

Faculty Work

Where does faculty work that supports the public good fit into faculty roles and rewards? Is it an add-on (that is, another category) or does it fit into the existing categories of teaching, research, and service? Such questions often stymie campuses in their efforts to connect faculty resources with needs that exist in the community, and addressing these questions calls for first defining faculty work in light of the public good.

Most colleges and universities make reference to teaching, research, and service in their mission statements and also in faculty contract and promotion and tenure guidelines. Identifying the teaching component is fairly clear—teaching is part of the very definition of what it means to be a faculty member. Faculty as teachers disseminate knowledge. As modern roles for faculty have evolved, another part of the faculty role that is clear, at least to those on the "inside" of academe, is research. The research component of faculty work encompasses the creation or discovery of knowledge and information (Boyer, 1990). Although more significant on campuses with a research focus, the research category is present in most definitions of faculty work regardless of institutional type to varying degrees. Teaching and research roles are shaped by institutional context, yet they are both mentioned in most definitions of faculty work.

When people refer to the service role of faculty, however, this component is less clear, perhaps rightly so, as the service role of faculty is expansive and oftentimes vague (Fear & Sandmann, 1995). The notion of service on many campuses today has come to mean committee work that supports the functioning of the campus, a definition that has been to the detriment of campus efforts to connect more to external audiences. Service viewed narrowly as committee work (what I call *internal service*; Ward, 2003) tends to go unrewarded. It's become a taken-for-granted aspect of faculty work. Historically, the service role of faculty was (and is) much more expansive. Service, depending on time and place, can mean service to the profession, service to the community, service to the institution, service to the public sector, service to the private sector, or service to society in general. While some of these service areas are tied to academic specialization and can easily be defined as "scholarly," some are not. The problem that exists for many institutions is how to acknowledge and reward service when it is not clear how faculty service is tied to academic specialization and to the institution (Fear & Sandmann, 1995). Service, even clearly academic, institutional service, has traditionally been the underappreciated stepchild of the triumvirate of academic work. It is easy to expect faculty to maintain their service responsibilities, yet it is the first to be overlooked come time for a raise. The difficulty inherent in identifying and rewarding less clearly "academic" service, variously described as outreach, engagement, and community service, among other terms, inhibits campus efforts to connect to external audiences and serve external needs (that is, the public good). Overcoming this mind-set is part of the work before us if we are to meaningfully connect faculty with their communities in ways that are integral to the lives of faculty members.

Elsewhere I have defined the service roles of faculty (see Ward, 2003) in an effort to link faculty service roles with campus missions for the public good. My intent in this chapter is to expand on the ways in which faculty work in the areas of teaching, research, and service can and do support the public good. It is necessary to see how faculty work addresses the public good if campuses as a whole see themselves taking on more prominent roles in their communities.

Teaching

In a passive sense, all teaching contributes to the public good through preparing students for life beyond college. Faculty as teachers work with students in class and out to help them learn particular subject material. It is assumed that these students will be educated and learned and that they will be, as they move on in life, contributing and informed citizens. Most of this preparation for civic life is done passively. That is, most faculty do not necessarily set out to make better citizens out of their students; instead they *assume* this will be the case as students become more educated and move on in their lives. Unfortunately, this is typically not the case. Traditional instruction does not typically challenge students to acquire deeper understanding and to apply it to larger contexts. "Lecture courses often do not support deep and enduring understandings of ideas and are even less well suited to developing the range of problem solving, communication, and interpersonal skills" (Colby, Ehrlich, Beaumont, & Stephens, 2003, p. 133) that support active citizenship.

Calls for higher education to more clearly act as a public resource challenge passive assumptions about teaching (that simply educating students serves the public good) and replace them with teaching strategies that are active and directly oriented to using the classroom as a way to prepare students for civic life, both in college and beyond. Colby et al. (2003) refer to these strategies as pedagogies of engagement and they include service-learning, other forms of experiential education, problem-based learning, and collaborative learning. To be certain these strategies are not mutually exclusive nor do they all always have the aim of civic education, yet they all can be used to support teaching goals that are focused on actively preparing students for a civic life that supports the public good.

Service-learning has been a focal point as a teaching strategy that directly prepares students for civic life. Service-learning connects academic learning with relevant community work. As Jacoby (1996) explains: "Service-learning is a form of experiential education in which students engage in activities that address human and community needs together with structured opportunities intentionally designed to promote student learning and development. Reflection and reciprocity are key concepts of service-learning" (p. 5).

Through service-learning, faculty are able to simultaneously meet classroom needs to learn a particular content area while also meeting community needs through student service. Service-learning is one form of experiential learning that has the explicit intent of addressing community needs and preparing students for civic life. Other forms of experiential learning can have a similar intent. Internships, simulations, and role plays are examples of other ways that can challenge students to apply their classroom learning to practical settings in ways that call for them to grapple with civic life.

Problem-based learning is another means that can be used to encourage students to bridge classroom theory with practical problems, which in turn can help students more realistically and readily deal with the challenges encountered in civic life. Problem-based learning poses real-world problems that students either individually or in groups grapple with in ways that connect classroom concepts to addressing the problem. To support civic aims, problem-based learning relies on problems that are derived from community concerns. Problem-based learning helps students translate what they know to what they do (Major, 1999).

Collaborative learning supports the civic aim of education in a slightly different way as it is more focused on process. Public problems are not solved in isolation. Collaborative learning prepares students for the process they need to undergo as active and problem-solving citizens. When used with a focus on civic life, these pedagogies of engagement work to actively prepare students to participate in a democratic society and to maintain active awareness of the public good.

Research

As with teaching, faculty as researchers are able to contribute to the public good in both passive and active ways. Most knowledge production via research has a link to the public good by furthering understanding of particular phenomena. A majority of research generated by faculty in academe, however, is conducted with the interest of furthering a particular discipline and is focused on meeting internal needs for knowledge production (and promotion and tenure). Again, calls for higher education to contribute more directly to the public good challenge traditional conceptions of research and make clear the need for making faculty research more applicable to community needs.

Community-based research is the terminology most often associated with research that directly and intentionally supports the public good (Couto, 2001; Strand, Marullo, Cutforth, Stoecker, & Donohue, 2003). Community-based research is "conducted *with* and *for,* not *on,* members of a community" (Strand et al., 2003, p. xx). Such an approach to research calls for partnerships with the community to meet pressing societal problems in deliberate and intentional ways. That said, traditional research can (and often does) meet community needs and support the advancement of the public good. This takes place through knowledge production (regardless of whether it was accrued through community collaboration—a primary tenet of community-based research) that contributes to the public good and also through taking the results of traditional research and translating them into findings that move beyond traditional academic venues to ones that are community oriented. The distinction lies in the primary goal of research and researchers. Traditional academic researchers typically have knowledge production and advancement as their primary focus, whereas researchers ascribing to a community-based tradition have the improvement of society, social change, or social justice as their primary goal (Strand et al., 2003).

There are three aspects to research focused on the public good—content, process, and outcome. In terms of *content,* research that addresses community needs and public concerns takes on topics that are not only important to the discipline (as is the case in traditional research) but also takes the next step by directly applying disciplinary expertise to community needs. For example, the nutrition professor who uses her expertise for a research project on causes and consequences of malnutrition in local migrant farm worker communities is simultaneously making a contribution to research in the field of nutrition while also gathering valuable information about the community, information that can be used to shape public policies and discussions.

The same example applies to *process.* Community-based research involves community members in the research process from problem identification to dissemination (Couto, 2001; Strand et al., 2003). For the nutrition professor to make her research on migrant farm workers meaningful to the community, she must understand the organizations and networks that affect and connect the community and the workers. If the professor were conducting focus groups, for example, there would likely to be greater participation if she included insider contact (that is, from the community) while conducting the interviews.

In terms of the *outcomes* of research focused on the public good, results need to be prepared and presented in ways that are meaningful to the community. Again, this is likely to involve working with community partners to understand how best to disseminate information so it is communicated effectively. Community-oriented research involves community partners as collaborators in the entirety of the research process (Kemmis & McTaggart, 2000; Strand et al., 2003). Community-oriented research does for traditional research what service-learning does for traditional classrooms.

Findings from such community-based research projects can also be presented in traditional academic venues to meet more traditional criteria for promotion and tenure. Just as not all traditional research addresses community needs, however, not all community-oriented research is likely to meet traditional standards of research. Faculty members must think creatively about how they can *simultaneously* meet their own personal needs to advance knowledge and to address community needs (and to also challenge institutions to recognize the scholarly contribution of both).

Service

The service category of faculty work is typically the most ambiguous. In general service has at least two meanings: (1) service to the institution and discipline, which I identify as internal service; and (2) service to the community, which I identify as external service (Ward, 2003). Like teaching and research, service has a long tradition as part of faculty work and institutional missions (Finkelstein, 1984). In terms of work in the service category that supports the public good, community service and consulting are the ways that faculty most often contribute to external service.

Many faculty engage in community service as private citizens. Most promotion and tenure documents ask faculty to list their community service as a way to highlight involvement with the local community. Campuses value faculty involvement in local communities as evidence of the good citizenship of the campus community. Cumulatively, as active community members, faculty can have quite an impact in a community. This is especially true in college towns where a significant portion of the community is college affiliated. In addition, much of what faculty do as private citizens (what I'm calling here community service) emanates from faculty disciplinary expertise. For example, if the nutrition professor mentioned above sits on the board of the local food bank, she will inevitably have the opportunity to contribute disciplinary expertise, and it is likely that this very expertise (in addition to her other involvement in the community through the research project) is what led to an invitation to be on the board. Involvement in community service can often open doors to other community opportunities that are more directly tied to faculty work (for example, service-learning and community research).

Although often overlooked as part of the outreach and service roles of faculty, consulting does play an important role in connecting campus resources with community needs. As with community service, consulting is often viewed as a private concern of faculty, yet nearly all consulting is grounded in faculty disciplinary expertise and is, therefore, an important part of the faculty role. Consulting is one way that faculty communicate their expertise in the discipline. Just as teaching is a means that faculty use to share knowledge about the discipline with students, so too is consulting a means to share knowledge with larger audiences. In terms of faculty work, service is usually included in campus descriptions of what faculty can do to fulfill their service roles. The place of consulting in the larger category of service is nebulous because faculty are typically paid for the work they do as consultants, raising the question: If you get paid, is it service? Campuses have multiple ways of dealing with the issue of consulting and pay, which are beyond the scope of this chapter. The point is that faculty consulting, paid or unpaid, can provide an important service to local communities through faculty work. Faculty as consultants can, and often do, contribute to the public good.

Integration

The example of the nutrition professor highlights how teaching, research, and service can overlap to meet the public good. In essence the public good can become the underlying link that ties faculty work together in ways that can meaningfully meet institutional needs and needs of the public. How much any given faculty member does of research, teaching, and service (to support the public good or not) is related to the type of institution, as well as the individual goals of a faculty member. Regardless, the "public good" can become an organizing scheme for a faculty member to organize his or her work where teaching, research, and service roles can be carried out in ways that are mindful of communities beyond the campus and discipline.

Cushman (1999) articulately summarizes how the link of service can manifest in all aspects of faculty work. In this framework, teaching, research, and service done in a community-oriented tradition contribute to each sector of faculty work simultaneously. Following are examples of how teaching, research, and service can be mutually reinforcing.

Teaching can contribute to research through classroom-based research. This may include being methodical about generating field notes, collecting class assignments, and taping class sessions and using these artifacts as forms of data. Teaching connects to service through involving community organizations in the classroom and through service learning.

Research has synergy to teaching through curriculum and course assignments that address class objectives, student learning, *and* community needs. Research can also reinforce a faculty member's involvement in service through extending research expertise to emerging community problems and by communicating the outcomes of research to not only academic audiences but community audiences as well.

Service relates to research by faculty that addresses problems with political and social salience to local communities. Service contributes to teaching by providing venues for faculty and students to "test" the utility of existing research in light of the everyday problems and challenges that communities face (Cushman, 1999).

Cushman's conceptualization illustrates the synergy that can exist between different faculty roles and how serving the public good facilitates the process. This integrated view of work is at the heart of what it means to serve the public good. Calls to meet the needs of the public in more and better ways do not necessarily mean that faculty members need to do more work; it is more a matter of doing work that is focused on community needs, and this focus, as discussed here, can be a source of integration of faculty work. Typically questions arise as to how to make the work of faculty fit a scholarly orientation, an issue I now address.

Scholarship

The professionalization of academic life was solidified in the post–World War II era when higher education and its faculty experienced unprecedented expansion. Jencks and Riesman (1977) refer to this time as an "academic revolution." What this revolution meant for faculty was the emergence and solidification of professional norms, many of which were dictated by faculty involvement in research (Finkelstein, 1984). The word *scholarship* came to be viewed as synonymous with research (Caplow & McGee, 2001; Ward, 2003). In terms of the public good, much of what faculty did (and continue to do) as researchers contributed directly to meeting public needs. And the intent of the genesis of the research role of faculty was to serve the public good through knowledge production. Unfortunately, however, traditional research on college campuses today too often has an "insider" orientation. That is, research is focused on meeting the needs of higher education (such as grant acquisition, research, and publication) at the sacrifice of meeting the needs of the public. The criticism currently leveled against higher education suggests that higher education's focus on research for self- and institutional promotion has overshadowed research that focuses on the public good (Strand et al., 2003). This criticism has led many campuses, and higher education as a whole, to think more about the role of research and to also expand notions of faculty work under the larger rubric of scholarship.

"Scholarship is considered to be creative intellectual work that is validated by peers and communicated, including: discovery of new knowledge; development of new technologies, methods, materials, or uses; integration of knowledge leading to new understandings; and artistry that creates new insights and understandings" (Weiser in Diamond, 1999, p. 45). As defined here, scholarship is *creative intellectual work that is validated by peers and communicated*. Scholarship is also grounded in a faculty member's expertise (Diamond & Adam, 1995). According to Diamond and Adam, to be "scholarly" faculty work (and the results of it) needs to:

• Break new ground and be innovative.
• Be replicated or elaborated.
• Be documented.
• Be peer-reviewed.
• Have significance or impact.

What these definitions of scholarship offer are means to consider a larger view of faculty work and to view this work as scholarly. Traditional definitions of scholarship equate it with traditional research. Seeing the essential components of the term *scholarship* allows one to see that scholarly work can go beyond a peer-reviewed article published in a top-tier journal. Instead these definitions provide a means to start to see faculty at work in classrooms as scholarly and also faculty at work enacting their service roles as scholarly. Does this mean that all teaching and service is scholarly? Certainly not, but using the guidelines put forth by Diamond and Adam (1995) (as well as others including Glassick, Huber, and Maeroff, [1997]) allows for expanded views of faculty scholarship.

Boyer's (1990) conceptualization of scholarship put forth in *Scholarship Reconsidered* is a reaction to his concerns that higher education was neglecting the public good, a consequence of *too much of a self-focus,* both of individual faculty members and institutions. From Boyer's perspective, the narrow definitions of scholarship that had come to pervade faculty work precluded even well-meaning professors from doing research (and other work as well) that directly addressed the public good. Boyer believed that for "America's colleges and universities to remain vital a new vision of scholarship is required" (p. 13).

Boyer (1990) called for thinking about traditional research as *one* form of scholarship, not as *the* form of scholarship. His expanded notion of scholarship included four aspects: discovery (which aligns with traditional research), integration (which aligns with an expanded view of research that "brings new insight to bear on original research" [p. 19] through integration and interdisciplinarity), application (which aligns knowledge with social problems), and teaching (which aligns teaching with not only the transmission of knowledge but the transformation and extension of it as well).

In later writings, Boyer (1996) began discussing another perspective on scholarship, that of engagement. The scholarship of engagement was not so much a distinct form of scholarship as much as a way to think about the other forms of scholarship (discovery, integration, teaching, and application) in ways that connected them with the public good. Engagement provided a vision, a way to think about the totality of faculty work in ways that connect it with the greater public good. Boyer talked about the scholarship of engagement this way:

> At one level, the scholarship of engagement means connecting the rich resources of the university to the most pressing social, civic, and ethical problems, to our children, to our schools, to our teachers, and to our cities, just to name the ones I am personally in

touch with most frequently. . . . at a deeper level, I have this growing conviction that what's also needed is not just more programs,
but a larger purpose, a larger sense of mission, a larger clarity of
direction in the nation's life as we move toward century twenty-one.
Increasingly, I'm convinced that ultimately, the scholarship of
engagement also means creating a special climate in which the
academic and civic cultures communicate more continuously and
more creatively with each other, helping to enlarge what anthropologist Clifford Geertz describes as the universe of human discourse and enriching the quality of life for all of us. (pp. 19–20)

Cumulatively, Boyer offers a big picture that points to the urgency
that we in higher education must use to make the work of the academy relevant and connected to community needs. Boyer's scholarship of engagement embraces all of the work of the university and its
connection to the world around it. For Boyer, engaged scholarship
means that faculty as scholars are taking on world problems through
disciplinary means, fulfilling campus mission, and incorporating
teaching, research, and service as vehicles to address the public good.
Boyer was also clear in pointing out the need for campuses to support faculty in their endeavors of expanded scholarship and engagement with the public good.

Reward Structures to Support
the Scholarship of Engagement

No matter how clear the mission statement or presidential procla-
mation to connect the campus with the community, if efforts to the
public good are unrewarded or seen by faculty as distracting from
the pursuit of the kinds of things that count on a dossier, either
those public service efforts will be set aside, or the faculty member
will be. Either way, community approaches to scholarship will not
be strengthened. If engagement is not supported, it becomes either altruism or an obligation, and either way it's seen as professionally compromising for faculty. Faculty reward structures need
to be aligned with institutional priorities for engagement of the
public good.

Boyer was instrumental in expanding the dialogue about the definition of scholarship as well as how to connect faculty work with the
public good. Institutions need faculty reward structures that value

the complexity of faculty work, including the important and unique contributions of teaching, research, and service that focus on the public good. Understandably, faculty are more likely to participate in activities that are supported and rewarded, thus calling for connection between campus missions related to the public good, faculty work that supports such a mission, and reward structures (Diamond, 1999; O'Meara, 2002; Spanier, 2001; Ward, 1996). Too often faculty work that operates using a model like Boyer's that seeks to engage community problems is viewed by faculty as a risky proposition, something that sounds well and good, but that is not likely to be rewarded come time for promotion and tenure (O'Meara, 2002). How can campuses address such concerns?

Campuses that want their faculty to work in connection to the community must define in their promotion and tenure guidelines and faculty handbooks what this work looks like, and how it will be evaluated and rewarded. Most promotion and tenure guidelines include examples of the type of work that is counted under each category. In the teaching category, for example, there are typically examples of types of teaching innovation that are encouraged and rewarded. On campuses looking to address the public good this might mean looking carefully at the guidelines and adding examples that accomplish this type of work (such as service-learning). Simply adding the example of service-learning as a form of teaching innovation is one way to put this type of work on the mind of faculty. Similarly, in the area of research, it might be helpful to provide examples of how one research project can lead to scholarly publication or a grant application *and* also to a community report. Granted, the latter, especially at an institution with a strong research focus, might not be given the same emphasis as the former, yet giving voice and value to work that is community oriented is one way to encourage faculty to attempt and explore it (the opposite is true as well—if community-oriented work is not mentioned specifically, it may well be rendered invisible).

Faculty work, whether teaching, research, or service oriented, that is tied to disciplinary expertise and community needs is often not neatly defined in terms of teaching, research, and service. The scholarship of engagement as defined by Boyer and later expanded on in my work (Ward, 2003) is by its definition integrated, and most promotion and tenure guidelines are compartmentalized. Without standards for evaluating and supporting engaged, integrated scholarship, much of this work might slip through the cracks of the traditional, tripartite evaluation.

Given the variability of campus missions and institutional types and the lack of uniformity of what constitutes faculty work, it may be helpful for campuses to establish committees or task forces that take on redefining promotion and tenure guidelines to assure that they are reflective of campus mission statements. For example, the University of Illinois at Chicago (UIC), in an effort to define the scholarship of engagement and its place in the reward structure, created a task force on scholarship that produced a report that defines the scholarship of engagement, makes recommendations for how to reward it, and aids faculty in making a case for the scholarship of engagement. The report provides specific directives for linking service to scholarship and for documentation to fulfill needs for promotion and tenure evaluation

The document is important as it provides very specific and useful information to faculty about the scholarship of engagement—definitions, examples, suggestions for documentation, and guidelines for rewarding such scholarship. The report is also important because it is tied to promotion and tenure standards—a crucial step as campuses endeavor to address community needs.

Another aspect of aligning campus reward structures with campus missions for the public good is faculty development. These structures may include fellowships, grants, release time, and cash awards for involvement in community-oriented work (particularly service-learning and community-based research) and are powerful motivation for getting faculty involved (Bringle & Hatcher, 2000). As with promotion and tenure guidelines, faculty development initiatives that include either a community-based orientation or include examples of community work send an important message about what the institution supports. For example, if a campus offers faculty grants to support teaching innovation, including examples of service-learning projects, then allowing funds to be shared with community partners is a way to elevate the importance of work that partners faculty with community needs. Some campuses have had entire cycles of faculty development grants for teaching and research focused on projects that support the public good. Again, tangible support of efforts to realize mission statements and serve the public elevates the importance of and participation in these activities.

Given the focus on the public good and higher education that is so prevalent in the discourse today, the acknowledgment that can be attached to public service can be an important extrinsic motivator for some faculty. External service can also receive recognition as faculty work is promoted in public venues. Many campuses have taken to highlighting faculty work that is tied to the community in campus publications as a way to communicate how the faculty work for the public good.

While rewards, awards, and other types of acknowledgment are not always incentive enough to encourage faculty involvement in public purposes, campuses can be proactive by providing recognition of activities that support campus missions aligned with the public good through promotion and tenure, establishing awards for outstanding service, and by bringing attention to service activities. Further, campuses with merit pay systems should recognize the scholarly contributions faculty make through work with the community (Finsen, 2002). If campuses value scholarship, then they should reward faculty work that uses the approach of the scholarship of engagement, which, by definition, calls for meeting the rigors of scholarship and community needs.

Conclusion

To fulfill the goals of the scholarship of engagement, scholars must link their teaching, research, and service to community problems, challenges, and goals, whether the community served is the department, the university, the town, state, nation, or the global community. Faculty must integrate their teaching with the needs of their students, their department and university missions, and the goals of their administrators. Finally, they must envision and enact their service roles, both internal and external to the university, to mean something more than sitting in meetings and generating memos, so that higher education can function more effectively internally as a means to function more effectively externally (Berberet; 1999, 2002; Lynton & Elman, 1987).

To fully realize what it means for a campus to serve the public good, an integrated view of faculty work is necessary. Without it, teaching will continue to stand in opposition to research and both in opposition to service. Professors will continue to feel that their service distracts them from their teaching and research obligations.

A scholarship of engagement links a scholar's service to his or her expertise and links teaching, research, and service activities to one another and to community needs. Connections between teaching, research, and service are what make engagement part of the mission of an institution (Singleton, Burack, & Hirsch, 1997).

Engagement encourages the synergy of teaching, research, and service, recognizing that the different parts of a faculty member's life can serve one another, rather than pulling in opposite directions. Huber (2001) notes that "faculty work has long been represented as comprised of some specified proportions of teaching, research, and service, including academic citizenship and outreach. But when faculty take a scholarly approach to teaching and learning, or to service in its various forms, the boundaries between conventional parts of academic life can easily blur" (p. 23).

It is easy to look longingly to the days of land-grant institutions and the Wisconsin Idea for what these ideas did for connecting higher education with social purpose, but even then the same challenges existed that face us today—that is, finding ways to encourage faculty to use their research to inform teaching and to use insights from both teaching and research to inform service. A synergy exists between the different components of faculty work, and the faculty member using the scholarship of engagement as an organizing framework for their work is one who can bridge and unify these components, and then use that unity of knowledge and service to bridge the gap between the academy and the community as to better address the public good.

Unless and until faculty members can pursue public service endeavors without jeopardizing their jobs and status, faculty will be unlikely to extend themselves to realize administrative calls for meeting the needs of the public good. Internal policies and procedures need to permit and reward work that supports the public good, and these policies can only be created when faculty are free to pursue their community work without fear that they have set their research agendas and teaching interests impossibly behind.

References

Berberet, J. (1999). The professoriate and institutional citizenship toward a scholarship of service. *Liberal Education, 85*(4), 33–39.

Berberet, J. (2002). The new academic compact. In L.A. McMillin & J. Berberet (Eds.), *The new academic compact: Revisioning the relationship between faculty and their institutions* (pp. 3–28). Bolton, MA: Anker.

Boyer, E. L. (1990). *Scholarship reconsidered: Priorities of the professoriate*. Princeton, NJ: Carnegie Foundation for the Advancement of Teaching.

Boyer, E. L. (1996). The scholarship of engagement. *Journal of Public Service and Outreach, 1*(1), 11–20.

Bringle, R. G., & Hatcher, J. A. (2000). Institutionalization of service learning in higher education. *Journal of Higher Education, 71*(3), 273–291.

Caplow, T., & McGee, R. J. (2001). *The academic marketplace*. New Brunswick, NJ: Transaction.

Colby, A., Ehrlich, T., Beaumont, E., & Stephens, J. (2003). *Educating citizens: Preparing undergraduates for lives of moral and civic responsibility*. San Francisco: Jossey-Bass.

Couto, R. (2001, Spring). The promise of a scholarship of engagement. *Academic Workplace,* 4–8.

Cushman, E. (1999). The public intellectual, service learning, and activist research. *College English, 61*(3), 328–336.

Diamond, R. M. (1999). *Aligning faculty rewards with institutional mission: Statements, policies and guidelines*. Bolton, MA: Anker.

Diamond, R. M., & Adam, B. E. (Eds.) (1995). *The disciplines speak: Rewarding the scholarly, professional, and creative work of faculty*. Washington, DC: American Association for Higher Education.

Fear, F. A., & Sandmann, L. R. (1995). Unpacking the service category: Reconceptualizing university outreach for the 21st century. *Continuing Higher Education Review, 59*(3), 110–122.

Finkelstein, M. J. (1984). *The American academic profession: A synthesis of social scientific inquiry since World War II*. Columbus: Ohio State University Press.

Finsen, L. (2002). Faculty as institutional citizens: Reconvening service and governance work. In L. A. McMillin & J. Berberet (Eds.), *The new academic compact: Revisioning the relationship between faculty and their institutions* (pp. 61–86). Bolton, MA: Anker.

Glassick, C. E., Huber, M. T., & Maeroff, G. I. (1997). *Scholarship assessed: Evaluation of the professoriate*. San Francisco: Jossey-Bass.

Huber, M. T. (2001, July-August). Balancing acts: Designing careers around the scholarship of teaching. *Change,* 21–29.

Jacoby, B. (1996). *Service-learning in higher education: Concepts and practices*. San Francisco: Jossey-Bass.

Jencks, C., & Riesman, D. (1977). *The academic revolution*. Chicago: University of Chicago Press.

Kemmis, S., & McTaggart, R. (2000). Participatory action research. In N. K. Denzin & Y. S. Lincoln (Eds.), *Handbook of qualitative research* (2nd ed., pp. 567–605). Thousand Oaks, CA: Sage.

Lynton, E. A., & Elman, S. E. (1987). *New priorities for the university: Meeting society's needs for applied knowledge and competent individuals.* San Francisco: Jossey-Bass.

Major, C. (1999). Connecting what we know and what we do through problem-based learning. *AAHE Bulletin, 51*(7), 7–9.

O'Meara, K. A. (2002). Uncovering the values in faculty evaluation of service as scholarship. *Review of Higher Education, 26,* 57–80.

Singleton, S. E., Burack, C. A., & Hirsch, D. J. (1997). Faculty service enclaves. *AAHE Bulletin, 49*(8), 3–7.

Spanier, G. (2001). *The engaged university: Our partnership with society.* Speech to the International Conference on the University as Citizen, University of South Florida, Tampa. Accessed January 28, 2003 from http://www.psu.edu/ur/GSpanier/speeches/engaged.html.

Strand, K., Marullo, S., Cutforth, N., Stoecker, R., & Donohue, P. (2003). *Community-based research and higher education.* San Francisco: Jossey-Bass.

Ward, K. (1996). Service-learning: Reflections on institutional commitment. *Michigan Journal of Community Service-learning, 3,* 55–65.

Ward, K. (2003). *Faculty service roles and the scholarship of engagement.* ASHE Higher Education Report, Vol. 29, No. 5. San Francisco: Jossey-Bass.

Chapter Thirteen

Institutional Differences in Pursuing the Public Good

Barbara A. Holland

Media reports and academic literature about higher education's infamous resistance to change, self-indulgent image, and apparent detachment from critical public issues can be pretty discouraging. The cliché is to claim that only the church and higher education have remained the same for hundreds of years while everything else has changed. Though writers may give a wink or nod to the vast diversity of institutional types, more often they quickly adopt a rhetorical frame that presents higher education as a uniform industry dominated by a small number of institutional types, primarily the prestigious research universities and the liberal arts colleges. Such generalizations fail to acknowledge or document the true experience of most academic institutions, both individually and collectively.

For example, many universities and colleges in the United States and abroad are exploring their conceptions of the civic mission of higher education. An examination of their experiences may suggest a way to enhance our understanding of institutional differences regarding how engagement is introduced and interpreted. Is engagement proving to be a force for greater diversification of institutional types? The growing engagement movement across postsecondary education is making it more important than ever to understand the distinctions among institutional types and to consider why engagement seems to take root in some institutional contexts more readily than in others.

The values and practices of engaged scholarship, student-centered learning environments, community-campus partnerships, diverse roles and rewards for faculty, and democratic practices in shared governance are not just abstract ideas or passing fads. They exist in higher education today across many kinds of universities and colleges. However, those who are making the most progress in developing these capacities are generally colleges and universities that are not pursuing a research-extensive mission. Their work therefore is less visible to policymakers and journalists who tend to follow the fortunes of the more visible research universities that are seen as the models of success and prestige.

In this chapter, I will share observations about differences in institutional responses to the idea of engagement and describe how internal and external stereotypes of higher education inhibit the recognition and transfer of engagement models from "lesser" institutions to wider practice across the sector as a whole. Further, I will argue that the need to generate wider acceptance and implementation of engagement is linked to (and being accelerated by) fundamental shifts in the nature of research and knowledge management on a global scale. I propose that engagement is a global trend in higher education that may yet challenge the preeminence of the United States' higher education system if we fail to integrate it more intentionally into our academic culture. Finally, based on observations from the field, I will make some assertions about what experience to date has revealed about the nature of engaged scholarly work and its impact on academic organizations and culture. These empirical observations may help explain why, in spite of wide interest in and apparent evidence of benefits of engagement as a tool for enhancing the performance and academic impact of some institutional types, obstacles and objections to recognition and legitimization of engaged scholarship persist.

What Evidence Supports This Essay?

Over the last decade, I have considered questions about organizational change in higher education, especially in regard to the notion that colleges and universities should each have a "civic mission"

(Boyte & Hollander, 1999). In particular, I studied how institutions make choices about their interest or non-interest in civic engagement strategies such as engaged scholarship or service-learning programs, and the ways they articulate and act on their sense of their institution's civic mission. Why does engagement seem to make more sense to some institutions than others? What organizational conditions, changes, or strategies are associated with capacity to implement and sustain engagement? What forces seem to foster or restrict organizational interest in or capacity for engagement? Case studies based on these questions led me to propose a matrix to illustrate how key organizational factors influence the level of institutional commitment to engagement (Holland, 1997). The organizational factors identified were:

- Mission
- Promotion, tenure, and hiring practices
- Organization infrastructure and funding
- Student involvement and curriculum
- Faculty involvement
- Community involvement
- External communications and fundraising

As I, and others, continue to gather data and improve on this model, some factors have been expanded and additional factors have been added (Bringle & Hatcher, 2000):

- Leadership
- Policy
- Budget allocation (internal)

These ten concepts represent common organizational elements that support all postsecondary institutions but which, when given different emphases or interpretations, can be used to describe and understand different levels of institutional commitment to engagement. The Holland Matrix identifies four levels of commitment to civic engagement based on demonstrated differences in levels of relevance of engagement to the core academic activities of an institution: low, medium, high, and full integration (Holland, 1997). In other words, examination of the different choices institutions make along these key organizational factors provides a way to measure the current state

of engagement and understand differences in individual and institutional reactions to the idea of engagement as scholarly work. This
is ongoing work because the field continues to evolve. Implied in
many of my assertions in this essay are fruitful questions and issues
for further and much-needed research on academic organizations,
higher education's societal roles, and the changing nature of faculty work.

In part, the theoretical framework underpinning this ongoing research is drawn from the work of Arthur Levine regarding the fate of
innovations in higher education. *Why Innovation Fails: The Institutionalization and Termination of Innovation in Higher Education* (Levine,
1980) offers a way to analyze data across many cases and recognize
patterns of organizational behavior that may explain differences in
institutional responses to innovative ideas.

According to Levine (1980), change can be introduced at different levels of scope and scale.

1. On rare occasions, entire *new institutions* are designed with
a clear change agenda in mind. This was the case, for example, for
some of the new campuses in the California State University system or for new colleges such as the Olin College of Engineering.

2. More often, *innovative enclaves* are introduced within existing organizations; examples include experimental units or changes
in a single course or even a whole department. Such changes are
relatively easy and inexpensive to implement, but they can become
isolated from the mainstream. These enclaves have the potential to
become demonstration projects, or they can become segregated
sanctuaries for dissatisfied faculty or students, or they can isolate
vital creative energy by walling it off from the rest of the institution.

3. A third kind of change entails *holistic changes* within existing
organizations. Change on this scale "involves the adoption of a
major institutional innovation characterized by a unified and coherent purpose" (Levine, 1980, p. 5). This form is the most efficient but the hardest to get adopted. "It is risky because it involves
already established institutions with built-in resources, habits, and
staff—and a staff at that usually lacking in consensus about institutional purpose" (p. 5).

4. Another form of change consists of *piecemeal changes* within
existing organizations. These fragmented attempts represent the

most common form of change. Change on this scale is easy to adopt because it is unlikely to perturb other units within the institution, but these islands of change are not likely to have significant impact. The initiators or "owners" of these isolated efforts rarely form a significant enough constituency to be able to undertake the complex political negotiations that must accompany the wider institutional adoption of a coherent plan or clear vision.

5. The final form of change consists of *peripheral activities* performed by units at the margins of existing organizations. Some institutions manage the energy behind demands for engagement originating within the organization or in the broader community by routing it to a continuing education unit or in cooperative extension or to a center for community engagement. These peripheral units can serve as a laboratory for innovation, but the movement of such innovations from the edges of the organization into the core can be very difficult, especially if they are the "designated service bearers" for the institution or seen as "pet projects" of particular faculty or administrators.

With this framework in mind, a pattern emerged across the institutional cases in my research work. When considering the relevance of civic engagement to their own academic priorities and values, institutions recognized for achievement for their traditional research or liberal arts mission, secure in their sense of mission and priorities, were more likely to take the route of piecemeal changes or peripheral activities. In contrast, other institutions were more likely to employ innovative enclaves or holistic strategies for enacting their civic mission. Here we see the early seeds of a rationale for differential institutional perspectives on engagement. Once institutions make some assessment of engagement's potential relevance, how is the implementation and actualization of that decision implemented and recognized in the organization?

Having articulated five different scales of implementation of innovations, Levine identifies four possible fates for innovations in academic organizations: *diffusion, enclaving, resocialization,* and *termination.* Diffusion means the innovation is intentionally dispersed broadly across the institution, which can either make it so diffuse as to have little impact or, more optimistically, it can be diffused and adopted into ongoing operations. Enclaving, used here as a strategic action rather than an organizational unit, seeks to contain innovative ideas in a bubble away from the rest of the organization. Resocialization (remember he was writing this during the Cold War) meant the innovation would be redefined and reshaped in terms and forms more familiar to the current organization's structure and values. Termination is exactly what it says!

In Levine's model, a particular innovation, however it was introduced, will proceed down one of these four pathways depending on individual and collective calculation of the *profitability* and *compatibility* of the innovation. In other words, organizational members assess an innovation in terms of its potential to generate positive impacts on themselves or the institution and its alignment with their own visions for the mission, goals, and culture of the organizational environment. The four options can be used to isolate and kill an innovative initiative, or the strategies could be used to allow an innovation to persist and succeed to at least some degree in that diffusion, enclaving, and resocialization can make it possible to disseminate, contain, or alter the innovation in ways that make it less threatening, at least until compatibility and profitability are more clearly demonstrated.

Levine's theory provides a helpful way to understand why engagement, certainly seen by most academics as an innovation that requires significant organizational change, has played out differently across various types of institutions. In other words, decisions and actions regarding levels of institutional commitment as measured by the Holland Matrix of organizational factors can be viewed as expressions of an institution's calculation of the profitability and compatibility of engagement. This perspective revealed that, across different institutional types, some organizational factors were more important influences on commitment to engagement than others.

In particular, clarity of mission seems to play the central role in shaping an institution's assessment of engagement's profitability and compatibility. Engagement remains most perplexing to institutions that are relatively self-assured about their current mission, priorities, and status, particularly institutions that are highly regarded in various ranking and classification systems. So far, engagement seems to resonate primarily with institutions that feel a fundamental need to clarify their mission, address competing institutional visions, or refocus on their core historic roots and purposes (Gelmon, Holland,

& Shinnamon, 1998; National Association for State and Land-Grant Colleges and Universities, 1999; American Association of State Colleges and Universities, 2002). Perhaps the concept of engagement has tapped into a reservoir of confusion and discontent among America's most generic, regional, public, and private institutions that, lacking the resources to become "real" research universities, find themselves questing for clear identity and pathways for recognizing comparative excellence and achievement.

Institutions that demonstrate the greatest interest in articulating and implementing a civic mission and engaged scholarship as compatible and profitable innovations exhibit the following dominant characteristics:

- A history of relatively comprehensive but unfocused academic and research programs
- Newer campuses serving specific regions and populations
- Large numbers of local students from—and who are likely to remain in—the region
- Located in economic hubs
- An emphasis on teaching and learning more than research but may also exhibit some confusion about their mission and priorities
- Located in communities with significant regional challenges and opportunities

Research and land-grant universities do not exhibit many of these characteristics to any great degree, except in some of their newer branch campuses created to serve specific locales (the new campuses of Washington State University and the University of Washington would be good examples of new branch campuses with signs of greater interest in and commitment to implementing a specific civic mission and engaged scholarship than their parent institutions).

The large, elite research universities (Association of American Universities members, for example) are successful institutions by many formal and informal measures and one must ask, what would motivate them to change from their current, respected models? Their record of achievement around a historically clear mission makes it hardly surprising that the major research universities have demonstrated much more caution in articulating or implementing a specific civic mission or considering reforms in the nature and priorities of faculty work. Their historic mission and strategies have brought them financial success and prestige. What additional profitability or compatibility would come with adopting an innovative form of scholarship? Their introduction of engagement most commonly resembles Levine's responses of enclaving or resocialization, perhaps because research university leaders and faculty see engagement as a piecemeal or peripheral activity. Not surprisingly, these institutions tend to articulate an engagement agenda that matches their past strengths and traditions, as demonstrated by the following common strategies:

- Creating centers or institutes to study community issues and needs, often with significant, named endowments
- Reforming the role or activities of cooperative extension
- Engaging in research on community
- Preparing future faculty with skills in community-based research
- Engaging in research on higher education and civic engagement; supporting one or more distinguished scholars of engagement
- Creating distinctive learning communities for some students that feature elements of civic education and service or service-learning

Applying the Holland Matrix to these institutions suggests engagement has medium to high relevance, with the land-grants more capable of demonstrating the latter level of commitment through their well-established infrastructure for outreach services. Based on Levine's theoretical framework, one could argue that this is all as it should be; each institution adopting the notions of civic engagement and engaged scholarship according to the relevance of those concepts to their particular institutional mission and capacity. However, the historic tradition of higher education has been to press for a narrow view of academic values and priorities, not distinctiveness.

The concern I raise here is not that research universities don't embrace engagement. For the most part they seem to be doing so in modes that reflect their mission, role, and strengths (NASLGCU, 1999). The problem is that so long as the research institution is seen as the ideal model, there is little opportunity to generate academic legitimacy and prestige for other types of institutions that find engagement much more compatible and profitable with their particular and very different missions and strengths. Thus, institutions that would better fulfill their regional missions through engaged scholarship may continue to view such a strategy as risky over a more traditional (if futile) ambition to expand traditional research work. The crux of my argument here is that higher education appears to be changing and diversifying in ways that may better respond to societal expectations for higher performance, accountability, and impact, but traditional cultural values and guidelines, at least for now, create persistent disincentives for new missions or modes of scholarship. Regenerating public support for postsecondary institutions, public and private, may depend a great deal on creating respect for a diverse array of institutional types responsive overall to societal needs and expectations.

The stereotypical description of higher education as a sector is that research is the ultimate priority, teaching is an afterthought at best, and external applications of knowledge are presumed important but occur in largely indirect ways (Ewell, 1985; Glassick, Huber, & Maeroff, 1997). Higher education is a competitive culture and does not yet offer recognition for alternative pathways to excellence and prestige that involve doing things that are different, such as engagement. The primary factors used to judge excellence in higher education continue to be: research funding for basic research in certain fields, the number of doctoral degree programs and graduates, selectivity in admissions (student quality), endowment level, and number of inventions and patents. These measures promote the status quo and provide no recognition of more diverse institutions that serve societal needs and expectations through different modes of scholarly work. As early as 1985, leading higher education scholars such as Peter Ewell argued that institutional diversity was a desirable strategy to build a postsecondary system able to meet society's diverse educational needs, and he understood that this meant that institutional effectiveness needs to be measured in several different ways. While pressures for accountability, and other forces such as changing demographics of the student body and the articulation of civic missions, have resulted in some movement toward institutional diversity, little progress has been made in identifying

244 HIGHER EDUCATION FOR THE PUBLIC GOOD

and implementing new indicators that recognize comparative performance and achievement in modes other than the research-dominated culture (Glassick et al., 1997).

But an additional force for change may soon inspire greater interest in the reform and differentiation of indicators of institutional success. As we gain deeper understanding of the impacts of technology and the Information Age on the generation and dissemination of knowledge, new conceptions of research and scholarship are emerging (Watson, 2003). Research models and conceptions of scholarly work seem to be evolving on a global scale, and this shift in the most fundamental role of higher education—knowledge generation—may create new competitive pressures for innovations in academic culture and the recognition of diverse institutional missions.

Understanding this possibility requires us to look at international discussions about the evolution of research and scholarship, including how other nations view the idea of engagement. "One thing is clear: more than ever before, in this age of globalization, Americans need to know more about diversity than uniformity; more about centrifugal forces than centrality; and more about other people's ideals, aspirations and anxieties in order to understand the rest of the world" (Graubard, 2004).

To the extent we believe that the United States' higher education system is the best in the world and that status ensures critical economic and political advantages, we must observe and reflect on the implications, if any, of academic changes occurring beyond our borders. Research universities may find it more interesting to consider recognition and regard for diverse forms of scholarship and academic cultures if it can be shown as helpful to sustaining their own prestigious position as world leaders in research. The following section offers a brief overview of international views of scholarship and engagement, and the potential implications for American higher education.

International Perspectives on Research, Engaged Scholarship, and Academic Excellence

Debates about the scholarship of engagement in this country center mostly on questions about its intellectual rigor and legitimacy in terms of the opportunity costs associated with doing scholarly work that may or may not contribute to personal and institutional prestige. What is its value if it is not measured by a traditional indicator of excellence in research? But are we fiddling around about the details of scholarly definitions while the rest of the world is burning up old traditions of academic excellence and building new visions of discovery and dissemination?

Recent research on higher education and changes in the nature and values of research and scholarship from international scholars reveals a perspective rather different from that of American academics. Impacted by technological advances and the new context of the European Union, higher education researchers in Europe are capturing evidence of fundamental shifts in conceptions of institutional missions, faculty work, the nature of scholarship, and the research process. In their view, the historic role of higher education as one of generating and transmitting knowledge to society through university-based research, teaching, and service is giving way to an emerging role where higher education contributes to a complex learning society through collaborative approaches to discovery, learning, and engagement (Watson, 2003). Sir David Watson, vice chancellor of the University of Brighton, has articulated something of a European interpretation of Boyer's model articulated in *Scholarship Reconsidered* (1990). He proposes a model of scholarship that aligns with new realities of how information is gathered and distributed, who frames critical research questions and owns valuable expertise, and who cares about the results and applies the findings. New modes and sources of knowledge production and distribution are requiring the academy to adopt new modes of research and communication. While the term *engagement* is not universally used outside the United States, Watson discusses integrative forms of learning and discovery, and the interaction of scholarship and public problem solving, as integral to his new model of research.

Watson draws in part on the work of Michael Gibbons, CEO of the Association of Commonwealth Universities, who began to see these changes in research paradigms as early as 1994 when he and colleagues articulated the emerging transformation of research practices as a set of epistemological challenges based on the ways that faculty as teachers and researchers view the world. Their analysis of approaches to knowledge production revealed an inexorable shift from the traditional mode of research—pure, disciplinary, homogeneous, expert-led, supply-driven, hierarchical, peer-reviewed, and almost exclusively university-based—to a new research mode that is more likely to be applied, problem-centered, transdisciplinary, heterogeneous, hybrid, demand-driven, entrepreneurial, and network-embedded (Gibbons et al., 1994). In this mode, historic values placed on disciplinary traditions, university ownership, subject-centered hierarchies, and boundaries across research organizations begin to melt like polar ice caps. Gibbons and Watson's vision suggests that academic excellence and institutional mission characteristics will need to be measured differently in such a dynamic context of collaborative work across societal sectors, organizations, and nations.

These changes in the way research is designed, conducted, and disseminated are global in their implications, and although some in the United States may continue to debate the wisdom or appropriateness of Boyer's reinvention of the separate arenas of research, teaching, and service into an integrated and interactive vision of scholarly work, the change is already in motion here and elsewhere. In particular, conceptions of community engagement, service-learning, and engaged scholarship are spreading around the world though the terminology varies across different nations. The examination of new forms of scholarship that link academic organizations to public problem-solving through collaborative, community-based research and teaching is, by far, not a uniquely American phenomenon.

For example, service-learning is expanding in South Africa, India, Southeast Asia, Australia, the Philippines, and Europe. An international service-learning conference was held in Thailand, and a Europe-wide meeting on service-learning in schools was held in France, both in early 2004. The University of Queensland in Australia organized international summits on engagement and community-university partnerships in 2001 and 2003. The International Consortium on Higher Education (ICHE), Civic Responsibility and Democracy (based at University of Pennsylvania) is conducting comparative studies of universities in fifteen other nations with fifteen American colleges and universities, focusing on questions regarding the capacity of higher education to model and enhance democratic practices within campus organizations as well as in communities

(General Report: European Sites Study of Universities as Sites of Citizenship and Civic Responsibility, 2002).

A task force of the Association of Commonwealth Universities wrote in 2001 that "engagement is now a core value for the university. . . .this implies strenuous, thoughtful, argumentative interaction with the non-university world in at least four spheres: setting universities' aims, purposes and priorities; relating teaching and learning to the wider world; the back-and-forth dialogue between researchers and practitioners; and taking on wider responsibilities as [institutional] neighbours and citizens" (ACU, 2001).

In other countries there is some replication of the American experience in the implementation of engagement in that the most elite research universities are more cautious than other institutional types in regard to integrating engaged scholarship into their culture and programs. However, to some degree this is less about being wedded to the research university as the sole model of academic prestige than it is about ensuring that each university focuses squarely on fulfilling its particular mission and role (Reid & Hawkins, 2003; Brown & Muirhead, 2003). Again, this makes sense when we consider Levine's model. Highly successful research universities already have great strengths and make considerable impacts on society directly and indirectly through research. Engaged scholarship seems to be a tool for enhancing the impact and knowledge role of other types of institutions, suggesting that engagement is a force for diversification of institutional types with each type making unique contributions to the connection between higher education and society.

In Australia, for example, the elite research universities have organized themselves into a coalition, the Circle of Eight. All the other (approximately thirty-one depending on how you count off-site centers) universities in the nation have missions that generally resemble those of the comprehensive masters universities in the United States. Their focus is on access, preparation of the workforce, and moderate, focused levels of research that contribute to community development and social improvement. Some of these institutions call themselves "The New Generation Universities" (Reid & Hawkins, 2003). As in the United States, the notion of engaged scholarship has resonated strongly with these comprehensive universities in Australia. In three short years since Australian academic leaders first convened as a group to consider the concepts of engagement, they have formed a national affiliate group, the Australian Universities Community Engagement Alliance (AUCEA). AUCEA holds annual national forums on engaged scholarship with blind-refereed papers, promotes peer learning among faculty through institutional exchange, and is planning to launch a refereed journal on engagement (AUCEA, 2004).

In South Africa, engagement is articulated as part of the mission of every university because higher education is expected to be deeply engaged in nation-building through the preparation of future citizens for a democratic society and engaged research that contributes to economic and community development. While some may worry that this means vocationalizing education (Adrianna Kezar, personal communication, 2004), others would argue that in an emerging nation, hopeful of building a democratic society, higher education has a legitimate role to play in responsibly demonstrating and modeling democratic practice through its methods of teaching and research. In a national policy paper written by the South African Council on Higher Education (CHE), it is suggested that "community service could become an overarching strategy for the transformation of higher education" meant in part to promote a community ethos for the nation (Council on Higher Education, 2002). In their context, the focus is on using engaged learning experiences and campus-community partnerships to develop students' commitment to service and to build community capacity by combining theory and practice. They define community-based learning, for example, as a "dynamic process linking real community problems with student learning, research and development" (Nuttall & Lazarus, 2000).

These few examples illustrate the growing international interest in creating diverse models of academic organizations and models of scholarship to match conditions and needs of a global information-driven society and economy. For America to continue to hold its pre-eminent reputation for excellence in higher education, our higher education sector is going to have to make more clear and specific decisions about these shifts in scholarly work, including the role and legitimacy of engaged scholarship. The rest of the world, while still working on aspects of implementation, seems more intrigued by and involved in new interpretations and diverse forms of scholarship as discovery, learning, and engagement. The importance of this to American higher education may be just beginning to emerge. A new report from the Carnegie Corporation articulates an American view of the changing nature of knowledge generation and dissemination and calls for changes in scholarship. In the Preface of this report, Vartan Gregorian (Graubard, 2004) observes that knowledge is increasingly fragmented as both the quantity of and access to information explodes. In response he argues there is an urgent need for scholarship "to reintegrate and reconnect the disparate, ever-multiplying strands of knowledge, to bring meaning to information and forge wisdom on the anvil of changing times" (p. 6).

A vital next step in advancing our nation's understanding of the role and import of global shifts in information management, knowledge generation, and academic culture is to consider what has been learned about the scholarship of engagement from institutional experiences to date, and thereby understand how traditional values esteemed in our current academic culture may be inhibiting institutional learning and adaptation to these new innovations in scholarship.

What Has Experience Revealed About the Scholarship of Engagement?

The scholarship of engagement is being embraced by many comprehensive colleges and universities as a mode of integrated teaching and research that aligns scholarly work with the institution's mission and is grounded in a web of campus-community relationships focused on reciprocal learning and discovery (Ramaley, 1997). At the more elite research and land-grant universities, engaged scholarship is still often seen as service or outreach, and even when the work has both intellectual value and public benefit, it is less likely to be recognized as scholarly work and less likely to involve reciprocal exchanges of knowledge (NASLGCU, 1999). This gap in experience and acceptance has obscured important lessons about engagement and the civic mission of higher education because the most advanced cases are institutions not traditionally seen as models worthy of emulation.

A diverse portfolio of institutions such as Portland State University, Florida Gulf Coast University, California State University Monterey Bay, Trinity College (Connecticut), or Columbia College Chicago, now have more than a decade's worth of experience at implementing their vision of a civic mission and the scholarship of engagement. From the experiences of these and other institutions actively interpreting the impacts of engagement on faculty work and academic culture, we can begin to draw some lessons about several key points of persistent confusion about the nature of engagement as scholarly work (Ramaley, 1997; Holland, 2001; Gelmon et al., 1998).

First, the scholarship of engagement is not just a new interpretation of service. The scholarship of engagement is a reflection of the institution's high interest in aligning academic strengths and assets with community conditions and expertise. Engaged faculty members are shaping their research and teaching as a reflection of the mission and commitment of the institution to connect scholarly work to public issues (Gelmon et al., 1998; Glassick et al., 1997; Holland, 1999).

Quality and rigor in engaged scholarship is an expression of and dependent on good teaching and good research. Engagement is a force for the greater integration of teaching and research. Mary Huber called for such an integrated view as she was working on *Scholarship Assessed,* the sequel to Boyer's *Scholarship Reconsidered* (1990). The scholarship of teaching like the scholarship of engagement calls for viewing academic work as an integrated whole instead of as a series of distinct parts (Glassick et al., 1998).

Engaged scholarship is not additive or extra work; linking it to service creates the impression that this is a new and additional burden on faculty. Rather, it is an integrated form of research and teaching that gives scholarly work a public purpose and gives faculty and students access to public sources of expertise. The scholarship of engagement recognizes that faculty attention to diverse research questions and public issues leads to different forms of research and teaching (Holland, 1999). Again, I assert that the scholarship of engagement is not a new interpretation of the role of service in the context of most institutions. The land-grant universities have articulated engagement as a reform of their historic roles of outreach and public service, and that is compatible with their unique mission (NASLGCU, 1999). For other institutional types, engagement has a more profoundly intellectual foundation that draws on the growing awareness that knowledge and information essential to discovery and learning is widely dispersed throughout society (Gibbons et al., 1994).

Service, as it has been historically and most widely known in higher education, continues everywhere in higher education as aspects of service to the campus, service to the discipline, and voluntary service in the community as an active citizen. Service to the campus and service to the discipline are largely administrative functions and rarely call on a faculty member's academic expertise. Service to the discipline and voluntary service in the community largely benefit the individual more than the institution.

The scholarship of engagement is an investment of the core assets of the institution, faculty expertise, in the exploration of critical public issues and opportunities. It allocates institutional attention, resources, and incentives toward the connection of research and teaching to the public good (London, 2003). At comprehensive, non-elite colleges and universities, this is more easily seen as relevant and valued (profitable and compatible in Levine's terms) scholarly work that is a core strategy for fulfilling the mission of the institution.

Second, the scholarship of engagement is not just a new form of applied research (as opposed to basic research), as it is not based on the one-way transference of academic knowledge to a public setting; it is a collaborative mode of inquiry (Strand, Marullo, Cutforth, Stoecker, & Donohue, 2003). Engaged scholarship is shaped to a great degree by the transformation of research traditions such as those as outlined by Gibbons and his colleagues (1994) in that this approach to research recognizes more collaborative approaches to issues such as who frames the questions, who will interpret and make sense of data, and who will make use of the findings.

In other words, engaged teaching and research recognizes that certain critical questions in the public marketplace present challenging opportunities to link the further development of theoretical understanding and student learning to the exploration of alternative solutions and understandings of public issues. It also recognizes that essential knowledge and expertise reside outside the university and require a networked approach to problem definition, data collection, analysis, and reporting. These are key features of participatory action research and community-based research that are growing models of engaged scholarship.

Third, engaged scholarship is inherently collaborative in that it depends on and connects to non-university-based expertise and wisdom. Therefore it requires a participatory and relational approach that shares design and reporting decisions with external partners. This is a direct move away from historic modes of applied research *on* community issues to a mode of research that is shared *with* community. Community as laboratory denigrates and ignores community knowledge and wisdom (Strand et al., 2003). Engaged scholarship recognizes, as Gibbons et al. (1994) does, that knowledge is dispersed in the Information Age, and exploration of critical public issues, conditions, and opportunities that does not include community-based expertise is likely to be inaccurate and misguided. Communities are savvy and are reluctant to be used as mere research guinea pigs.

Collaborative research is therefore "messy," long term, and because it involves multiple perspectives and partners, makes attribution difficult. This has raised questions about the scholarship of engagement in more traditional academic settings in that it makes attribution and impact, key components of the evaluation of faculty performance, more difficult. However, many institutions have overcome the complex challenges of evaluating and rewarding the scholarship of engagement and Ward summarizes some of these strategies in Chapter Twelve. In addition, there has been success in creating academic capacity for one of the core traditions of faculty evaluation—peer review. Created with support from the Kellogg Foundation, the Clearinghouse for the Scholarship of Engagement has launched a National Review Board comprised of engaged faculty across diverse disciplines (National Review Board, 2004). The review board provides a ready resource for institutions and individual faculty who must identify appropriate external peer reviewers for scholarly portfolios that include elements of engaged research and teaching. This has helped to ensure one of the core elements of rigorous review of faculty work and demonstrates that the scholarship of engagement can be judged by the most traditional standards of the academy.

The partnership relationship is central to the scholarship of engagement and requires commitment on the part of both faculty and the academic institution to an external relationship that influences academic work and outcomes. Because engagement is different from traditional modes of service or outreach, it is not a one-way application of knowledge to public issues. Engagement is an interactive mode of community-based research and teaching meant to lead to insights and enhanced capacity for faculty, students, and community participants in the process. The nature of engaged teaching and research requires reciprocal, mutually beneficial interactions between campus and community in order to ensure that the work is based on the full array of expertise and knowledge, and that findings are of greatest value and impact for all involved (Gelmon et al., 1998; Garlick, 2003).

The most effective models of these partnership relationships operate as learning communities. Participants are constantly exchanging knowledge, questions, expertise, and wisdom as they work collaboratively to explore critical issues and enhance their individual and collective capacity. Learning is the connection that binds campus and community together in partnerships that support research and teaching activities that develop new insights for communities, enhance the learning and civic development of students, provide faculty with access to new data sources that lead to publications and enhanced theoretical frameworks, and perhaps most importantly, build trust and mutuality between the institution and its communities (Ramaley, 1997; Wiewel & Lieber, 1998; Holland, 2001).

As these lessons emerge in both literature and practice, we see that the empirical evidence for the key features of civic engagement come from the experience of institutions not generally recognized as role models for leadership, prestige, and quality. While institutions such as the examples mentioned above are sometimes complimented for their achievements, they are often described as "special" or "unique" cases from which little wisdom can be transferred to the setting of other institutions, especially larger, more mature and elite research institutions. Thus, we face a core question. If we accept (or at least want to test the idea) that engagement is an effective strategy for creating more diverse and high-performing institutions, how will engaged scholarship gain legitimacy when it is not being modeled, respected, and practiced as widely by the "gatekeeper" universities as by "lesser" institutions?

Conclusion

Different institutional responses to engagement are predictably logical and compatible with the mission, history, purpose, and capacity of different types of institutions (Holland, 1997). However, the lack of standard valuation across different institutional types creates a problem for institutionalization in that so long as research universities continue to define core values of academic culture and public impressions of higher education, then their approach tends to dominate internal and external attitudes toward the scholarship of engagement. This gap between levels of institutional acceptance of engagement as a form of scholarship perpetuates the perception that engaged scholarship lacks legitimacy as scholarly work even though many institutions experience engagement as a valuable and rewarding mode of research and teaching essential to their core mission.

In this chapter I have made a series of assertions about the greater relevance and scholarly role of engagement in comprehensive, regionally-oriented universities and colleges and argued that the lack of greater interest in engaged scholarship among more elite institutions has a critical dampening effect on the wider institutionalization of engagement by raising persistent questions that fail to consider what has been learned and documented about engagement. Even though comprehensive university faculty and academic administrators find engagement "profitable and compatible" (Levine, 1980) with their culture and mission, and have developed standards and practices that ensure rigor and quality, they continue to be concerned about the attitudes and judgments of their research university colleagues who find engagement less relevant in their institutional contexts. In the absence of wider affirmation that pursuing different forms of scholarship will not harm their funding, reputation, accreditation, and so on, even the most advanced examples of engaged faculty and institutions still express reservations about the level of regard for engaged scholarly work.

The lack of wider support for engaged scholarship and teaching as a valued institutional and faculty priority in the research university may be limiting the capacity of engaged colleges and universities to create a new and unique academic culture that supports their true mission and their potential to serve society through engaged discovery and learning. That this is a problem may be further demonstrated by recent, emerging signs of beneficial impacts on academic culture and practices that may possibly be attributable to increased campus commitment to engagement. If these apparent impacts prove to be related to engagement, a notion that must be tested, the connection to enhanced institutional performance may offer additional reasons for institutions to consider their level of interest in enhancing their civic mission through an agenda of engaged scholarship. Two examples of potential impact on academic culture are especially worthy of further consideration and study.

First, institutions working intensely on building the scholarship of engagement seem to show signs of strengthened shared governance. University of Pittsburgh's faculty senate took the initiative to launch a revision of promotion and tenure guidelines to create a more specific mode of recognizing engaged scholarship. At Florida Gulf Coast University, administrators and the faculty senate worked together on iterative drafts of their service-learning definition and curricular models, and associated infrastructure decisions. At California State University San Bernardino, a community engagement council brings administrators, faculty, and community members together to work on grant proposals, grant management, faculty recruitment, and project management. In these and many other campus settings, I observe faculty and administration talking together with energy and enthusiasm as they work together to articulate their vision for linking the institution's scholarly work to public issues. Engagement seems to generate some sense of common purpose and positive impacts on morale, at least for campus members who participate in engaged teaching and research efforts. Could it be that the results-oriented, partnership-driven nature of engaged scholarship creates a larger context of trust and shared purposes that might strengthen shared governance further? These are certainly testable observations.

A second example of the surprising impact of engagement, especially on comprehensive universities, is its apparently positive influence on the research capacity and performance of the institution. In these institutional contexts, a focus on engaged scholarship seems to contribute to the development of a more focused research agenda that can lead to greater extramural research funding. There are at least two possible explanations. A focus on engagement may help concentrate research energy on a more specific set of topics that help the institution build strength in certain fields. Lacking this kind of focus, the research agendas of comprehensive universities can be very individualistic and scattered. A second possibility is that clarifying specific elements of scholarly work and developing a more clear definition of what is and isn't scholarly work may help each faculty member be more successful by accommodating diverse faculty interests and talents. In other words, if the scholarship of engagement is recognized as a form of research and teaching, it may open the door for a more robust research agenda for some faculty. Alternatively, reward systems that change to accommodate more diverse faculty portfolios may allow some faculty to emphasize their teaching more than research and thus liberate other faculty to give greater emphasis to research. Portland State University is an interesting example of engagement's apparently positive impact on research. Immediately following the revision of faculty reward guidelines to more clearly define categories of scholarship and criteria of quality, research activity and funding (in traditional research-oriented disciplines) expanded from less than $10 million a year to more than $20 million and has continued to grow. Of course, this could be purely coincidental, but it is not an isolated case (though certainly the most dramatic one I have observed) and is worthy of further study so we can expand our understanding of the impacts of engagement on academic culture and organizations.

The point is that engagement not only has differential relevance to different institutional types, but the experience of implementing a civic mission is playing out differently in diverse institutional settings with both intended and unintended consequences that need to be better understood through further research.

If we think of engagement as an innovative concept in higher education, Levine would remind us that there is no reason to expect that the innovation would meet the same fate at every university or college. Regionally-oriented comprehensive institutions, seeking to refine and focus their specific missions and move away from imitating an elite model they will never be funded to achieve, have been more successful at diffusing engagement as an innovation across their organizations. This signals an inherent view of the innovation as profitable and compatible with the culture and mission of the institution, at least to some degree. It may also signal that institutions with a more fuzzy and generic culture and mission have less commitment to a set of traditions, and may find it easier to consider the value of innovations and to diffuse them. In many ways, especially in regard to organizational change, elite research universities are extremely challenged by the fact that they are enormously large, complex organizations. Building consensus for change in such a massive environment is a daunting proposition, even if those institutions felt motivated to consider significant changes.

Further cross-institutional research is urgently needed to explore many of these propositions so that higher education can move toward ensuring the opportunity to create a vision of excellence for every institution. I propose that the exciting current challenge for higher education is to consider whether we are ready to accept and embrace that there is no single model of engagement, or even more boldly, no one model for scholarship generally, and that no model is "better" or more prestigious than another. They are different expressions of different institutional missions that together must serve our nation's students and communities with a comprehensive and diverse agenda of discovery, learning, and engagement. Engagement has variable levels of profitability and compatibility for different types of institutions (and in different international contexts) because it must be aligned with the organization's mission and capacity, and its quality should be rigorously assessed in the context of each of those institutional cultures and environments. Acknowledging the importance and legitimacy of the fundamental differences in institutional relevance of this form of scholarship could move the higher education sector forward in inventing multiple pathways to institutional excellence and prestige, break up old stereotypes that inhibit innovation, and enhance overall capacity to serve the public good.

References

American Association of State Colleges and Universities (AASCU). (2002). *Stepping forward as stewards of place: A guide for leading engagement at state colleges and universities.* AASCU Task Force on Public Engagement. Washington, DC: Author.

Association of Commonwealth Universities (ACU). (2001). Engagement as a core value for the university: A consultation document. http://www.acu.ac.uk.

Australian Universities Community Engagement Alliance (AUCEA). (2004). Homepage: http://www.uws.edu.au/about/adminorg/devint/ord/aucea.

Boyer, E. L. (1990). *Scholarship reconsidered: Priorities of the professoriate.* Princeton, NJ: Carnegie Foundation for the Advancement of Teaching.

Boyte, H., & Hollander, E. (1999). *Wingspread declaration on renewing the civic mission of the American research university.* Providence, RI: Campus Compact.

Bringle, R. G., & Hatcher, J. A. (2000). Institutionalization of service learning in higher education. *Journal of Higher Education, 71*(3) 274–289.

Brown, L., & Muirhead, B. (2003). The civic mission of Australian universities. *Metropolitan Universities, 14*(2), 18–32.

Council on Higher Education (CHE). (2002). A new academic policy for higher education programmes and qualifications in higher education. Discussion Paper prepared for the South African Department of Education. Pretoria, South Africa: Author. Available at: http://www.che.ac.za/documents/d000049/New_academic_Policy.pdf.

Ewell, P. T. (1985). *Levers for change: The role of state government in improving the quality of postsecondary education.* Denver: Education Commission of the States.

Garlick, S. (2003). Creative regional development: Knowledge-based associations between universities and their places. *Metropolitan Universities, 14*(2), 48–70.

Gelmon, S. B., Holland, B. A., & Shinnamon, A. (1998). Health professions schools in service to the nation: Final evaluation report, 1996–98. San Francisco: Center for the Health Professions, University of California San Francisco.

General report: European sites study of universities as sites of citizenship and civic responsibility. (2002). Available at http://iche.sas.upenn.edu/reports/Final%20report%20European%20sites%20with%20appendices.pdf.

Gibbons, M., Limoges, C., Nowotny, H., Schartzman, S., Scott, P., & Trow, M. (1994). *The new production of knowledge: The dynamics of science and research in contemporary societies.* London: Sage.

Glassick, C. E., Huber, M. T., & Maeroff, G. I. (1997). *Scholarship assessed: Evaluation of the professoriate.* San Francisco: Jossey-Bass.

Graubard, S. R. (2004). *Public scholarship: A new perspective for the 21st century.* Foreword by Vartan Gregorian. New York: Carnegie Corporation.

Holland, B. A. (1997). Analyzing institutional commitment to service. *Michigan Journal of Community Service Learning, 4,* Fall 1997, 39–41.

Holland, B. A. (1999). Factors and strategies that influence faculty involvement in public service. *Journal of Public Service and Outreach, 4*(1), 37–43.

Holland, B. A. (2001). Toward a definition and characterization of the engaged campus: Six cases. *Metropolitan Universities, 12*(3), 20–29.

Levine, A. (1980). *Why innovation fails: The institutionalization and termination of innovation in higher education.* Albany: State University of New York Press.

London, S. (2003). *Higher education for the public good: A report from the national leadership dialogues.* Ann Arbor, MI: National Forum on Higher Education and the Public Good.

National Association for State and Land-Grant Colleges and Universities (NASLGCU). (1999). *Returning to our roots: The engaged institution.* Washington, DC: Author.

National Review Board (NRB). (2004). Clearinghouse and National Review Board for the Scholarship of Engagement. www.scholarshipof engagement.org.

Nuttall, T., & Lazarus, J. (2000). *Community-based learning: A policy statement.* Unpublished manuscript.

Ramaley, J. A. (1997). Shared consequences: Recent experiences with outreach and community-based learning. *Journal of Public Service and Outreach, 2*(1), 19–25.

Reid, J., & Hawkins, R. (2003). The emergence of the new generation university. *Metropolitan Universities, 14*(2), 7–17.

Strand, K., Marullo, S., Cutforth, N., Stoecker, R., & Donohue, P. (2003). Principles of best practice for community-based research. *Michigan Journal of Community Service-Learning.* Special Issue, Summer 2003, pp. 5–15.

Watson, D. (2003). *Universities and civic engagement: A critique and prospectus.* Keynote address to the Second Biennial International InsideOut Conference, Ipswich, Queensland, hosted by the Community Service and Research Centre, the University of Queensland, Australia.

Wiewel, W., & Lieber, M. (1998). Goal achievement, relationship building, and incrementalism: The challenges of university-community partnerships. *Journal of Planning Education and Research, 17,* 291–301.

Part Five

Individual Leadership for the Public Good

Chapter Fourteen

Leading the Engaged Institution

James C. Votruba

The major focus of my career for over twenty-five years as a faculty member, academic administrator, and president has been the role of higher education in advancing the public good. Over these many years, I have worked with hundreds of institutional leaders representing every dimension of higher education from community and technical colleges to research-intensive universities concerning one fundamental leadership challenge: In an age when campuses are being asked to be a full partner in advancing preK–12 education, supporting economic development, improving environmental quality, enhancing governmental effectiveness, improving nonprofit management, addressing unresolved issues around race and class, and a host of other public concerns, what can we do to make this work a more integral part of our core academic mission? My intent in this chapter is to share what I believe are the key strategic elements for addressing this question.

First, some history. A defining quality of American public higher education has been both its willingness and capacity to advance the public good through what I will call *public engagement*. Over the past 140 years, America's colleges and universities have brought science to agriculture, provided the workforce for industrial expansion, offered the principal pathway for intergenerational mobility, strengthened national defense, and pushed back the frontiers of knowledge in every dimension of our lives. In return, *the public has provided enormous financial support for American higher education, not because it was seen as an end in itself, but because it was seen as a vehicle for achieving a broader set of social and economic purposes.* This understanding is an important backdrop for the discussion that follows.

Recently, a university president said to me, "I've given speech after speech concerning the importance of public engagement in the life of our campus. We've reorganized our public engagement efforts under the provost and hired a new vice provost to provide leadership. Still, nothing seems to have changed! Public engagement remains at the margin of our campus rather than at the core. What's wrong?"

What I have found over the years is that most campus presidents embrace the importance of public engagement. They understand how public engagement can not only serve the public good but also enrich and expand the experience of both their students and faculty while also helping to build public support. Their problem is not a lack of commitment to public engagement. Rather, it is how to act on that commitment in a way that translates into campus behavior.

In their 2002 book, *Built to Last,* Jim Collins and Jerry Porras studied eighteen companies that achieved and maintained a very high level of performance over many years. They found that these companies had two qualities in common. First, they were very clear about the outcomes that they wanted to produce (products, services, and so on). Second, and this may be the most important message in this chapter, *every element of the organization was aligned to support those outcomes.*

To draw an example from higher education, America's top research universities have evolved over the past fifty years to a point where all elements of the campus, from faculty incentives and rewards to organizational structures, policies, and procedures, reinforce the importance of externally funded research as a core institutional mission. Presidents, provosts, deans, and chairs come and go, but the importance of research as a core institutional outcome remains deeply rooted in the campus and continues uninterrupted. Moreover, state and federal policy reinforces this focus, providing significant funding opportunities for both individual scholars and the institution itself.

In contrast, public engagement is generally much less deeply rooted in the life of most campuses, is much more person dependent, and enjoys far less support from funding streams created through the state and federal public policy process. Higher education is replete with stories of public engagement flourishing under a particular dean, provost, or president, but the commitment diminishes when the leader departs. From this perspective, the key leadership challenge is to weave public engagement so deeply into the fabric of the campus that it remains strong, even when key leaders move on. We turn now to steps that campus leaders can take to address this challenge.

In 2001, the American Association of State Colleges and Universities (AASCU) asked me to chair a task force on public engagement that would offer recommendations to campus leaders, primarily presidents and provosts, on how to more fully integrate public engagement into the fabric of their institutions. Published in 2002 under the title *Stepping Forward as Stewards of Place,* the report used a study of over 350 universities to describe strategies that can be used to align colleges and universities to more deeply support public engagement as a core campus activity. While the study focused on comprehensive universities, the message and the strategic elements are equally relevant for any type of higher education institution.

In the AASCU (2002) report, public engagement was defined as follows: "The publicly engaged institution is fully committed to direct, two-way interaction with communities and other external constituencies through the development, exchange, and application of knowledge, information, and expertise for mutual benefit" (p. 9).

Some examples of public engagement include such things as

Applied research designed to help increase understanding of a client or community problem

Technical assistance involving the direct application of faculty and student expertise to design strategies for problem resolution

Demonstration *projects* designed to test new models and approaches or apply "best practice" to problems within community settings

Impact assessment designed to measure the effect of programs and services with reference to their intended outcomes

Policy analysis directed at framing new policy approaches or assessing the impact of current policy initiatives

Seminars, lectures, and essays designed to engage the public around issues of public concern

Lifelong learning opportunities designed to meet the public's diverse and ongoing learning needs

Formulated in this way, public engagement cuts across and draws upon the full breadth of an institution's mission to discover, transmit, and apply knowledge.

Key Questions for Campus Leaders

For campus leaders, building a strategy for strengthening institutional support for public engagement involves knowing the right questions to ask. For campus leaders, the following questions are both a good diagnostic and a good framework for strategy formulation:

1. To what extent is public engagement part of the campus mission and vision statement? How about the mission statements of the colleges and departments? Can you find in the strategic priorities of the campus explicit reference to priorities related to community engagement? Is public engagement defined clearly in a way that enhances and supports the other dimensions of the campus academic mission? Is it guided by a coherent philosophy?

2. Is campus and community interaction institutionalized? Are campus leaders active and visible in community educational, civic, and cultural life? Does the campus involve the community in its strategic planning and its selection of key academic leaders? How about involvement in program review?

3. Is the ability to lead in the public engagement arena a criteria for the selection and evaluation of key campus leaders including the president, provost, deans, and chairs?

4. Does the campus have adequate infrastructure to support the public engagement mission? Are there "boundary spanning" units that help link campus with community? Is there a campus "front door" that allows the public to conveniently access campus resources?

5. Do campus policies and procedures serve to either enhance or inhibit faculty involvement in public engagement activities? (A good way to answer this question is to ask the faculty.)

6. Do faculty and unit-level incentives and rewards support public engagement? Is this work an important criteria for annual salary decisions, promotion, and tenure? Are there clearly under-

stood criteria for evaluating the quality of a faculty member's public engagement activities? Are there incentives and rewards for *academic units* that make a commitment to engagement as a core unit mission? Are there revenue streams that act as incentives for faculty and units to involve themselves in engagement activities?

7. Is there a clear expectation that each academic unit is responsible for serving the full breadth of the teaching, research, and public engagement mission? Are units expected to set goals for public engagement and are they measured against those goals? Do campus information and reporting systems provide for the reporting of public engagement activities?

8. Does the process of faculty recruitment, orientation, and ongoing professional development make clear that public engagement is an important element of the overall academic mission? In particular, are faculty members provided the opportunity to deepen their understanding of how to work effectively with communities and other external clients?

9. Does the campus planning and budgeting process reflect the importance of the community engagement process? Is there opportunity for budget allocations to support engagement efforts? What percentage of the overall campus budget is associated with the public engagement mission?

10. Is public engagement built into the curriculum? Are there opportunities for students to gain experience in public engagement through service-learning and other forms of community-based learning?

11. Do campus communications and key communicators reflect the importance of community engagement? How about campus rituals, ceremonies, and awards? Is community engagement prominent in the public remarks of governing board members, the president, provost, and other key campus leaders?

12. Are the campus facilities and environment designed to welcome community involvement? Is campus signage and parking reflective of an environment that welcomes the public?

Different types of institutions will address these questions in different ways, and not all campuses, no matter how committed they are to public engagement, will score high on each cluster. However, it has been my experience that these are the key alignment questions that must be addressed if an institution wants to embed public engagement in the life of the campus.

Key Questions for State Systems Leaders

Colleges and universities do not exist in a vacuum. Many have state-level coordinating and governing boards with whom they interact. If public engagement is to thrive at the campus level, it must be supported at the systems level as well. Systems leaders must also address several key questions:

1. Is public engagement prominent in systemwide planning and priority setting? Have we established statewide priorities for campus public engagement?
2. Have we created a clear expectation that our campuses should be involved in public engagement activities?
3. Have we made public engagement (as well as enrollment growth and research) a priority in our political advocacy at both the state and federal levels?
4. Have we established measures that can be used to assess campus productivity in public engagement?

Key Questions for State Policymakers

Unlike traditional forms of instruction and research, each of which have both federal and state resource streams to support them, *public engagement is a cost center* for most colleges and universities. With few exceptions, public engagement is conducted in partnership with community clients who cannot afford to pay the full cost of the program or service. Granted, there are sometimes funds allocated by local foundations to support at least a portion of the work, but these are generally available to cover only the direct program costs, not overhead. In difficult financial times, the tendency is for organizations, including colleges and universities, to focus on expanding their revenue centers and reducing their cost centers. This places the public engagement mission at considerable risk.

There is no doubt in my mind that campus public engagement will never reach the full measure of its potential without support from the public policy process. With a few exceptions, this public policy support does not currently exist. In this spirit, I offer the following key questions for state public policymakers:

1. Does the state have a "public agenda" focused on the needs of its population? For example, are there priorities for economic development, education, health, and crime prevention?

2. Are colleges and universities held accountable for addressing the public agenda through their teaching, research, and public engagement efforts?

3. Have we articulated the importance of public engagement in both rhetorical and financial terms?

4. Have we developed criteria that allow us to measure the quantity and quality of campus public engagement activity?

5. Have we created resource streams to support higher education's engagement of our most important public priorities?

In the area of state policy, there are some positive signs. The Kentucky Council on Postsecondary Education has created the Regional Stewardship Trust Fund designed to provide each regional university $1 million annually to address challenges that confront the communities that they serve. We can only hope that more states will follow this lead and that the federal government will explore similar options.

Five Cautions Related to Public Engagement

When done well, public engagement can advance the public good, enrich the experience and learning of both faculty and students, and strengthen public support and advocacy on behalf of the campus. However, there are also dangers related to public engagement. I close with five cautions that leaders should always consider. I have the scars to prove it!

1. *Be careful to define who owns the problem.* I have seen colleges and universities, with their hearts in the right place, assume ownership for community problems that are far beyond their capacity to resolve. At our best, campuses can be indispensable partners in helping to address complex and persistent community problems. However, when ownership for the problem is transferred from community to campus, it will, more often than not, lead to frustration and disillusionment for all.

2. *Be sure that faculty are prepared.* There is very little in faculty members' academic preparation that prepares them for public engagement. Faculty who are good at this work know how to listen, are sensitive to context, see themselves as learners as well as teachers, speak in a language that the community can understand, and always seek first to understand, then be understood. Sending forth faculty who are unprepared to engage the public is a slippery slope for all.

3. *Define clearly the engagement project scope, duration, and outcomes as well as the contribution that each partner will make.* An ill-defined engagement project allows both campus and community to infer expectations that may not be valid. Who will do what? When? How will progress be monitored? What will each partner contribute financially as well as in-kind? What will constitute project completion? Being specific at the front end will help prevent disagreements along the way.

4. *Beware of political alignment.* Public engagement can often place a campus in the middle of powerful political forces that have fundamental differences over how to address a particular community problem. Years ago, my university was involved in helping a community address several school improvement issues that required buy-in from a local parents group, school administrators, and corporate and political leaders. The schools in question served a predominantly lower income African American population while the corporate and political leadership was predominantly middle- to upper-income and white. The challenge was to find common ground among all of the groups, build trust, and work toward a solution. In circumstances like these, colleges and universities must be sure that their representatives are savvy in their understanding of how to position the campus in a way that does not get co-opted by any one group.

5. *Have a disengagement strategy.* Public engagement efforts should always have a start and end point. Absent any message to the contrary, community partners often assume that the campus is committed to a permanent partnership on behalf of a particular program or service. If this isn't the case, it should be made clear at the outset so that misunderstandings are avoided later on.

Conclusion

Higher education has a unique and indispensable role to play in fostering the public good. What this chapter has suggested is that, in addition to our traditional research and instructional role, we have an obligation to extend and apply our vast knowledge resources in the public arena for the public good. At its best, this process, which I've referred to as public engagement, improves lives and strengthens communities at the same time that it enriches the knowledge and understanding of our students and faculty.

The key leadership challenge is to align all elements of our colleges and universities to support public engagement as an important institutional priority. Campus leaders cannot do this alone. It requires not only internal campus alignment but also support and alignment at the state and federal level. Absent the recognition of campus public engagement as a major public policy priority, university involvement in public engagement is not likely to increase.

Having key campus and public policy leaders advocate on behalf of public engagement is necessary but far from sufficient. What is needed at every level are leaders who roll up their sleeves and address the questions posed in this chapter. The stakes for both our campuses and our communities are too great for us to fail.

References

American Association of State Colleges and Universities (AASCU). (2002). *Stepping forward as stewards of place: A guide for leading public engagement at state colleges and universities.* Report of the American Association of State Colleges and Universities' National Task Force on Public Engagement. Washington, DC: Author.

Collins, J. C., & Porras, J. (2002). *Built to last: Successful habits of visionary companies.* New York: HarperCollins.

Chapter Fifteen

Preparing Doctoral Students for Faculty Careers That Contribute to the Public Good

Ann Austin, Benita J. Barnes

One way to strengthen the commitment of higher education institutions to serving the public good is through the work of the faculty. With many retirements occurring now and in the near future, graduate students who are preparing for the faculty and new faculty members beginning their careers will be those who are working with students, leading higher education institutions, and taking up responsibilities for the public good in the coming decades. This chapter considers how doctoral programs can guide aspiring faculty members to develop an appreciation for the important role of higher education institutions in serving the public good, as well as to gain the abilities and skills needed to create careers that express commitment to serving the civic good. To address these goals, the chapter is divided into three parts. First, we highlight findings from recent studies on graduate education that hold implications for preparing doctoral students to appreciate and incorporate a commitment to the public good. Second, we suggest some of the abilities and skills that aspiring faculty members should develop in graduate school necessary for careers that contribute to the broader society. Third, we offer suggestions for specific strategies for preparing graduate students to value their role in serving the public good. The third section provides examples of foundation efforts, institutional initiatives, and strategies used by faculty members that help prepare doctoral students for this important aspect of their future work.

Highlights from Recent Studies

Over the past decade, researchers have examined the strengths and weaknesses of graduate education and the experiences of doctoral students, including the problems, barriers, and concerns they encounter (Antony & Taylor, 2004; Austin, 2002; Fagen & Suedkamp Wells, 2004; Golde & Dore, 2001; Lovitts, 2004; Nerad, Aanerud, & Cerny, 2004; Nyquist et al., 1999; Nyquist & Woodford, 2000; Wulff & Austin, 2004; Wulff, Austin, Nyquist, & Sprague, 2004). In addition, research that has examined the experiences and challenges of new faculty members (Rice, Sorcinelli, & Austin, 2000; Sorcinelli & Austin, 1992; Tierney & Bensimon, 1996; Trower, Austin, & Sorcinelli, 2001) suggests difficulties which may relate partially to shortcomings in their preparation in graduate school for their faculty roles. Since graduate school is the location for much of the socialization for the faculty career (Van Maanen, 1976), the experiences of aspiring faculty members during this period are likely to affect how they conduct their work once they are in faculty positions. Here we summarize and discuss several research-based themes that offer implications relevant to how graduate education can prepare aspiring faculty for valuing and pursuing careers that contribute to the public good.

Theme 1: Doctoral students often complete their graduate preparation with limited understanding of the full range of responsibilities involved in faculty work, the history of higher education and its role in the broader society, and the different missions and cultural characteristics of the various higher education institutional types.

Doctoral programs focus much attention on cultivating the research skills of graduate students. They work in laboratories, serve as research assistants, and collaborate with individual faculty or on research teams to research and write papers. Students who are teaching assistants often gain some teaching experience as they assist professors or teach sections. In many doctoral programs, however, preparation for teaching responsibilities is far less extensive than for research and not very systematic (Austin, 2002; Wulff et al., 2004). In recent years, programs such as Preparing Future Faculty (PFF) have offered ways through which universities can more fully prepare their students for the teaching responsibilities they will face in their careers, often in institutions different from the research universities in which they were prepared (Gaff, Pruitt-Logan, & Weibl, 2000; Pruitt-Logan & Gaff, 2004; http://www.preparing-faculty.org/; http://www.preparing-faculty.org/PFFWeb.Contents.htm). In addition, attention to teaching assistant training has increased in the past decade, which has enhanced the opportunities for graduate students to develop understandings and skills as teachers (Marincovich, Prostko, & Stout, 1998; Nyquist, Abbott, Wulff, & Sprague, 1991; Nyquist & Wulff, 1992).

Preparation for the public service dimensions of faculty roles seems to have been largely neglected in the preparation of graduate students, however. When asked about how they understood public service, engagement, or outreach in a qualitative, longitudinal study of graduate students in a range of disciplines, the aspiring faculty had little notion of the meaning of these terms and their relevance to faculty work (Austin, 2002; Wulff et al., 2004). Also, graduate students typically do not learn about the particular missions of different institutional types, such as the commitment felt in community colleges to serve the needs of the surrounding city or region in specific and direct ways. It is likely that many are not encountering courses or discussions that enable them to learn how the academy has related to society over time or the various ways in which a faculty member may contribute to the public good (ranging, for example, from including service-learning in a course, to engaging in action research with a community group, to finding avenues for translating complex research findings into language accessible to the public, to bringing scholarly perspectives into public debates).

Theme 2: Doctoral students and new faculty members perceive mixed messages about what is valued in their professional work.

As they watch faculty members, read institutional documents, engage in formal and informal conversations, and observe who is most respected and honored within the institution and profession, doctoral students and new faculty members perceive mixed messages about what is valued and rewarded (Austin, 2002; Nyquist et al., 1999; Wulff et al., 2004). For example, a president or provost may emphasize the importance placed on excellent teaching for undergraduates, but graduate students may observe that the faculty members receiving the most respect in their departments are the researchers with national reputations. In discussing the nature of doctoral education, including the mixed messages graduate students perceive about what kind of scholarship is valued, Austin (2002) concluded that "preparation for the faculty career stands in direct contrast to the national discussion about the importance of various kinds of scholarship (including teaching and service/outreach), institutional calls to encourage a balance between teaching and research, and the likelihood that many graduates will find positions in master's- and bachelor's-granting institutions" (p. 108).

Of relevance to this chapter, graduate students may hear that contributing to the public good is important, but they may not see examples of faculty members engaging in this kind of work. Doctoral students and new faculty also may wonder whether the institutional reward structure honors faculty members who engage in such work, for example, as spending time on action projects with community groups or writing for popular news outlets. The mixed messages within many universities about what work is most highly respected are barriers to the process of preparing faculty members who value and know how to engage in the range of possible work that serves the public good.

Theme 3: Doctoral students and new faculty are concerned about the quality of life in the academy.

Doctoral students observe that their faculty members work long hours, with multiple demands, and in some cases juggle (or sacrifice) personal relationships and interests—and they question whether they want to adopt similar lifestyles. The data from several studies show that they wonder whether they can create lives characterized by balance and integration across their personal and professional responsibilities (Austin, 2002; Golde, 1997; Golde & Dore, 2001; Rice et al., 2000; Trower et al., 2001). Doctoral students and new faculty report that they are willing to work hard, but that they also want personal relationships and interests to be integrated into their daily lives.

Closely related to concerns about time and balance are the feelings of loneliness and isolation and the yearning for community that nag at newcomers to faculty work (Menges & Associates, 1999; Rice et al., 2000; Sorcinelli & Austin, 1992; Tierney & Bensimon, 1996). They observe that the press of time demands and multiple responsibilities interfere with faculty members' time for informal collegial interactions. As they make these observations, doctoral students sometimes experience conflicts between their own values and what they perceive as the emphases and quality of life in the academy. In a study conducted more than ten years ago, Anderson and Swazey (1998) explained that "nearly a third of respondents agreed with the statement that graduate education was changing them in ways they did not like" (p. 2). Even while they express such reservations about the lifestyle that they observe often characterizes academic careers, doctoral students and new faculty often nurture a different vision. Responding in a study about the perceptions of aspiring and new faculty sponsored by the American Association of Higher Education several years ago, one doctoral student mused: "What I want most in a faculty career is a profession that makes me feel connected to my students, to my colleagues, to the larger community, and to myself" (Rice et al., 2000, p. 16). Many newcomers to the academy bring a vision of a work environment characterized by the kind of connections and caring that is often part of engaging in work that serves the public good.

Theme 4: Many new and aspiring faculty members are deeply committed to doing what they call *meaningful work.*

Results of several studies show that aspiring and new faculty members are motivated to enter academic careers because they want to pursue their disciplinary interests, carry out creative work, interact with interesting and diverse people, make a positive impact on students and the development of the future generation, and contribute to the betterment of society (Anderson & Swazey,

1998; Austin, 1992, 2002; Rice et al., 2000). Golde and Dore (2001) found in their extensive quantitative study that more than half the graduate students responding said that they wanted to provide community service, but relatively few said they felt prepared to do so. In Nyquist and Woodford's project on Re-envisioning the Ph.D., doctoral students interviewed about their graduate experiences expressed concern about the narrow ways in which professional work in their fields often seems to be understood (Nyquist & Woodford, 2000; Nyquist, Woodford, & Rogers, 2004). All in all, graduate students and newcomers entering the faculty ranks are enthusiastic (often passionate) and rather idealistic about how they will make a contribution to their disciplines, their students, and the broader society. Yet the research also has shown that they do not see the academic career as the only way in which to enact their values, pursue their passions, and fulfill their dreams. Some are willing to consider other career areas outside higher education, and some even wonder aloud if they can find the balance, integration, and opportunity within the academy to find meaning in their work and to make the kind of significant contributions they envision (Austin, 2002; Nyquist et al., 1999; Rice et al., 2000; Wulff et al., 2004).

In sum, then, graduate students often complete their degrees and begin academic careers with only limited understanding of the roles and responsibilities of colleges and universities to the broader society and the ways those responsibilities can be carried out by faculty members. Many also have not been introduced to the different kinds of universities and colleges with their diverse missions and expectations for faculty roles. Second, doctoral students often perceive mixed messages about the kind of scholarly work that is valued and may have little exposure to explicit discussion or examples of scholarly work to serve the public good. Third, aspiring and new faculty members often express concern about the quality of academic life, hoping to find greater professional and personal balance and more opportunities for connections and collegiality. Fourth, doctoral students and new faculty are often motivated by a desire to make significant contributions to their students, disciplines, and communities. They want to make a difference, and they want to do meaningful work.

Overall, graduate education is not explicitly preparing students to understand and engage in work for the public good. However, the data suggest that aspiring and new faculty members are looking for balance and integration, collegiality, and meaningfulness in their work and lives. Opportunities to learn about and engage in work that explicitly serves the public good could help them achieve these goals.

Abilities and Skills Related to Serving the Public Good

Explicit attention could be given by faculty advisors and program curriculum committees to prepare doctoral students for faculty careers in which they value the role of the university in serving the public good, understand the range of work that addresses this goal, and know how to engage in such scholarly work. This section outlines the abilities and skills that we suggest doctoral programs should help students develop as they prepare to assume faculty positions. (Some of these skills have been discussed in earlier work by Austin, 2003.)

Appreciation of the Core Purposes and Values of Higher Education Institutions

Doctoral students should gain some understanding of what Levine calls the "essential purposes and core values" (Levine, 2000, p. 17) of higher education. They should be introduced to the history of higher education and the role of universities and colleges in educating citizens with appreciation for and skills necessary in a democratic society, addressing significant societal needs in such areas as urban, environmental, health, and educational fields; preparing leaders for civic life; and serving as home to scholars who have the expertise to raise difficult questions and speak as social critics on issues of import to the society. Doctoral students should consider not only the organizational role of the academy in society, but also the roles and responsibilities of those individuals who accept the role of faculty member. They should be invited to reflect on how their research and teaching can contribute in many different ways to the public good. As an example, in the context of international affairs today, faculty members in philosophy, geography, government, literature, languages, history, sociology, and a number of other fields can play a very helpful role in enhancing the knowledge and understanding of the population about current national and world issues.

Understanding of Different Institutional Types and Their Missions

While doctoral students are prepared in major research universities, they assume positions in community colleges, liberal arts colleges, comprehensive institutions, and elsewhere. Programs such as Preparing Future Faculty (PFF) are introducing doctoral students to a range of institutions (Gaff et al., 2000; Pruitt-Logan & Gaff, 2004; http://www.preparing-faculty.org/; http://www.preparing-faculty.org/PFFWeb.Contents.htm). Yet it is still the case that many doctoral graduates are unfamiliar with the kinds of institutions that compose the higher education spectrum in the United States. Doctoral students who are preparing for careers in which they will serve the public good need to understand the particular missions of each institutional type. They also should know how historically the range of institutional types emerged to meet national needs. Then, when taking a position at a comprehensive university, for example, new faculty members will have enough awareness to inquire about how the institution's mission relates to regional employment and social needs and how they can relate their own work to those institutional missions and commitments.

Understanding of What Public Service, Outreach, and Engagement Mean

As mentioned, aspiring faculty members, though often committed to engaging in meaningful work, are not always familiar with terms such as *public service, outreach,* or *engagement,* nor have they considered what these aspects of their faculty life might involve. Thus, if students are to be prepared to envision their work in relation to the public good, graduate education should provide opportunities for them to encounter these terms, learn how to relate theory and practice, discuss different ways to incorporate commitment to the public good into one's work, and interact with faculty members who offer diverse examples of ways to lead a scholarly life that contributes to the public good. They need to understand that such work might take a range of forms: for example, action research with community groups, working with students on service-learning projects, helping students learn skills of cooperation, teamwork, and conflict resolution necessary for civic engagement, working with agencies to apply knowledge to a specific problem, engaging in basic research on critically important societal problems, writing for government agencies or for the popular press in their areas of expertise, and working within the university to ensure that processes, interactions, and habits model effective democratic practices.

Research Skills

While doctoral students typically learn a great deal about conducting research in their fields, preparation for a career of service to the public good requires a broadening of research preparation in many cases. Certainly virtually all research contributes to the public good by expanding human knowledge or by adding new elements of basic knowledge that advance science, medicine, or other fields. Those who want to contribute to the public good in more direct ways benefit from learning about strategies, philosophical principles, and ethics concerning action research, community-based research, and applied research (Smith, Willms, & Johnson, 1997; Strand, Cutforth, Stoecker, Marullo, & Donohue, 2000; Strand, Marullo, Cutforth, Stoecker, & Donohue, 2003; Stringer, 1999; Zuber-Skerrit, 1996). Many societal problems require interdisciplinary or cross-disciplinary perspectives, so graduate students would do well to learn how to work with colleagues in other disciplines and appreciate different ways of framing and researching problems. Golde and Dore (2001) reported from their survey of doctoral students that only 27 percent believe that their programs prepare them to collaborate with people from other disciplines.

Teaching Skills

Doctoral students today are more likely than a decade ago to experience some preparation for teaching responsibilities. Preparing Future Faculty (PFF) programs (Gaff et al., 2000; Pruitt-Logan & Gaff, 2004; http://www.preparing-faculty.org/; http://www.preparing-faculty.org/PFFWeb.Contents.htm), teaching certificates, and well-conceptualized training programs for teaching assistants are in place at many universities (Nyquist et al., 1991). We encourage such programs to give particular attention to the abilities that will help future faculty integrate a commitment to the public good into their teaching. For example, future faculty can learn ways to encourage students to deepen their understanding of the meaning of being a good citizen and strategies to help students enhance their critical thinking skills. Other important teaching skills involve knowing how to integrate service-learning into one's course development plans and how to help students use service-learning experiences as opportunities to examine their values and develop lifelong commitments to contributing to the broader society.

Teamwork and Collaboration Skills

In order to work on projects that address complex societal problems, prospective faculty members need to know how to work collaboratively with others who have different disciplinary perspectives and epistemological and methodological approaches. They must also be comfortable when interacting with others different from them in race and ethnicity, with faculty members holding different kinds of appointments (part-time or contract appointments), and with individuals from various walks of life. Skills for collaborating and working in diverse groups and knowledge of strategies for handling conflict resolution are helpful also (Austin, 2003; Rice, 1996).

Communication Skills

Future faculty prepared to contribute to the public good also should be comfortable engaging in dialogue characterized by mutual respect and respectful listening. Knowing how to share one's expertise while also being open to others' knowledge and perspectives is a talent that sometimes must be cultivated. Prospective faculty should be able to communicate effectively with diverse audiences, including policymakers, government leaders, community members, foundation officers, and members of the community. While graduate education typically teaches aspiring faculty how to write and present in scholarly venues, preparation also should be offered in writing for newspapers and the popular press, developing succinct briefs and memos appropriate for policy groups or government leaders, and talking with individuals not professionally involved in one's area of expertise.

Appreciation for Institutional Citizenship Responsibilities

One way in which universities and colleges serve the public good is by providing examples of democratic communities. When faculty members model the abilities of committed, thoughtful citizens in their work within the university, students have examples useful to their own growth as citizens. In order to preserve and advance this important contribution that higher education institutions can make, faculty members must understand, appreciate, and be willing to participate as citizens of their academic institutions. Furthermore, through their participation on committees and in leadership roles as institutional citizens, individual faculty members can influence the role of their institutions in contributing to the public good. Thus, doctoral students should learn what institutional citizenship means, the responsibility one assumes when taking on a faculty role, and how faculty members and administrators can work together through institutional governance structures. Since they may be department leaders and committee members in the future, aspiring faculty members also should have opportunities to develop skills in time management, strategic planning, effective group processes, meeting management, and, as already mentioned, conflict resolution.

Strategies for Improving Doctoral Education to Prepare Faculty Committed to the Public Good

In this final section, we suggest strategies for preparing doctoral students more explicitly and fully to be faculty members who appreciate the important role and responsibility of higher education in contributing to the public good and who have the inclinations, abilities, and skills to do so—in a range of ways—through their own work. We organize these strategies in four categories. First, we describe the efforts of two foundations with projects involving multiple universities designed to reform graduate education in ways that will strengthen the preparation of graduate students in their understanding and abilities to serve the public good. Second, we highlight a particularly comprehensive institutional plan for improving graduate education. This institution's work is distinctive in its explicit and extensive efforts to prepare graduates to interact with constituencies outside the university. Third, we suggest that universities can identify and then build on resources already in place to offer courses, workshops, and other opportunities that help graduate students develop some of the skills needed to become faculty members with abilities useful for working with wide audiences. Finally, we suggest strategies that departments and individual faculty members can take to strengthen the preparation of their doctoral students for connecting their work with the public good.

Foundation Initiatives

Foundations can influence the direction of academic work through the programs they initiate or support. Here we highlight two foundation initiatives aimed at reforming graduate education. Each explicitly addresses the preparation of Ph.D. students for contributing to the public good.

The Responsive PhD

The Woodrow Wilson Foundation, under the leadership of Robert Weisbuch, has committed itself to a new vision of doctoral education through its program entitled The Responsive PhD (Weisbuch, 2004; http://www.woodrow.org/responsivephd/responsive_phd.html). The program has brought together fourteen universities to envision and experiment with new approaches to doctoral education. Four themes guide the innovations of the institutions participating in the Responsive PhD initiative: new partnerships, new paradigms, new practices, and new people. First, the program encourages conversations and partnerships among those inside and outside the university to consider how graduate education should change. Second, the program encourages "adventurous scholarship" (Weisbuch, 2004, p. 224) that crosses disciplinary boundaries to foster the kind of interdisciplinary work necessary to address contemporary social problems. Third, there is a focus on new practices, including more attention in doctoral education on teaching experiences that enable students to develop teaching expertise in systematic ways, and opportunities for students to become acquainted with issues in K–12 as well as higher education. This programmatic focus also emphasizes that doctoral education is "guiding the next generation of intellectual leaders"

(Weisbuch, 2004, p. 228), not only academic leaders, who accordingly must know how to use their expertise and knowledge in the broader society. In addition to the Responsive PhD program, the Woodrow Wilson Foundation's Humanities at Work program carries out this commitment by providing grants for doctoral students to work in nonacademic settings in the summer where they can use their scholarly expertise. For example, an American studies student helped create archives and an exhibit through his work with an East Los Angeles graphic arts cooperative (Weisbuch, 2004). Fourth, The Responsive PhD is working to bring new participants into doctoral education and to support their success. Part of the motivation for this effort is recognition of "the desire of people from oppressed groups to give back, to stay connected to their communities, and to make their individual success helpful for others in that population" (Weisbuch, 2004, p. 231).

While the Responsive PhD initiative is still in process, it is one of the national programs committed to reform in graduate education that is explicitly seeking ways to prepare doctoral graduates to use their scholarly expertise beyond the academy. Over the next few years, the institutional initiatives that emerge in conjunction with The Responsive PhD are likely to offer some good examples of strategies for preparing doctoral students more fully for careers that contribute to the public good.

The Carnegie Initiative on the Doctorate

The Carnegie Foundation for the Advancement of Teaching is in the midst of a five year (2001–2006) project entitled The Carnegie Initiative on the Doctorate (CID) (www.carnegiefoundation.org/CID). This project is organized to address the purpose of the doctorate and advances the concept that doctoral programs are preparing "stewards of the discipline" who have responsibility for "generation, conservation, and transformation" (Walker, 2004, p. 238). That is, the holder of the Ph.D. should have the ability to: (a) "generate new knowledge by conducting research and scholarship"; (b) "critically conserve history and foundational ideas of a discipline"; and (c) "effectively transform existing knowledge and its benefits to others through application, teaching, and writing" (Walker, 2004, p. 238). The third ability (transformation) that the Carnegie Initiative emphasizes as critically important for every Ph.D. graduate to gain is particularly pertinent to the preparation of faculty committed to contributing to the public good.

The CID initiative encourages graduate programs to develop "a cadre of scholarly leaders or stewards of the discipline who are able to function . . . effectively in diverse environments" (Walker, 2004, p. 246). Such graduates should be creative problem solvers, effective participants in interdisciplinary teams, and good communicators. The Carnegie Foundation has brought together six to eight departments in six fields who currently are engaged in in-depth study of their graduate programs, reform efforts, and assessment of the impact of their work. Their ideas and initiatives are helping to advance at universities across the country improvements in graduate education that should more fully prepare Ph.D. graduates with the understanding, abilities, and skills to use their scholarly expertise in ways that explicitly contribute to the broader community.

A Comprehensive Institutional Initiative

The University of Texas at Austin has an exciting and comprehensive program entitled the Professional Development and Community Engagement Program (PDCE) to prepare graduate students for a range of future careers. According to its Web site, this program "supports and encourages graduate students in becoming leaders and innovators both at the university and around the globe" (http://www. utexas.edu/ogs/development.html). Students can participate in community engagement projects enabling them to contribute to and impact the local or global community through research, consulting, and other projects. Internships outside the university also are available. In addition, "synergy groups" bring together graduate students with faculty members and community citizens to focus the intellectual resources of the university on issues within the community concerning health, education, race relations, the environment, and technology. Such opportunities enable students to learn analysis and communication skills necessary for linking their areas of expertise with community concerns. The PDCE also includes courses and workshops on such topics as collaboration, team building, networking, consulting, entrepreneurship, ethics, and professional and academic writing.

Building on Institutional Resources

Developing a comprehensive institutional plan takes time, planning, and involvement from many people and offices on a campus. Components of the institutional plan at the University of Texas such as the community engagement projects, the internships, the synergy groups, and the courses are examples of possible strategies for institutions to consider. Universities might begin their efforts by conducting a campus audit to identify interested faculty members or units on campus where courses or resources already available might be adapted to prepare graduate students to learn about serving the public good. For example, faculty members in a department of communication might be willing to adapt or develop graduate courses or workshops focused on communicating to diverse audiences. Faculty members teaching courses involving service-learning could be invited to provide internships for graduate students who want to learn how to incorporate service opportunities into their teaching. Faculty working in interdisciplinary programs—for example, programs concerning environmental studies or family, youth, and children—might be willing to offer workshops or give lectures targeted to graduate students that explore ways to integrate public service into one's scholarly work.

We offer two other examples here of courses and workshops that graduate schools could offer to help students develop some of the skills necessary to interact with citizens and groups in the broader society. In each case, the faculty members who developed these opportunities were drawing on long experience and scholarly expertise to help graduate students develop skills relevant to serving the public good.

Conflict Resolution Workshops

Michigan State University, with support from FIPSE, the Fund for the Improvement of Postsecondary Education, has developed a well-conceptualized and tested approach to teach faculty members and students effective strategies for setting expectations and resolving conflicts (Klomparens & Beck, 2004; www.grad.msu.edu/conflict.htm). Situated in the graduate school, the program involves workshops for students and faculty that utilize short video vignettes to trigger dialogue and learning. Participants learn to use interest-based approaches to setting expectations and resolving conflicts that have been found successful in labor-management relations, environmental disputes, and international relations. Students, faculty members, and graduate deans at a number of campuses where this approach has been introduced have evaluated the workshops very positively. Such a workshop approach is an example of how a graduate school could offer opportunities for graduate students to learn some of the skills essential for working successfully and effectively both within the academy and with citizens, community groups, political leaders, and others in the broader society.

Informal Education Course

The second example is a course developed by The Center for the Integration of Research, Teaching, and Learning (CIRTL), a National Science Foundation–sponsored five-year program specifically designed to prepare graduate students in science, technology, engineering, and mathematics (STEM) fields for successful careers that integrate excellent research and superb teaching and learning (http://www.wcer.wisc.edu/cirtl/). Part of the purpose of CIRTL is to help graduate students, post-docs, and faculty find ways to ensure the broader impact of their work, which is a key emphasis of the National Science Foundation. The center, which soon will include a network of ten universities, is developing courses, workshops, and opportunities that can be adapted at universities throughout the country interested in better preparing future faculty in STEM fields. One of these courses focuses on *informal education,* a term used often within science fields to denote communication and education outside traditional educational venues. Graduate students participating in the course have the opportunity to interact with faculty members on projects that link their disciplinary expertise to the community, such as work with museums or with popular news magazines. A key outcome of the course is for students to learn forms of communication that are effective in helping lay audiences understand complex issues in science, technology, engineering, and mathematics.

Department and Faculty Initiatives

Of equal importance to the efforts made through foundations, comprehensive institutional programs, and institutional courses and workshops are the efforts of departmental and academic program faculty members to help their doctoral students appreciate their responsibilities for contributing to the public good. At the department level, chairs and faculty members can review the curriculum to determine whether program requirements, courses, and options provide doctoral students with opportunities to gain relevant skills. For example, a program review might examine where and how students learn about such issues as the meanings of public service, the history of the university in society, the diverse roles and responsibilities of faculty members, how to work with diverse groups, how to communicate effectively to various audiences and for different purposes, and ethical issues concerning faculty work. The earlier section on abilities and skills doctoral students should learn if they are to be prepared to serve the public good could be a starting point for faculty discussions about the breadth and depth of the program's curriculum and the graduate experience available to students.

Individual faculty members can assess their roles as advisors. As an advisor, do I discuss with my doctoral advisees how I think about my faculty role and the impact of my work? Do I discuss different kinds of careers available to a Ph.D. graduate in my field and the array of ways in which one might use one's expertise and talents to contribute to the field, the academy, and the broader society? How do I respond when students bring up their passions, interests, and goals? Do I share ideas about the ethical issues or implications of the work in my field? Do I offer opportunities for graduate students to engage in self-reflection about the kind of work they want to do and lives they want to live? Through formal advising and informal interactions in classrooms, laboratories, and hallways, faculty members convey expectations and offer possibilities to doctoral students about how their work can matter and make a difference.

Conclusion

What doctoral students learn in graduate school will affect how they do their work as faculty members. Therefore, if serving the public good is to be a priority for higher education institutions in the twenty-first century, the preparation of doctoral students during their graduate school experience must provide explicit emphasis on how to value and engage in such work. Doctoral students need faculty members who model commitment to serving the public good and provide examples of the range of research, teaching, and outreach activities through which such commitment can be expressed. As suggested in this chapter, the various studies that have examined the doctoral experience have shown that students typically do not learn about the place that public service, civic engagement, and outreach could play in their academic lives. Yet, as also discussed in this chapter, a number of nationally recognized programs, such as The Responsive PhD, The Carnegie Initiative on the Doctorate (CID), and The Center for the Integration of Research, Teaching, and Learning (CIRTL), are working to find ways to prepare doctoral students more fully for the range of their responsibilities as scholars and academic citizens, including their responsibilities to the broader society. In addition, this chapter has suggested a variety of strategies and programs through which universities, departments and programs, and individual faculty members can help doctoral students develop the variety of skills and abilities—in their research, teaching, collaboration, and communication skills—that will enable them to become future faculty who are professionally prepared, socially aware, and personally committed to serve the public good.

References

Anderson, M. S., & Swazey, J. P. (1998). *The experience of being in graduate school: An exploration.* New Directions for Higher Education, No. 101. San Francisco: Jossey-Bass.

Antony, J. S., & Taylor, E. (2004). Theories and strategies of academic career socialization: Improving paths to the professoriate for black graduate students. In D. H. Wulff & A. E. Austin (Eds.), *Paths to the professoriate: Strategies for enriching the preparation of future faculty* (pp. 92–114). San Francisco: Jossey-Bass.

Austin, A. E. (1992). Supporting junior faculty through a Teaching Fellows Program. In M. D. Sorcinelli & A. E. Austin (Eds.), *Developing new and junior faculty.* New Directions for Teaching and Learning, No. 50 (pp. 73–86). San Francisco: Jossey-Bass.

Austin, A. E. (2002, January/February). Preparing the next generation of faculty: Graduate school as socialization to the academic career. *Journal of Higher Education, 73*(1), 94–122.

Austin, A. E. (2003, Winter). Creating a bridge to the future: Preparing new faculty to face changing expectations in a shifting context. *The Review of Higher Education, 26*(2), 119–144.

Fagen, A. P., & Suedkamp Wells, K. M. (2004). The 2000 National Doctoral Program Survey: An on-line study of students' voices. In D. H. Wulff & A. E. Austin (Eds.), *Paths to the professoriate: Strategies for enriching the preparation of future faculty* (pp. 74–91). San Francisco: Jossey-Bass.

Gaff, J., Pruitt-Logan, A., & Weibl, R. (2000). *Building the faculty we need: Colleges and universities working together.* Washington, DC: Association of American Colleges and Universities and Council of Graduate Schools.

Golde, C. M. (1997, November). *Gaps in the training of future faculty: Doctoral student perceptions.* Paper presented at the annual meeting of the Association for the Study of Higher Education, Albuquerque, NM.

Golde, C. M., & Dore, T. M. (2001). *At cross purposes: What the experiences of doctoral students reveal about doctoral education* (www.phd-survey.org). Philadelphia: The Pew Charitable Trusts.

Klomparens, K. L., & Beck. J. P. (2004). Michigan State University's Conflict Resolution Program: Setting expectations and resolving conflicts. In D. H. Wulff & A. E. Austin (Eds.), *Paths to the professoriate: Strategies for enriching the preparation of future faculty* (pp. 250–263). San Francisco: Jossey-Bass.

Levine, A. (2000). *Higher education at a crossroads.* Earl Pullias Lecture in Higher Education, Los Angeles: Center for Higher Education Policy Analysis, Rossier School of Education, University of Southern California.

Lovitts, B. E. (2004). Research on the structure and process of graduate education: Retaining students. In D. H. Wulff & A. E. Austin (Eds.), *Paths to the professoriate: Strategies for enriching the preparation of future faculty* (pp. 115–136). San Francisco: Jossey-Bass.

Marincovich, M., Prostko, J., & Stout, F. (Eds.). (1998). *The professional development of graduate teaching assistants.* Bolton, MA: Anker.

Menges, R. J., & Associates. (1999). *Faculty in new jobs: A guide to settling in, becoming established, and building institutional support.* San Francisco: Jossey-Bass.

Nerad, M., Aanerud, R., & Cerny, J. (2004). "So you want to become a professor!": Lessons from PhDs–Ten Years Later study. In D. H. Wulff & A. E. Austin (Eds.), *Paths to the professoriate: Strategies for enriching the preparation of future faculty* (pp. 137–158). San Francisco: Jossey-Bass.

Nyquist, J. D., Abbott, R. D., Wulff, D. H., & Sprague, J. (Eds.). (1991). *Preparing the professoriate of tomorrow to teach: Selected readings in TA training* (pp. 295–312). Dubuque: Kendall Hunt.

Nyquist, J. D., Manning, L., Wulff, D. H., Austin, A. E., Sprague, J., Fraser, P. K., Calcagno, C., & Woodford, B. (1999). On the road to becoming a professor: The graduate student experience. *Change, 31*(3), 18–27.

Nyquist, J. D., & Woodford, B. (2000). *Re-envisioning the Ph.D.: What concerns do we have?* Seattle: Center for Instructional Development and Research and the University of Washington.

Nyquist, J. D., Woodford, B. J., & Rogers, D. L. (2004). Re-envisioning the Ph.D.: A challenge for the twenty-first century. In D. H. Wulff & A. E. Austin (Eds.), *Paths to the professoriate: Strategies for enriching the preparation of future faculty* (pp. 194–216). San Francisco: Jossey-Bass.

Nyquist, J. D., & Wulff, D. H. (Eds.). (1992). *Preparing teaching assistants for instructional roles: Supervising TAs in communication* (pp. 100–113). Annandale, VA: Speech Communication Association.

Pruitt-Logan, A. S., & Gaff, J. G. (2004). Preparing future faculty: Changing the culture of doctoral education. In D. H. Wulff & A. E. Austin (Eds.), *Paths to the professoriate: Strategies for enriching the preparation of future faculty* (pp. 177–193). San Francisco: Jossey-Bass.

Rice, R. E. (1996). *Making a place for the new American scholar.* New Pathways Inquiry No. 1. Washington, DC: American Association for Higher Education.

Rice, R., Sorcinelli, M., & Austin, A. E. (2000). *Heeding new voices: Academic careers for a new generation.* New Pathways Working Papers Series No. 7. Washington, DC: American Association for Higher Education.

Smith, S. E., Willms, D. G., & Johnson, N. A. (Eds.). (1997). *Nurtured by knowledge: Learning to do participation action research.* New York: Apex Press.

Sorcinelli, M. D., & Austin, A. E. (1992). *Developing new and junior faculty.* New Directions for Teaching and Learning, No. 50. San Francisco: Jossey-Bass.

Strand, K. J., Cutforth, N., Stoecker, R., Marullo, S., & Donohue, P. (Eds.). (2000). *Community-based research and higher education: Principles and practices.* San Francisco: Jossey–Bass.

Strand, K., Marullo, S., Cutforth, N., Stoecker, R., & Donohue, P. (2003). Principles of best practice for community-based research. *Michigan Journal of Community Service, 9*(3), 15–15.

Stringer, E. T. (1999). *Action research.* (2nd ed.). Thousand Oaks, CA: Sage.

Tierney, W. G., & Bensimon, E. M. (1996). *Community and socialization in academe.* Albany: SUNY Press.

Trower, C. A., Austin, A. E., & Sorcinelli, M. D. (May, 2001). Paradise lost: How the academy converts enthusiastic recruits into early-career doubters. *AAHE Bulletin, 53*(9), 3–6.

Van Maanen, J. (1976). Breaking in: Socialization to work. In R. Dubin (Ed.), *Handbook of work, organization, and society* (pp. 67–130). Chicago: Rand-McNally College Publishing.

Walker, G. E. (2004). The Carnegie Initiative on the Doctorate: Creating stewards of the discipline. In D. H. Wulff & A. E. Austin (Eds.), *Paths*

    to the Professoriate: Strategies for Enriching the Preparation of Future Faculty (pp. 236–249). San Francisco: Jossey-Bass.
Weisbuch, R. (2004). Toward a Reponsive PhD: New partnerships, paradigms, practices, and people. In D. H. Wulff & A. E. Austin (Eds.), *Paths to the professoriate: Strategies for enriching the preparation of future faculty* (pp. 217–235). San Francisco: Jossey-Bass.
Wulff, D. H., & Austin, A. E. (Eds.). (2004). *Paths to the professoriate: Strategies for enriching the preparation of future faculty.* San Francisco: Jossey-Bass.
Wulff, D. H., Austin, A. E., Nyquist, J. D., & Sprague, J. (2004). The development of graduate students as teaching scholars: A four-year longitudinal study. In D. H. Wulff & A. E. Austin (Eds.), *Paths to the professoriate: Strategies for enriching the preparation of future faculty.* San Francisco: Jossey-Bass.
Zuber-Skerrit, O. (Ed.). (1996). *New directions in action research.* London: Falmer.

Chapter Sixteen

Let Us Speak

Including Students' Voices in the Public Good of Higher Education

Stephen John Quaye

In this chapter, I argue for the value of capitalizing on students' voices as a means of engaging them in the public good of higher education. I open with a personal experience that enabled me to see the necessity of listening to students' perspectives and experiences in order to fulfill higher education's public good. Next, I define the public good and note my responsibility to it. I then outline how students develop a voice for the public good and their role in fulfilling it. Finally, I offer some concluding comments on the public good. Throughout this chapter, I also repeatedly mention three smaller subthemes within the overarching theme of voice: (1) the public good demands a more diverse and inclusive faculty, (2) the public good necessitates a keen attention to students' voices, and (3) the public good revolves around public intellectuals who connect their practice to the needs of people in society.

Personal Experience of the Public Good

I recently attended a brown bag discussion on the public good of higher education presented by Adrianna Kezar and Guilbert Hentschke, faculty members at the University of Southern California (USC) where I recently began my tenure as a doctoral student. I walked into the room a few minutes after the presentation had begun, took an empty seat in the back, and quickly scanned the faces in the room searching for other persons of color. I have engaged in this common routine for as long as I can remember. Though USC has the second most racially and ethnically diverse undergraduate enrollment among top-tier, private institutions in the nation (Burgin, 2004), my tendencies to search for other people "like me" in the room remain strong, often unconscious. I have attended predominantly white educational institutions my entire educational experience. USC's blossoming ethnic diversity is a far cry from my homogeneous K–12, undergraduate, and graduate experiences. Being the only African American student, or person of color for that matter, in the vast majority of my classes up until now, I frequently pondered the notion of participation in America's professed egalitarian society. Yet it was not until this presentation that I began to think about this in terms of "public" and "good."

I am not certain who held the title of "faculty," "administrator," or "staff" at this particular discussion; nonetheless, I recall perhaps only one faculty member of color. This astounded me. I began to wonder, "If USC is so much more diverse than Miami University of Ohio (where I obtained my master's degree) or James Madison University (my undergraduate alma mater), then should there not be a greater percentage of faculty of color at this institution?" The number of faculty of color across higher education institutions in the United States is abysmally low. In fact, in a recent publication titled "The Road Ahead: Improving Diversity in Graduate Education," William Tierney, Dean Campbell, and George Sanchez (2004) argue for the necessity of increasing the number of graduate students of color who go on to assume faculty positions. The authors specifically noted: "Higher education ought not to differ from the rest of American society: those who participate in postsecondary education should reflect the demographic changes that are occurring in the United States. Yet one of the more vexing problems for many faculty and administrators who work in higher education has been the continued under-representation of faculty of color" (p. 1).

Higher education cannot fulfill its vow to the public good unless it amplifies its commitment to increasing its number of junior and tenured faculty of color. An increasingly multiracial and multiethnic American democracy demands that a more diverse group of scholars educate students and support them in developing their voices with respect to their cultural backgrounds.

Though the paucity of faculty of color in the room troubled me, I was even more disconcerted when Kezar and Hentschke opened the floor for questions and discussion at the conclusion of their presentation. I immediately noticed the lack of student voice and participation in this segment. I listened to interesting commentary from the faculty, staff, and administrators in the room on key issues such as the extent to which higher education is a public good; the irony of the social stratification that both an exposure to education and a lack of opportunity to education produces; the neoliberalist philosophy that views higher education in terms of its profit, competitive nature, and relation to the market and economy (Kezar, 2004; Stromquist, 2002); and ways to measure higher education's societal benefit. Yet I felt silenced, overcome by my inability to engage in this timely and critical discussion. Why did I not contribute by offering my perspectives on this topic? Why did I allow those who held more power than I control my behavior? Why did I as a doctoral student, four years removed from securing my own faculty position, return to my undergraduate days where my professors commonly rewarded students' passivity and conformity? Why did I feel so intimidated in this environment, so intimidated that I could not even adequately organize the thoughts in my head? Why did I not feel comfortable exercising my right to free speech?

As I left the discussion an hour and a half later, my feelings of inadequacy and fear turned into anger as I reflected on squandering an opportunity to interject my views. Though I still have no concrete answers to my abovementioned queries, I did make a valuable observation about the lack of student voice in that particular discussion on the public good of higher education. Therefore, when one of the editors asked me if I would like to write a chapter for this text, I seized the opportunity. I did not want to again allow my voice as a student to remain unheard, especially in a discussion of the public good, a context where all voices, particularly those that remain often unheard, deserve space, recognition, and merit.

In what follows, I, as a student, argue for the importance of engaging students in this dialogue. As a sensitive, compassionate, African American, heterosexual male, I use my personal narrative to portray how my educational experiences, particularly my graduate experience at Miami University, contributed to my current conceptualization of and passion for the public good of higher education. I also offer examples of how the inclusion of students in these conversations by engaging and caring educators aids in fulfilling the public good. Writing this chapter enabled me to reflect on and come to a more informed understanding of myself and my role in fulfilling higher education's commitment to the public good, and I hope readers use this chapter as a means to reflect on their own lives as students, educators, parents, and community members. Before I continue, it is important that I clarify my conceptualization of the *public good*.

Defining the Public Good

During my two years as a graduate student pursuing my M.S. in college student personnel from Miami University, I became interested in making sure that my future work benefited society. Yet it was not until a meeting with my advisor at USC, Adrianna Kezar, that I began using the terminology *public good*. In two short years at Miami University, I grew and changed immensely as I explored my African American ethnic identity and began to critically think and reflect on ideas from books, authority figures, and the media rather than accepting all knowledge as truth. As I did, I began to recognize and name the vast inequities and injustices brought on individuals simply because of the shade of their skin.

In Miami University's predominantly white context, I did not feel comfortable. There were many days when I could walk across campus and not see any other students of color. I felt isolated, lonely, and awkward; simply put, I felt out of place. In this seemingly public space of the campus, I did not belong. Reflecting on my past and current experiences, for the first time in my life, I was able to name the pain I felt and attribute it to concrete occurrences. That naming process was a critical piece of my personal and intellectual development. As such, I desired to continue my education and become a faculty member so that I could support other students in naming their pain, particularly students of color whose voices and personal selves are often marginalized in largely white contexts. This, in my mind, is the fundamental way I can help shape the public good. If I can aid students in discovering their voices in a nonpatriarchal manner, then together, we can collectively combat the multiple forms of oppression that pervade college and university campuses and American society today. What a humbling, powerful, and significant way to contribute to the public good of higher education!

Allow me to more specifically detail my understanding of the term *public good*. In Chapter Two of this book, Adrianna Kezar pointed out faculty's long-standing role as social critic. Though Cornel West does not explicitly define the *public good* in *The Future of the Race* (Gates & West, 1996), I find his usage of the "public intellectual" similar to that of a social critic, highly relevant in making sense of the public good: "The fundamental role of the public intellectual—distinct from, yet building on, the indispensable work of academics, experts, analysts, and pundits—is to create and sustain high-quality public discourse addressing urgent public problems which enlightens and energizes fellow citizens, prompting them to take public action" (p. 71).

Dovetailing with West's idea of a public intellectual, bell hooks (1995) notes the role of African American intellectuals: "Black intellectuals who choose to do work that addresses the needs and concerns of black liberation struggle, of black folks seeking to decolonize their minds and imaginations, will find no separation has to exist between themselves and other black people from various class backgrounds" (p. 234).

The eloquent words from West and hooks enhance my understanding of the public good. A public good is a public good in the sense that extending it to one person does not mean it cannot be similarly extended to another. In other words, the rights of equality, liberty, free speech, and justice do not disappear or dwindle in size if they are offered to a few people or to an entire society. Therefore, these rights constitute public goods because they involve all citizens and benefit their lives. As West claimed, public intellectuals partner with citizens in addressing challenges to the public good. My definition of a public good connects with Denise Greene and William Trent's assertions that the inclusion of more racially and ethnically diverse voices is a precursor to fulfilling the public good (see Chapter Seven of this book).

Our current capitalistic society and our ideals of democracy often run counterintuitively to each other, for the very notion of capitalism means that some individuals will be "losers" and others "winners." Competition and individualism drive capitalism, not the public good. Capitalism seeks to profit at the expense of others. The white, supremacist, capitalistic, patriarchal culture of American society manifests itself in tension with the public good. The hierarchical structure of society is precisely why many individuals in academe struggle to connect with those outside of it and vice versa, as hooks (1995) insightfully noted. With the power structures that pervade our "democracy," public good is not equally offered to all. Yet this does not mean that we do not strive to fulfill this aim. Accordingly, we must develop a responsibility for moving higher education's focus back to the public good.

Responsibility to the Public Good

I am a privileged citizen. The very fact that I am pursuing my doctoral degree and have the opportunity to write this chapter deems me a privileged member of society. Some would say that with privilege comes an obligation to give in return to others; however, I see this as an incomplete view of responsibility. I do not agree that *solely* with my privilege comes a certain level of responsibility to others. I do, however, argue that it is my *willingness* combined with my *responsibility* to society that enables me to contribute to the public good of higher education. Responsibility void of willingness breeds inaction and cynicism.

Similarly, expecting higher education to simply respond to society's needs is not a complete picture of its duty. In Chapter One, Tony Chambers introduced the notion of the charter between higher education and society. In return for public funding of much of higher education's pursuits and knowledge production, this charter predicated that higher education would contribute positively to society's various communities and prepare an engaged and informed student body who would participate fully in the ideals of American democracy.

It is higher education's willingness merged with its responsibility to society that enables it to fulfill its charter. This is a fuller view of responsibility. With higher education's current movement toward a capitalistic, self-centered agenda, its responsibility to larger society still remains; the willingness is missing. It is this disinclination to respond to the needs of its citizens that I note as the fundamental issue facing colleges and universities in the twenty-first century.

Higher education is a public good when it connects its mission with the ideals of a democracy (for example, freedom and equality of all people regardless of race, gender, or sexuality; equality of opportunity in jobs and education; and participation in democracy by all people) and prepares students who have explored their own values and beliefs in and outside of the classroom as a means of developing their voices to fully take part in this democracy. As Henry Giroux (2002) noted: "Higher education must be safeguarded as a public good against the ongoing attempts to organize and run it like a corporation, because . . . it is one of the few public spaces left where students can learn the power of questioning authority, recover the ideals of engaged citizenship, reaffirm the importance of the public good, and expand their capacities to make a difference" (p. 450).

Surely, if students are to see themselves in this process of the public good, educators must provide them with multiple opportunities to develop this power of challenging authority and exploring their beliefs. In essence, this describes their ability to develop their voices, to which I turn next.

Developing Voice and Resistance for the Public Good

I have always felt different, like I did not belong, in all educational contexts of which I have been a part. I rarely spoke unless asked a direct question by a teacher, for my education socialized me to believe that my voice did not matter. It did not take long for me to learn that the perspectives and insights offered by my teachers, the sole authority figures, were of utmost importance. No one ever exposed me to the notion of the public good and higher education's relation to it. At Miami University I began for the first time to critically analyze (Marcuse, 1964) and engage in hooks's (1994) notion of transgressing and Paulo Freire's (1970) problem-posing education, which "bases itself on creativity and stimulates true reflection and action upon reality, thereby responding to the vocation of persons as beings who are authentic only when engaged in inquiry and creative transformation" (p. 84). I often describe this experience as my intellectual awakening, which woke me up from my metaphorical deep sleep and began the development of my voice.

However, in the brown bag discussion, I retreated to my old ways and succumbed to expectations that silenced my voice. Through finding and developing my voice, I began to exemplify my resistance to this neoliberalist underpinning that expects students to simply be consumers and not critically reflect on the product—that is, education—that they purchase (Giroux, 2002; Marcuse, 1964; Stromquist, 2002). As I speak out against and write about the injustices higher education's shift to responding to capitalism and the market poses for society (for example, an amplification of the gap between the privileged and the poor; the commodification of education; and the silencing of discourses that oppose this neoliberalist philosophy, to name a few) (Giroux, 2002), I reveal my voice.

Resistance efforts (Castells, 2004; Hebdige, 1979; Rhoads, 1994) have aided me in understanding my role in the public good. As I reflected on my past educational experiences prior to Miami, I began to understand the concept of hegemony. Hegemony describes a situation created and sustained by the dominant culture (in this case, the neoliberalist assumption that the purpose of higher education is to prepare students for the job market in the aim of profit-making and gaining a competitive advantage over others) in which it exerts its influence in ways that seem normal and natural. The key characteristic of hegemony is that those subordinate groups who do not necessarily agree with the views of this ruling order "buy into" it because they believe the dominant culture's power is legitimate and natural (Hebdige, 1979).

Neoliberalism has become so common, and hence, natural and normal, that those who challenge it are seen as "fanatics" or "extremists." Hegemony retains its power because it requires the consent of the subordinated class. After all, as this hegemony asks, what other way of life is there than to seek the utmost wealth for one's individual purposes? As Giroux (2002) articulated: "Neoliberalism wraps itself in what appears to be an unassailable appeal to common sense" (p. 428). Nelly Stromquist (2002) analyzed hegemony in the context of globalization when she wrote: "Opposition by NGOs [nongovernmental organizations] to globalization processes is often misunderstood, particularly by the media, which tends, for instance, to describe the work of small groups protesting unwanted economic policies as the machination of anarchists bent on unproductive disorder" (p. 12). So, when President Bush states that those who oppose the war on terror have sided with the terrorists and are unpatriotic, he is perpetuating this hegemony. When I do not challenge such a claim, I am also preserving the hegemony. It is precisely these "lunatics" or "anarchists" that warrant keen attention, for these are the individuals (many times students) who seek to subvert the cunning hand of hegemony and shift higher education and society's focus to the public good.

African Americans are often excluded from reaping the so-called gains of higher education's alliance with capitalism. When I observed those African American individuals in my educational experience who were cast aside because of the color of their skin and their lack of economic privileges that I was fortunate enough to have, I wondered what role they could play in the public good. Did they not deserve to have their voices heard as well?

At Miami University for the first time in my education, my educators expected that I think critically, challenge authority figures, and express my views in a classroom context. It was in my initial Student Development Theory class that for the first time an educator asked me to tell my story. I then realized that my educators and peers valued my personal experiences not only in that class but in all the others during my graduate experience, which provided me with ample opportunities to have my story heard. My educators at Miami, in effect, linked higher education to the public good. A public good in our American democracy is that all people have a right to speak. Higher education should encourage this societal good through providing room for students' voices in the classroom. Not doing so oppresses and dehumanizes them (Freire, 1970) and takes away one of their fundamental rights as human beings in a democracy.

I am not neutral nor do I pretend to be. Similarly, education is not a neutral endeavor but is subjective and political. As such, when we do not encourage students to speak in the classroom, we make a political decision, just as we make a political decision when we do provide opportunities for students to share their stories. How can we expect students to fulfill the aims of responding to the needs of people in society if their educators have not asked them to tell their stories as a means of developing their ideas? How can students respond to and develop compassion for the needs of others if they have not had opportunities to hear their peers' views in the classroom? To become full participants in the democracy, students must interject their voices into classroom discussions (developing voice) to build up the skills necessary to challenge neoliberalism's basic tenets (developing resistance) and respond to the public good. This process is essential in enabling them to cultivate their voices and resist the passive and acquiescent method of education that is commonly expected of them.

Students' Role in the Public Good

I have listened to many politicians and pop culture icons in the media claim that today's students are passive and uninterested in participating in bettering the American democracy. I am reminded of the many conversations with my dad where he began with that all-too-common phrase I am sure those reading have heard as well: "Young people these days don't . . ." Yet Giroux (2002) paints a different picture of students in his analysis of higher education and the public in "Neoliberalism, Corporate Culture, and the Promise of Higher Education: The University as a Democratic Public Sphere." In this essay, Giroux traces many forms of student involvement in democracy such as protesting and responding to the money-driven, competitive, individualistic, and market-oriented forces now shaping higher education. Specifically, he noted: "Students recognize that the corporate model of leadership shaping higher education fosters a narrow sense of responsibility, agency, and public values because it lacks a vocabulary for providing guidance on matters of justice, equality, fairness, equity, and freedom" (p. 454). When I witnessed the number of young people protesting at the 2004 Republican National Convention, or when I engaged in discussions outside of class with my peers about ways to involve and educate ourselves on the crucial issues in the 2004 presidential election, I know that students are not apathetic about the political and public sphere shaping higher education. In fact, the students with whom I have spoken crave a space to insert their voices into a discussion that often belittles or ignores them. This, in my mind, is one way students connect higher education with the public good.

The brown bag discussion on the public good did not provide the public space for students' voices in the discussion. Perhaps my peers and I did not have anything to say on the matter (which I highly doubt, given our past discussions). Maybe we did not understand how to insert our voices into the conversation or were afraid to do so, as I was. In "The Civic Mission of Higher Education: From Outreach to Engagement," Scott London (2001) claimed that "bringing students together in a structured setting to explore pressing social and political questions brings about not only a heightened awareness of the issues but also a richer and more complex understanding of their contribution as citizens. In some cases, it also leads to greater involvement in campus and community affairs" (p. 4).

I cannot count the numerous times during my graduate assistantship in the Office of Learning Assistance at Miami University that I engaged in a discussion of politics and other societal and global concerns with the other graduate assistants in the office. Though this was not a structured setting per se, it enabled us to develop our values, beliefs, and voices to critically analyze how to effect change among the public.

As London (2001) noted, "for students to become actively engaged in the process [of discussing political and social concerns], they have to feel that their voices matter and that the conclusions they arrive at carry some weight" (p. 7). London's remarks dovetail with that of hooks's (1994) notion of education as the practice of freedom. In my classes at Miami, I knew that my voice mattered. I knew that faculty did not simply ask for my opinion to appease me but because they honestly valued it. As a result, I learned to value it myself. Furthermore, in my less structured discussions with other graduate students, I knew that they also respected and expected to hear my views. Since the telling of my narrative was reinforced in multiple settings, I learned that my voice counted, and that has been the most noteworthy process in enabling me to understand my role in the public good.

Students play a special role in the public good because, like me, they often cling to an idealized, yet not naïve, sense of change. The debilitating forces of society have not yet shattered our hopes and dreams. Students connect higher education to the public good when they challenge authority and readings in the classroom, serve the community when they participate in service-learning opportunities outside of class, organize protests and resistance efforts, defy the commodification of education by demanding that the curriculum respond to their cultural needs, participate in study abroad programs to learn more about the impacts of neoliberalism globally, and so on. Moreover, students may hold a hunger strike, write letters to the editor in school newspapers advocating for domestic partner benefits to couples of the same sex, sleep on the lawn outside of the president's office to protest low wages of staff, explore admissions access to their college or university, participate in a bilingual education program at a Los Angeles community college, or organize a rally to discuss the exploitation of graduate student employees. In taking these actions, students refuse to accept neoliberalism's aim of focusing on the individual and ignoring the public good.

Educators should pay special attention to these resistance efforts and not merely label them as trivial or as ways students are "being difficult." Resistance efforts should never be taken lightly, for in them, students are often trying to exert their influence on a hegemonic system that refuses to see them as human beings but instead as pawns who can be bought, commodified, and exploited. Educators can purposefully facilitate students' understanding of their participation in the public good and their oppositional efforts through providing forums for students to pose questions and share their reflections and experiences with one another (Mathews, n.d.; London, 2001; "The Work of the Kettering Foundation," 2003).

Conclusion

In the opening of this chapter, I noted the lack of faculty of color present at the brown bag discussion on education and the public good. In the monograph on improving the diversity in graduate studies, Tierney, Campbell, and Sanchez (2004) emphasized: "American society is increasingly diverse. As the country becomes more diverse, however, inequities remain. Latinos and African Americans are disproportionately poorer than their White counterparts, for example, and they are less likely to vote and to participate in the public sphere. A key challenge, then, is to ensure that everyone has the possibility to be full participants in the United States of the twenty-first century" (p. 1).

Unfortunately, not everyone (particularly, people of color and those without economic advantages) has the opportunity to fully partake in American democracy. At times, when I envision my doctoral studies over the next four years, I become frightened and overwhelmed. As I begin to ponder my role as a future academician, I recognize the seriousness of my doctoral studies and the potent and influential role of a faculty member in higher education. I realize the growing cynicism among some of my African American peers because of educators who have not committed themselves to becoming public intellectuals like bell hooks and Cornel West (Brown, Kingston, & Levine, 2004; Gates & West, 1996; hooks, 1995). Given the lack of faculty of color on college and university campuses, I am terrified to enter that realm in the near future, for fear of personal failure, but more significantly, for fear of failing to fulfill or losing sight of my philosophy of connecting my teaching, service, research, and scholarship to the public good in ways that refashion society in a more egalitarian manner.

In writing this chapter, I reflected on my feelings and fears that prevented me from speaking during the brown bag presentation. As an African American, I still struggle daily with my own self-esteem and confidence, despite my current place in life. This ongoing, internal struggle will likely be the most significant limiting factor to my continued success. Given the pervasive negative portrayals of African Americans in the media and the daily assaults on black beauty, intelligence, significance, and humanity, it is still challenging for me to resist those false notions and display my intelligence. I believed I did not have an adequate perspective to offer in a discussion about the public good. I now realize that by remaining quiet, I did not foster the opportunity for others to hear my voice and allowed the discussion to be dominated by those in academe who are regularly heard—the faculty.

This will likely be my initial entrance into the public discourse on the public good. As a student, it is essential that I contribute to this dialogue and not continue to allow my voice to remain unheard. Likewise, faculty members cannot permit their students' speech in the classroom to remain hushed for fear of losing control or uneasiness with facilitating a discussion that at times may drift from the prescribed topic of the day or the textbook. One of the paramount ways to realize higher education's charter to society is to provide the space for students to develop their voices as a means of also participating in the public good. Not doing so exploits students, limits their capabilities, and in turn oppresses them by not enabling them to develop Freire's (1970) notion of praxis—personal reflection combined with action.

I began this undertaking by stressing the necessity of using higher education, and more specifically the classroom, as one avenue for enabling students to develop their voices. In defining the public good as a societal benefit that is rightfully and equally extended to all, I have argued that not affording students their right to speak in the classroom precludes them from being full participants in democracy. Ultimately, I have noted that students involve themselves in this process through developing their voices and defying the current neoliberalist movement in higher education that ignores its responsibility to the public good.

I will close this chapter with a thought-provoking quote by Pastor Martin Niemöller[1]: "First they came for the socialists, and I did not speak out because I was not a socialist. Then they came for the trade unionists, and I did not speak out because I was not a trade unionist. Then they came for the Jews, and I did not speak out because I was not a Jew. Then they came for me, and there was no one left to speak for me."

Who will speak out for the public good of higher education if its members do not? Who will speak out for students, like me, if we do not speak out for ourselves? Who will create avenues for students to speak out if we in academe do not invite them to speak? In this era, neoliberalism and those who embrace its tenets are coming for those committed to the public good of higher education. Unless we collectively forge mechanisms to resist neoliberalism's commodification, individualistic tendencies, capitalistic, profit-driven desires, its game of winners and losers, and its "brand-naming" of education and develop voices that speak out against its influences, there will be no one left to speak out against it. We must combine our responsibility as privileged citizens with our willingness and renew the public's confidence that what we do in academe is beneficial to the common needs of all citizens.

---

[1]After searching for the whereabouts of this quotation, I found that there are many variations of this statement from Niemöller with one version opening with: "First they came for the communists, and I did not speak out because I was not a communist."

References

Brown, D., Kingston, R., & Levine, P. (2004). What is "public" about what academics do? *Higher Education Exchange,* 17–29.

Burgin, A. (2004, August 25). USC ranks high in diversity. *Daily Trojan,* pp. 1, 10.

Castells, M. (2004). *The power of identity* (2nd ed.). Malden, MA: Blackwell.

Freire, P. (1970). *Pedagogy of the oppressed.* New York: Continuum International.

Gates, H. L., Jr., & West, C. (1996). *The future of the race.* New York: Vintage Books.

Giroux, H. A. (2002). Neoliberalism, corporate culture, and the promise of higher education: The university as a democratic public sphere. *Harvard Educational Review,* 72(4), 425–462.

Hebdige, D. (1979). *Subculture: The meaning of style.* London: Routledge.

hooks, b. (1994). *Teaching to transgress: Education as the practice of freedom.* New York: Routledge.

hooks, b. (1995). *Killing rage: Ending racism.* New York: Henry Holt & Company.

Kezar, A. (2004). Obtaining integrity? Reviewing and examining the charter between higher education and society. *Review of Higher Education,* 27(4), 429–459.

London, S. (2001). *The civic mission of higher education: From outreach to engagement.* Dayton, OH: Kettering Foundation.

Marcuse, H. (1964). *One-dimensional man.* Boston: Beacon Press.

Mathews, D. (n.d.). *Creating more public space in higher education.* Washington, DC: Council on Public Policy Education.

Rhoads, R. A. (1994). *Coming out in college: The struggle for a queer identity.* Westport, CT: Bergin & Garvey.

Stromquist, N. P. (2002). *Education in a globalized world: The connectivity of economic power, technology, and knowledge.* Lanham, MD: Rowman & Littlefield.

Tierney, W. G., Campbell, C. D., & Sanchez, G. J. (Eds.). (2004). *The road ahead: Improving diversity in graduate education.* Los Angeles: Center for Higher Education Policy Analysis.

The work of the Kettering Foundation: An overview. (2003, February). *Kettering Foundation.*

Chapter Seventeen

Presidential Leadership for the Public Good

Martha W. Gilliland

Given the centrality of public good in the history of public higher education, the fact that we are writing a book on higher education for the public good may suggest that we, as leaders, have veered off track. I hope this book inspires others, just as it signals the end of doubt and confusion about what the twenty-first century demands of leaders in higher education. A rekindling of higher education's distinctive and honorable call is needed—a call that summons leaders to deliver a bold response. That response centers in a movement of transformation for public universities as we serve the public good in our communities, our states, this nation, and the world.

I have tried to set a bold, yet careful and deliberate course for the University of Missouri-Kansas City (UMKC). We have made much progress in four years and had some disappointments. As I reflected on both, two leadership principles emerged as central to my leadership in moving UMKC toward a focus on the public good.

The University of Missouri-Kansas City (UMKC)

A vital defining feature for UMKC is that, while our public mission is statewide, we are in a city. In my view, leading a public research university in a city is a special privilege, because cities are where a diverse group of individuals in America resides, cities are where economies are growing, and cities are the domain of the great social issues of our times. And public universities have, as their core mission, to educate mainstream America, drive economic development, and support social progress.

UMKC has 14,200 students in a college of arts and sciences, a conservatory of music, and schools of business and public administration, computing and engineering, education, law, medicine, dentistry, pharmacy, nursing, and biological sciences. In fact, 43 percent of our students are professional or graduate students, an unusual profile for a public research university. UMKC's mission, as defined by the University of Missouri Board of Curators, is to focus programming in the visual and performing arts, health sciences, and urban affairs. Of our degree-seeking students for whom ethnic origin is known, approximately 32 percent are minorities or nonresident aliens. Of the total, 12 percent are African American, 6 percent are of Asian-Pacific Islander descent, 4 percent are Hispanic, 1 percent is American Indian-Alaskan Native, and 9 percent are nonresident aliens.

Leadership Principles

As I reflected on the principles that served me well, each relate either to vision or values, to inspiring as a leader with vision, or to reaching inside for a guiding moral principle for decision making as a leader with values. That, in turn, requires knowing yourself.

Vision

Presidential leadership for the public good for me meant that "the public" had to be very present in the expression of the university's vision. Little will unfold relative to the public good if the importance of the public good is not expressed powerfully in the vision for the institution. UMKC's vision is: *A community of learners making the world a better place.* The public good matters in our vision in the word *community,* as we have discovered how much people want to be part of a community working together, and in the phrase *making the world a better place,* as it expresses our relationship to the public.

In *The Creation of the Future: The Role of the American University,* Frank H. T. Rhodes (2001) describes the role of the president as one who "should devote his or her best skills to dream the institution into something new, to challenge its greatness, to elevate its hopes and extend its reach, to energize it to new levels of success and galvanize it to high levels of achievement in every area of its institutional life" (p. 223).

A vision that includes public good was not enough. It also had to be owned by a critical mass of the campus and was essential to our success. Our process of formulating a vision took eighteen months and engaged nearly one thousand people in a somewhat chaotic but creative planning process. This was *not* a consensus-building process, rather we referred to it as an alignment-building process. The leader or, in this case, a group of eighty leaders, "planted a stake in the ground" with a draft vision. That same group then engaged the campus and the community in dialogue sessions about what they thought might be possible within this vision. Over many months, a vision emerged around which people aligned. By the time it emerged, most already owned it because they had already explored for themselves what might be possible in their work in the context of that vision. At the time this process seemed painfully slow; in retrospect, fostering campus ownership of the public good as a reason to exist was essential.

Equally important, I had to take a stand for the vision over and over and over (and over) again. As a campus changes, the old culture is like an immune system trying to dominate and expel the new vision. That immune system operates unconsciously, voluntarily, and relentlessly. Thus, the changes we experienced required the leaders to (1) talk about the vision all the time, literally all day, every day in every meeting and every set of remarks, (2) make decisions from that vision, always using it as the context for the decision, and (3) make clear to others in communications the relationship of decisions to the vision.

The leadership team at the top matters. The leadership team I developed had as their moral compass the public good, in our case a university making the world better. Not all leaders are interested in the public good. Success, defined as real outcomes, depends on a top leadership team that is genuine and transparent in their commitment to the public good. That said, I discovered that when a vision speaks powerfully to the public good, it causes incredible leaders to show up who want to be a part of it, leaders who want to contribute their wisdom, passion, and energy to make the world better. From a personal perspective, I have been extremely fortunate, and I am grateful for the leaders who have shown up at UMKC.

Moreover, the distinction between *accomplishing* the vision versus *fulfilling* the vision was and still is vital. Accomplishing can be prescriptive. Fulfilling is emergent and embraces the creativity of others. Success depended on tapping the creative spirit of people and allowing people to design for themselves what actions should be taken to fulfill the vision. Rather than prescribing what is to be, access the wisdom, passion, and creativity of others to produce actions far better than those you might prescribe. On reflection, my biggest successes occurred when I created the "clearing" for others to "show up" with that creativity. People want to make a difference; they want to be part of something that makes the world better; they will create to the extent the leaders provide the clearing for it.

Finally, results do matter and they matter a lot. The results that we produced early in the process demonstrated a vision for public good and helped greatly with building momentum. Since alignment around a vision and values requires at least a year or more in a large university, we learned that credibility and momentum depend on results that actually demonstrate the rhetoric about the public good. We identified twelve breakthrough projects on which to produce results quickly even as we carried out the dialogues about vision and values. For example, because we are in a city, it was natural for the Center for the City to be launched as a breakthrough project, which is designed to leverage the intellectual and human resources of the university with the challenges, issues, and needs of the urban core. Its advisory board is comprised of ten UMKC faculty and administrators and an equal number of civic leaders. The center engages students, faculty, staff, and the Kansas City community in partnership connections, research projects, and student learning opportunities.

Values

The personal impact of leading an institution that is always looking to leadership for guidance can only be felt from experience. A set of core values is all you have ultimately for guidance. Spending the time to develop them, communicate them, and live them was even more important than I thought. While vision inspires people to act, values are just as important in inspiring discussion about how to act. This is obvious to most leaders, but rarely are we able to bring values alive in a public institution.

At UMKC our core values were developed using the same process of iterative alignment as was the vision. By the time we finished the dialogues about a set of values, there was "ownership." The value that has proven the most powerful is open and candid communication. As we faced the withdrawal of state revenue support for our institution, relying on that value caused us to communicate the flaws, mistakes, special deals, and issues with the budget and the budgeting system. That, in turn, produced the trust that is such a vital element in serving the public good. In fact, a cross-campus team redesigned the budgeting processes in accordance with the values and won a national award for that design.

Values can be used in a destructive fashion, and we were guilty of that occasionally. We learned that values are to be used to create possibilities, not to judge. We were effective when we used the values to create discussion about what might be possible if we behaved in accordance with the values or if we redesigned a procedure in accordance with the values. The university's values came to life, quite literally, in conversations about possibilities. We got into trouble with values when we succumbed to the temptation to judge someone's behavior as out of step with the values and, therefore, judged their ideas as invalid. Several of our values include respect, collaboration, and accountability. When designing a process, a procedure, a goal, or when considering how to handle a situation, ask what might be possible if we (or I) were accountable, demonstrated respect, collaborated, and so on. The conversation that results produces remarkable creativity and outcomes.

The domain of leading for the public good that we still struggle the most with is alignment of management practices, vision, and behaviors with the values. Moving the public good into the architecture and infrastructure is a long-term proposition, but it must occur if the public good focus for the institution is to be sustained. Reward systems, promotion guidelines, performance evaluation processes, budgeting, planning, revenue development, compensation guidelines, procurement, technology plans, scheduling, and the many other business, administrative, facilities, human resources, and academic processes that exist in a university eventually must undergo scrutiny framed by the question: What might be possible if this process were aligned with the vision and values? At UMKC, we have only begun to examine management practices in the domain of what might be possible. We do know because of the award-winning budget process that the scrutiny and change are worth doing.

Finally, for me, all of the above depends on knowing myself. Only if you know yourself can you stay the course through the challenges and breakdowns that are inevitable. Kahlil Gibran (1994) said, "Self is a sea boundless and measureless." However, we all have beaches and reefs with which we are quite familiar. The power that resides in leadership positions is dangerous in its ability to seduce leaders into believing they are right. The demands made on our time, character, and courage provide further psychological justification for "being right" and having it our way. Thus, the ultimate challenge in leadership for the public good is the challenge to examine one's own life all the time. Yet that challenge is also the ultimate opportunity and privilege for, as Socrates said, "the unexamined life is not worth living." In the domain of leadership for the public good, make no mistake about it—a leader does have the privilege of examining her life.

External Challenges

Many challenges external to our individual universities act against our work inside. In particular, the pressure for faculty to be judged successful by their professional associations rather than by their impact on the public good is enormous. Adjusting our internal policies can help, but this breakthrough requires a change much greater than that which can be brought about by any one university. Secondly, the shift of the cost of public higher education from the general taxpayer to the students and their families is a shift away from the public good. Again, no one university can handle this challenge. Indeed, it is unlikely that any one state can shift it. This requires a federal initiative, but as leaders of higher education we can impact that conversation dramatically.

Conclusion

For this leader, the term *higher education* is synonymous with the phrase *higher education for the public good*. If we are not educating people and creating knowledge for the public good, then what are we doing? No one has much doubt that American democracy depends on educated citizens, the American economy depends on the discovery of new knowledge, and the human spirit requires nourishment from the arts and the humanities. Not so obvious is the *how*—how to bring about a powerful conversation among leaders and how to work inside our campuses as leaders such that outcomes shift to the public good.

References
Gibran, K. (1994). *The prophet*. New York: Knopf.
Rhodes, F.H.T. (2001). *The creation of the future: The role of the American university*. Ithaca, NY: Cornell University Press.

Part Six

Concluding Thoughts on the Public Good

Chapter Eighteen

Creating Dialogue
A New Charter and Vision of the Public Good
Adrianna J. Kezar

Higher education has traditionally been a social institution. As noted in earlier chapters, social institutions have long-standing missions, supporting values, and a specific historical pattern of rights and responsibilities that are constantly renegotiated. Since the founding of Harvard in 1636, there has been a social charter between higher education and society. From time to time, the charter was renegotiated, and a new version of the charter dominated. For over two decades, the trends and forces described in Chapter Two (as well as other chapters) have been at the forefront of conversations about the new social charter for the twenty-first century. The version of the charter promoted by neoliberalists is one that devalues the public service mission of higher education with potentially devastating effects for society. We must make sure that the voices emphasizing the public good, some of which were outlined earlier, are part of the discussion and negotiation.

How can we create a new charter for higher education? I believe that no one person can or should define the public good. Instead, this is a collective responsibility. As a result, society needs intentionally designed conversations or dialogues about how higher education can serve the public good. Having read this volume, you may think there is a fairly clear picture of how the public good is (or should be) served, or you may resonate with a particular voice described in one of the chapters. Certainly, we have tried to present a set of ideas for what we think might make up the elements of a new vision for the way higher education can serve the public good. Some may feel I am abdicating my voice or the voice of the metamovement by saying that a new vision has not emerged. Others may feel that I am being disingenuous since the authors in this book have expressed concern about the industrial model of higher education and provided ideas from various movements about re-creating a broader reaching social charter, emphasizing a wider range of benefits over only those that are individual and economic. Indeed, the purpose of the book was to interject another perspective in the dialogue that has been silenced in recent years or that has not been encouraged as much as other dialogues. The emerging vision presented in Chapter Three is one we feel should be described and articulated at dialogues about the role higher education might play in society.

Ultimately, we believe in the importance of deliberation in a democratic society and for a collective process for defining the public good. In Chapter Three, I noted that various movements, such as service-learning, are encouraging for a new vision but are not enough as they rarely engage society in a reciprocal conversation. Society's commitment and input are needed to complete the vision; the vision cannot be derived only from higher education. I also noted that it is likely that these various movements will be thwarted by economic interests that are quite powerful, if larger networks and support for a public charter are not garnered. The notion of the importance of dialogue has also been voiced by many chapter authors such as David Mathews (trustees), James Votruba (institutional leaders), David Longanecker (policymakers), and Tony Chambers. The purpose of this chapter is to review some strategies for establishing dialogues and to articulate a set of questions (based on the ideas presented in this book) for consideration within these dialogues. The dialogue and questions described in this chapter complement those offered in other chapters for specific groups such as institutional leaders or policymakers. In this chapter, I suggest how to frame a broader dialogue among various interested groups in society. In summary, part of the work of building the role of higher education for the public good is to create dialogues about the social and public purposes of higher education. Developing dialogues also expands the network involved in defining and creating higher education for the public good.

Why does a discussion of the charter between higher education and society matter? The social charter is the foundation of higher education institutions' missions and values, and it affects choices made by all individuals in the system of higher education from policymakers to parents to faculty to students. For example, if policymakers and the public do not have a clear picture of why investment in higher education matters, including the social and public benefits, other public policy priorities may end up gaining more support than higher education. Critics suggest the following may result if a divestment from higher education is made: growing economic and social disparities, increased expenditure on social welfare programs, inability to compete in an increasingly technological world economy, declining quality of living, and diminished civic engagement. Also, policymakers need to understand the potential dangers of relying on private and corporate sources for supporting higher education as has been the practice and encouragement over the last two decades. Books such as Bok's *Universities in the Marketplace* (2003) demonstrate how corporate values have resulted in secrecy and corruption in research, conflicts of interest, cheating among college students, and commitment conflict among faculty, to name a few.

A Process for Rethinking the Charter

Two approaches have been offered for rethinking the social charter, both of which focus on creating an open dialogue between groups within higher education and interested parties in society. This book was designed with both of the following approaches in mind.

Derek Bok (1982) suggests a comprehensive strategy for creating a new vision of higher education and support to implement the vision. First, since higher education is a decentralized system, planning or policy will be less important than leadership. Presidents and boards can rally both human and financial resources across the nation. Yet such leadership is becoming rarer as government spending lags and presidents spend all their time lobbying and fundraising. Professional associations can influence the nature of dialogues, asking questions about the public good among various groups such as faculty or administrators. Foundations can alter funding priorities to focus on areas that serve the public good. And government can have a significant influence by implementing policies such as forgiving loans for students who enter professions that serve the public good or altering funding patterns for research. Each of these groups needs to be brought into the dialogue about the public good, since the problem is systemic and complex, crossing the entire enterprise. A systems approach was represented in the outline of this book in which various groups and levels of the enterprise have been included in the conceptualization of the issue. Bok's approach could be characterized as structural in which we can create a new vision by reoriented goals, providing appropriate rewards and resources, and developing a plan.

Hollander and Hartley (2000) suggest that a national network or metamovement needs to be created. In order to develop such a movement, groups need to understand that they share a common set of values, they need to understand the opposition, and they need to interact to form an agenda or vision. Dialogue is critical throughout this process. This political approach is also represented within this volume through the writings that encourage the splintered movements to see they have a common vision. Chapter Three, focused on creating a metamovement, was the main articulation of this approach. In addition, Chapter Two focused on outlining the opposition; many chapters also supported this goal, including Chapters Eleven and Twelve. The book itself is an attempt to provide interaction of ideas across the various, often isolated movements. We hope that those of you who are passionate about service-learning might now also consider the importance of community-based research or civic engagement. Those interested in civic engagement might also rethink the importance of public service. We hope that a metamovement is growing around the public good, in opposition to a purely industrial model of higher education. Yet we worry about creating a political and dialectical atmosphere in which varying ideas about the public good are not considered. Although political support is important for building a voice and platform, it can also result in breaking down genuine dialogue and collaboration toward a shared vision of the public good. Admittedly, a shared vision is difficult to develop, but one that is informed by more voices and perspectives is possible.

Both a structural approach and political approach are likely needed to move forward in the creation of a new charter. Whichever path is taken, dialogue is the key underlying strategy. A discussion about the social charter is critical for developing a new vision related to higher education's mission and values. Dialogues about the social charter need to consider many important questions. The first dialogue may engage a set of questions about public policy, public support, and public understanding related to the social charter:

1. At what level should higher education institutions adapt to market forces and to what level should they retain historic functions and longer term public interests? What aspects of the social and public missions of higher education need to be maintained? What traditional academic values are necessary to support these social and public missions? How can we create a social charter for higher education that honors economic, social, private, and public goods? Should human and community priorities maintain equal importance to the other goals or outcomes of higher education as they have in the past?

2. What are some of the historic social functions that need to be considered in this dialogue? How can new social functions, such as educating for a diverse democracy and creating reciprocal partnerships with community, be incorporated?

3. To what degree should higher education become private and what is the impact of this shift? Is public higher education part of the state or is it independent? What type of autonomy or regulation should be exerted?

4. How can we reconcile market-oriented values with traditional academic values? For example, within the traditional academic environment, academic freedom, access and equity, excellence and integrity, and dedication to inquiry are important to meet the public mission. Which values should be upheld and reinforced as higher education partners with other groups representing different value systems? How can they be maintained?

5. How can we think about private and public in complex ways that still maintain the social role of higher education? It is important not to completely dichotomize public and private or social and economic interests. Various studies have illustrated how private goods benefit the public in substantial ways, such as higher salaries and stability of employment, improved health of college graduates, and better consumer decision making among college graduates.

6. To what degree is the dilemma of values and priorities internal and institutional rather than external and corporate?

7. How can the public be engaged in a reciprocal relationship around the social charter?

8. How can current movements be aligned and a collective vision of higher education for the public good be developed?

In addition to the broader set of questions around balancing public, social, private, and economic interests related to the social charter, several focused issues need attention and can be an emphasis at the later dialogues when there is some consensus around broader issues of the public good:

1. Perhaps the most influential area that can affect the trend toward a more public and social charter is the financing of higher education. Although multiple influences shaped the current charter, declining finances and encouragement to seek external, private sources was the major influence. How can federal, state, and local legislators, alumni, foundations, and parents work together to rethink their support of public higher education? Yet the entire burden cannot be on the taxpayers and public to simply provide higher education with more money to meet the social charter. What choices should institutions make related to priorities to ensure the entire mission and social charter in higher education are met with limited funds?

2. Since the corporatization of governance and leadership has affected the mission and values of the academy significantly, these areas need attention. How can the trend toward corporatization of governance and leadership in colleges and universities be reversed? The Association of Governing Boards of Colleges and Universities could play a role in working with legislators to reconcile business and academic values around the administration of campuses.

3. Trends toward privatization of research need to be addressed. How might the general public be better served if research discoveries remained public rather than private, commercial enterprises? Should basic or applied social research be a priority over commercial research? How can a system of priorities be established and encouraged? If universities continue commercial research, how do they reconcile the values of academe (knowledge development, long-term

orientation, accountability to society, broad view of worth, peer re-view) with those of industry (profit, short-term orientation, account-ability only to shareholders, narrow view of worth around profit, no peer review)?

4. A tipping-point trend (growing close to that of athletics) might be the growth of part-time and contract faculty. The entrepreneurial work conditions where faculty are encouraged to bring in their own salary, essentially subsidizing their institutional salary without outside grants and contracts, is rampant on some campuses. Faculty have been driven from traditional commitments and are choosing new paths, since the commitment to autonomy, stability, equitable pay, and tenure have been compromised. This change compromises many aspects of the public good from the quality of undergraduate education to the advancement of knowledge in this country. The American Association of University Professors, the National Educa-tion Association, and the American Federation of Teachers should be engaged and brought to the table with administrators and legis-lators who have effected these choices.

5. How can a balanced curriculum representing all disciplines be maintained? How can interdisciplinarity be encouraged? Sev-eral disciplinary societies have issued papers and reports that focus on the importance of the humanities and social sciences for teach-ing, democracy, and knowledge creation. Institutional leadership is needed to support these movements.

6. How can we encourage and support approaches to learning that maintain critical and higher order thinking necessary for cit-izenship? The Association of American Colleges and Universities' American Commitments Project outlines several strategies and ap-proaches that need more attention. Furthermore, several of the movements, community service-learning and learning communi-ties in particular, support relational, higher order, and whole stu-dent learning.

7. In a time of diminishing funds, how do we support the role of college-community partnerships? How can the notion of the engaged campus be institutionalized? How can the notion of collaboration be used in order to create more public service? Regional collaboratives provide some ideas and opportunities for the future.

8. How can conflicts of interest around industry-university partnerships be negotiated? In what circumstances should these

partnerships be engaged? How can they be used to support social or public goals? The Business–Higher Education Forum Report (2001) provides a foundation for such a discussion.

9. How can public policy be developed that support students' entering low-paying careers? How can states lower tuitions for students to ensure access to education and maintain the public good?

These questions will help us to rethink higher education. Yet many of these questions are focused on informed policymakers and leaders and relate to very specific concerns within the academy. The dialogue must also occur among the general public, as well as between the general public and higher education. Howard Bowen's (1982) questions for each of us in society to reflect upon provide a more basic entry point into the discussion of the public good. The answers to these questions may lead ultimately to realizing the kind of social covenant and charter we seek.

- What kind of people do we want our children and grandchildren to be?
- What kind of society do we want them to live in?
- How can we best shape our institutions to nurture those kinds of people and that kind of society?

There will be opposition to answering these questions. Some will argue that the service role (whether as commercially or publicly defined) itself is problematic and that the university should return to being an ivory tower, in which pure research is emphasized, government and private support for research diminished so that teaching can become more prominent again, and service is defined as internal governance. Myself and others writing in this volume do not support such a retreat; the problems of marketization and commercialization need to be confronted without a retreat to a romanticized golden age for universities and colleges in which they primarily focused on the interests of the elites and maintaining the status quo in society.

Furthermore, some individuals herald the triumph of markets and management and the metaphor of higher education as an industry, believing no dialogue is necessary (Zemsky, 1993). They believe this is the only way for higher education to remain a central enterprise within the new world order and to ensure the funds needed to maintain world-class status. They remind us that higher education has always been market driven and this is what has facilitated the innovations that make it the premiere higher education system in the world. In addition, they note that higher education has long been diverted from the teaching mission toward research; vocationalism has been a trend since the early nineteenth century. Yet the historical context reminds us that market forces have never been allowed to operate unfettered. It is this challenge that faces the movement—to be the voice that tempers market forces and engages the nation in a dialogue that will ensure that higher education continues to emphasize the public good, however that is defined.

References

Bok, D. (1982). The corporation on campus: Balancing responsibility and innovation. *Change, 14*(6), 16–25.

Bok, D. (2003). *Universities in the marketplace: The commercialization of higher education.* Princeton, NJ: Princeton University Press.

Bowen, H. (1982). *The state of the nation and the agenda for higher education.* San Francisco: Jossey-Bass.

Business–Higher Education Forum. (2001). *Working together, creating knowledge: The University-Industry Research Collaboration Initiative.* Washington, DC: American Council on Education.

Hollander, E., & Hartley, M. (2000). The civic renewal in higher education: The state of the movement and the need for a national network. In T. Ehrlich (Ed.), *Civic Responsibility and Higher Education* (pp. 345–366). Washington, DC: American Council on Education and Oryx Press.

Zemsky, R. (1993). Consumer markets and higher education. *Liberal Education, 79*(3), 14–18.

Chapter Nineteen

Pondering the Social Charter
Critical Reflection for Leaders

Tony C. Chambers

This volume has been focused on two central questions: *What does society need from higher education?* and *Can higher education deliver it?* These questions are also at the center of the fragile relationship between colleges and universities and the broader publics that they serve and are a part. Throughout this book various authors have considered these questions and offered suggestions about answering these quandaries. In Chapter One, I suggest that multiple informed networks of individuals and groups are forming around an emerging sense of what a diverse democracy should look like and what role higher education could and should play in realizing that new vision. Many of the authors in this volume echoed this observation. In Chapter Eighteen, Kezar stressed that no one movement or even meta movement should define the charter; the dialogue is ongoing and needs to happen among various groups within society. In this closing chapter, I consider the meaning behind the questions about society's needs and higher education's ability to address those needs. I suggest that the answers to these questions may shift several times and should be responsive to changes in society, some of which are noted within this chapter. However, being responsive to changes in the society and context is different from being driven by a particular philosophy such as neoliberalism that heralds market forces. The responsiveness and reflection suggested in this chapter is one informed by human wisdom that carefully examines each force in society to see its effect. I view the current acceptance of market forces as reactive and with very little thought to circumstances. Most important, I encourage leaders to routinely reflect on higher education's role and responsibility in addressing society's needs as a part of their goal setting, work plan, and life accomplishments.

The 1993 Wingspread Group on Higher Education responded to the question *What does our society need from higher education?* as follows:

> It needs stronger, more vital forms of community. It needs an informed and involved citizenry. It needs graduates able to assume leadership roles in American life. It needs a competent and adaptable workforce. It needs very high quality undergraduate education producing graduates who can sustain each of these goals. It needs more first-rate research pushing back the important boundaries of human knowledge and less research designed to lengthen academic resumes. It needs an affordable, cost effective educational enterprise offering lifelong learning. Above all, it needs a commitment to the American promise—the idea that all Americans have the opportunity to develop their talents to the fullest. (1993, p. 2)

They go on to say, "Higher education is not meeting these imperatives." In 1999, the then chancellor of the University of California-Berkeley, Robert Berdahl, echoed the Wingspread group's concerns in a speech to the National Press Club with his sense of what is needed from higher education by a democratic society:

> The legitimacy of the public university's claim as an instrument of progress in a democratic society hangs in balance on the question of access—and not only on access, but quality and purpose. Are we providing the broadest possible cross-section of America's population access to the best possible education? Are we excluding by any means anyone who has the right to be included? Are we serving society—with our research and by teaching people to serve as leaders and citizens? Are we thereby, in answer to all of these questions, meeting our highest obligation, clearly spelled out in our charge to fulfill the public trust?

While Berdahl was speaking about the public university, it is clear that private and other colleges and universities can be considered in the same vein.

Many who are directly affiliated, as well as those who have distant, yet enduring affinities, with higher education would say that higher education is delivering all that the public wants and needs. If this is true, why then do we have ongoing discourse about the disconnect between higher education and the role it plays in addressing critical public issues in a democratic society? How can institutions better align their practices and values with the needs of the domestic and global societies of which they are a part? How do various communities within and around colleges and universities engage in transformative exchanges about social and institutional prosperity? What needs to happen in order for more diverse publics to see, believe, and act toward colleges and universities as resources committed to the public good? What are the societal and institutional obligations to prepare students for public and private leadership? How do we create educational institutions that prepare students to deal with the complexities of an expanding society after they leave the confines of our classrooms and campuses? The answers to these, and many other questions, lie somewhere in the middle of the broader dialogue between society and higher education. In the new social movement to strengthen the public relationship between higher education and society, there needs to be more creative and collaborative efforts to understand the needs of those partners in the relationship. These efforts of understanding will require different forms of communication and interaction, as well as different assumptions about power, privilege, and where knowledge and information exist.

To paraphrase the often-quoted Yogi Berra, "The future ain't what it used to be." The current and anticipated realities confronting social institutions are unparalleled in the history of this nation. Independently, many of the challenges seem familiar, but the confluence of complex conditions is unprecedented in our democratic experiment. Nor have the advancements in technology, science, medicine, humanities, telecommunications, and human consciousness been so promising and accessible to so many. The potential for incredible progress, as well as the potential for unimaginable devastation exist in parallel tension for this and future generations in our nation and around the world. The social and global context in which higher education exists changes drastically with unpredictable turbulence and impact. Higher education, as a social institution, is charged with holding its central mission close to its heart while honorably serving the needs of this rapidly changing society. The challenge is to hold the same values but act on those values differently in this very different world.

The demands confronting higher education as it attempts to serve the public demands of a rapidly changing social landscape are, in most ways, the same demands that all of society faces in trying to realize the potential of our diverse democracy. More and more, it is becoming clear that all of our intractable social problems, such as humane, affordable healthcare, urban K–12 public education, and escalating poverty, are complex, systemic, and interconnected. Further, it is becoming painfully clear that in order to mitigate the current and future manifestations of these problems, networks of all types of people and institutions need to confront the problems with the same complex, systemic, and interconnected frame that inspired and prolonged the problems. A recent article by Vartan Gregorian, president of the Carnegie Corporation in New York and former president at Brown University, puts it this way:

> As a society, we tend to pay lip service to the complexity of problems and then continue to gamble on simplistic solutions, such as building prisons to solve the crime and drug problems. But as Bela H. Banathy, a systems theorist, writes: "A technical problem of transportation, such as the building of a freeway, becomes a land use problem, linked with economics, environmental, conservation, ethical, and political issues. Can we really draw a boundary? When asked to improve a situation, particularly if it is a public one, we find ourselves facing not a problem, but a cluster of problems . . . and none of these problems can be tackled using linear or sequential methods." (2004, p. B12)

These public problems are not those of a single social domain, nor are there singular solutions to the cluster of problems embedded in each identified problem. These realities impact every corner of society and the world, without discrimination. By not accepting and operating on these realities, higher education and other institutions run the risk of repeating or worsening the very conditions that we seek to improve.

Finally, at the end of the day, the movement to build a more prosperous, just, and progressive society is about people—their ideas, their fears, their capacity to imagine and work together toward a different future (Green, 1997, p. 2). The notion of who is part of the discussion and movement is expanding. As a result, new visions of the public good are allowed to emerge. Can we achieve higher education for the public good? Should our aim be broader and more encompassing?

Partnerships, complexity, changing demographics, social innovations, networks, systems, fears, changing patterns of knowledge and information, and many other conditions will affect the meaning of the public good. Before and as the dialogue occurs, we cannot know what the outcome will be. It is likely that the charter will look different based on the changing social contexts. Hopefully, the changing social contexts will not divorce the charter from its important historical roots that have proven important for society in the past and will be important to the future. Thoughtful and caring leadership and stewardship is needed to realize the enormous potential present in the charter between higher education and society. Within the pages of this book, we hope you find the sustenance necessary to actively engage in the movement to strengthen the charter between higher education and the multiple publics that feed it and that it serves.

References

Berdahl, R. M. (1999). *The public university in the 21st century*. Address to the National Press Club. Washington, DC, June 2, 1999.

Green, M. (1997). *Transforming higher education*. Phoenix: American Council on Education and the Oryx Press.

Gregorian, V. (June 6, 2004). Colleges must reconstruct the unity of knowledge. *Chronicle of Higher Education, 50*(39), B12.

Wingspread Group on Higher Education. (1993). *An American imperative: Higher expectations for higher education*. Racine, WI: Johnson Foundation.

Name Index

Weibl, R., 274, 280
Weintraub, S. C., 156
Weisbuch, R., 283, 284
Wellman, J. V., 90, 99
Wergin, J., 154
West, C., 297, 306
Wiewel, W., 253
Willms, D. G., 280
Witt, D., 111, 113
Wolfe, A., 80, 83, 84
Womack, F. W., 88, 92
Woodford, B., 273, 275, 277
Wulff, D. H., 273, 274, 275, 277, 280

Y

Yff, J., 152
Yosso, T. J., 116
Young, R., 36, 37

Z

Zemsky, R., 38, 58, 325
Ziegert, A. L., 152
Zinn, H., 163
Zlotkowski, E., 146, 154
Zuber-Skerrit, O., 280

Subject Index

A

Academic freedom, and corporatization of higher education, 36–37

Academic-community partnerships, 323; academic values and, 30, 36–38; barriers to, 155; benefits and conflicts of interest in, 29–30; curriculum-project integration in, 210–212; disciplinary-level, 148–162; diversity-related, 157; engagement model of, 175–176; funding for, 160; historical roots of, 147–148; as learning communities, 48–49, 253; professional associations and, 47–48; research for the public good in, 221; resources for, 154–162; scholarship of engagement and, 251–253; service-learning in, 204–212; technology-based, 160–161

Academic—student affairs partnerships, 49, 51

Access to Democracy initiative, 19

Access to education, 95, 108–109, 327–328; and financial support for higher education, 90–91

Accountability: public demands for, 15, 91; and institutional change, 112

Accreditation: and civic development, 45; and service-learning, 1, 161

Administrators, and corporate management practices, 27, 37–38

Affirmative action debate, 110

American Association for Higher Education (AAHE), 18–19, 50, 151

American Association of State Colleges and Universities (AAC&U), 98, 131, 132–133, 134, 135, 137–138, 140, 141, 176, 177, 241, 265; American Commitments Project, 323; *Stepping Forward as Stewards of Place* (report), 265

American Association of University Professors (AAUP), 82–83, 323

American College Personnel Association (ACPA), 19

American Council on Education, 35

American Democracy in an Age of Rising Inequality (report), 135

American Democracy Project, 135

American Educational Research Association (AERA), 19, 110

American Institute of Biological Sciences, 150–151

American Political Science Association (APSA), 132, 135, 152

American Psychological Association, 150

American Sociological Association, 133, 148

Arts and humanities, civic engagement programs in, 157–159

Association of American Colleges and Universities, 131, 150, 159; American Commitments project of, 46

Association of American Geographers (AAG), 149

Association of American Universities, 341

Association of Commonwealth Universities (ACU), 247

Community-Campus Partnerships
for Health (CCPH), 157–158
Conflict resolution workshops,
286–287
Corporation for National Service, 48
Corporations, and racial diversity, 115
Council of Independent Colleges, 47
Covenant, defined, 6–8
Creating Common Ground (CCG),
157
*Creation of the Future: The Role of the
American University, The* (Rhodes),
309–310
Critical race theory, diversity narra-
tive and, 115–117
Critical thinking: support for develop-
ment of, 323; and vocationalized
teaching, 28
*Cultivating the Sociological Imagina-
tion: Concepts and Models for Service-
Learning in Sociology* (Howery), 147
Curriculum: design, outsourcing
of, 62; for engaged learning, 177;
exclusionary, 108; privatization
of, 61; vocational orientation in,
27–28
Customized worker training, 61–62

D

Democratic society: capitalistic
power structure of, 298; collective decision making in, 73–74;
and critical race theory, 115–117;
higher education's mission in,
9, 187–189, 191–194, 200, 248;
liberal education and, 130, 131,
135; and lifelong learning, 178;
as public good, 102; racial/ethnic
diversity paradigm for, 102–115;
and service-learning, 190–191
Disciplinary majors, development of
civic capacity in, 133
"Disciplinary Toolkit" 156–157
Disciplines, 146–164; civic engagement ethos in, 147, 15, 156; culture of self–referentiality and

influence of, 146–147, 154; engagement strategy/resources in,
151–162; professional associations
and, 148, 149–151, 156–162; and
public scholarship ventures, 78;
research focus in, 150, 151, 159
*Disciplines Speak: Rewarding the Schol-
arly, Professional, and Creative Work
of Faculty, The* (Diamond & Adam),
149–150
Distance education, 28
Diversity: civic education movement
and, 46; institutional, 243. *See also*
Racial/ethnic diversity
Diversity programs/studies, 104, 139
Doctoral education: communication
skills development in, 281; and
institutional resources/strategies,
286–288; public service preparation in, 274, 276–289; reform
initiatives in, 283–285; research
preparation in, 280; strategies for
improving, 282–288; strengths
and weaknesses of, 273–278;
teaching preparation in, 274,
280–281; and teamwork/conflict
handling skills, 281

E

Economic development, as public
good of higher education, 57–58
*Educating Citizens: Preparing America's
Undergraduates for Lives of Moral
and Civic Responsibility* (Colby &
others), 198–199, 200
Educational institutions: evolving
concepts of, 170–175; hegemony of research in, 171–172;
ideal, 166–167; "multiversity"
form of, 171–172; for profit
activities of, 65; research-teaching-
service triad in, 170, 175; self-
government projects in, 77–78.
See also Higher education; Institutional engagement; Mission,
institutional

theory of, 195–196; disciplinary fallacy in, 198–199; external policy models for, 38–39; and financial aid policy shifts, 32; historic public purposes of, 191–194; hypocrisy of, 201–203; idealist versus materialist function of, 186; and job attainment, 35; market- and consumer-oriented culture of, 24–26; 32–33, 51–52; measures of excellence in, 243; Plato's idealist theory of, 171, 195–196, 199; privatization/corporatization of, 24, 25, 27, 322–323; as public good, 299; public view of, 8–9; social charter of, 298; social and individual outcomes of, 10–12; students as consumers of, 300. *See also* Educational institutions

Holland Matrix of organizational factors, 237–238, 240–242

I

"Idea of a University" (Bollinger), 186
Imagining America (IA), 158–159
Informal education courses, 287
Information management, global shifts in, 249
Institute for Higher Education Policy (IHEP), 31, 35
Institutional engagement, 172–175; barriers to, 173–174; civic aspirations/goals for, 169–170; as cost center, 268; formulating strategy for, 266–268; funding for, 83, 97; Holland Matrix of organizational elements and, 237–240; and institutional characteristics, 240–241, 247, 249, 250–251; and levels of commitment, 237–238; manifestations of, 174; mission clarity and, 240–241; model, 172–175; pathways for innovation in, 239–240; potential problems in, 269–270; presidential leadership for, 308–325; public policy support for,

268–269, 271; research university model of, 242–243, 253–254; scope and scale considerations in, 238–239; system level support for, 268
Integrative learning, social problems in, 136
Intentional learners, 176–177
Interdisciplinary research movement, 49
International Consortium on Higher Education (ICHE), 246

J

Justice, as academic value, 38

K

Kellogg Commission on the Future of State Universities and Land-Grant Universities, 50, 91, 175
Kettering Foundation, 45, 75
Knowledge, privatization of, 38
Knowledge production: through faculty research, 221–222, 226; and practical wisdom, 74–75. *See also* Research; Scholarship
K–12 education: engagement reform strategy for, 173; service-learning in, 157
K–16 movement, 49–50

L

Land-grant institutions: creation of, 14; engaged scholarship in, 241, 249, 250; extension model of, 172–173; founding purpose of, 79, 192–193
Leadership, academic: and civic education movement, 44; and diversity efforts, 110–111, 115–120; and exclusionary academic traditions, 111–114; guiding principles for, 309–313; privatization and, 68; and public engagement strategy, 265–268; and public good discourse, 119–120; and